Millennials Speak.

Millennials Speak.
Essays on the 21ˢᵗ Century

Edited by R.P. Thead
with Sabith Khan

Contents

Introduction
R.P. Thead, with Sabith Khan and Deven Walther Thead i

Part 1
Foreign Policy and International Relations

Global Youth: Why this Group is More Important
than Ever
Sumithra Rajendra and Shoaib Rahim **1**

The Arab Spring and 'Generation 2011':
Succeeding Where Others Failed
Hamza Safouane **13**

Pushing Past the Talk: Evaluating the Strengths
of Youth as Potential Problem-Solvers
Andrew Leon Hanna **30**

The Young, the Educated, and the Restless
Makda Getachew **38**

The Future of the Sino-U.S. Relationship:
A Chinese Millennial Perspective
Owen Liu **56**

Riches, Wrinkles, and Rallies:
Societal Changes Shaping China's Future
Jeremy Peters **66**

Which Way Forward?
The Role of International Organizations in
World Politics
Jillienne Haglund   **76**

Is it Time to Re-Imagine U.S. Foreign Policy
in the Middle East?
Sabith Khan   **90**

Part 2
Popular Culture

The New Economics of Digital Content
R.P. Thead   **103**

Making it in the 21ˢᵗ Century Music Industry
Michael Young   **116**

The Artist, Incorporated.
The Creative Culture of the Millennial Generation
Rachel Kerwin   **127**

No Aliens in the Basement:
Popular Culture's Take on State Secrets versus Reality
Anonymous Contributor   **139**

Blending the Old School and the New School:
The Intersection of Social Networking with
Old Fashioned Grassroots Organizing
Paula Fynboh   **150**

Part 3
Food, Consumption, and Global Health

Building a New Global Food System
Sara Nawaz   **163**

The Effects of Large Scale Land Acquisitions on
Global Food Security: The Case of Brazil
Mieke Dale-Harris   **179**

Consumption, Climate Change, and the Environment
Nick Santos   **196**

Global Health in the 21st Century
Anne-Marie Jamin, Paxton Bach, and Kimberly Williams   **206**

Part 4
United States

Taxes in America
Benjamin Ross   **225**

The Student Loan Crisis and the Next Generation of
American Capitalists
R.P. Thead   **241**

America's Religious Diversity:
Challenge or Opportunity?
Sabith Khan   **255**

About the contributors

Paxton Bach is a medical student at Queen's University in Kingston, Ontario, Canada. He has been involved in global health advocacy for several years, most recently serving as the Vice-President of Global Health at the Canadian Federation of Medical Students and representing Canada within the International Federation of Medical Students' Associations. He will graduate in 2013 and pursue a residency in internal medicine with a focus on caring for underserved and marginalized populations.

Mieke L Dale-Harris grew up in Devon, UK, and graduated with B.sc. in psychology from Goldsmiths College, London University. Since then she has worked in Ecuador and Bolivia, where she did an internship at the Institute of Advanced Development Studies (INESAD). In October she will be starting a Masters in development economics and international cooperation at Rome University Tor Vergata. You can find her at mieke_@hotmail.co.uk.

Paula Fynboh has more than 15 years of experience in implementing, developing, managing, and consulting on community, legislative, public policy, grassroots governance, and electoral and private sector campaigns in areas such as youth leadership and engagement, community cohesion, and sustainability. Originally from the United States, she relocated to Bogota, Colombia in 2011 to purse her dream of working internationally and finally learning Spanish. You can find her at @PaulaFynboh

Makda Getachew lives in Addis Ababa, Ethiopia where she was born and raised. She attended university in Germany and the U.S. and has a B.A. in Integrated Social Sciences and a Master in Public Policy. Getachew currently works at the International Labour Organization, Regional Office for Africa. She has a keen interest in the issues relating to youth development, and in particular youth employment.

Jillienne Haglund is a Ph.D. candidate at Florida State University. She received her B.A. in Political Science from Montana State University in 2007, her M.A. in Political Science from the University of Memphis in 2009, and her M.S. in Political Science from Florida State University in 2010. She expects to complete her Ph.D. in summer 2014. She is particularly interested in human rights, international organizations, and domestic political institutions. She grew up in Montana, but has migrated south and currently resides in Tallahassee, FL. You can find her at www.jill-haglund.com or on Twitter at @jillhaglund.

Andrew Leon Hanna is a third-year undergraduate at Duke University, where he serves as President of Duke Partnership for Service, an organization that oversees 65+ youth-led service initiatives in the areas of education, health, environment, and more. Locally, he is the Founder and Co-Director of IGNITE Peer Mentoring, an organization working in his hometown of Jacksonville, Florida and in Durham, North Carolina. Globally, he has represented the U.S. at the UNESCO Youth Forum and global youth at the UN High Level Panel on the Post 2015 Development Agenda. He is a "Global Changemaker" and has spent time on projects in Haiti, India, and South Africa, and will relocate to Atlanta, Georgia as a Summer Business Analyst at McKinsey & Company.

Anne-Marie Jamin is completing her Masters in Public Health at the University of Alberta. She is committed to working towards health equity and sustainable development, with related experience in Canada, Africa, Guatemala, and Mexico. She currently resides in Edmonton.

Rachel Kerwin is a D.C.-based artist. She grew up in Chicago and graduated with a B.F.A. in painting from Cornell University. Her work has been shown New York, Virginia, Chicago, and the D.C. metro area. She can be found online at www.rachelkerwin.com.

Sabith Khan is pursuing his Ph.D. at Virginia Tech and has over eight years of experience in public affairs, strategic communications, and non-profit management across India, UAE, and the U.S. He is a graduate of the Maxwell School of Syracuse University, where he earned an M.P.A. and M.A. in International Relations. His research and career interests include philanthropy, religion, civil society, international relations, and non-profit governance issues.

Liu Chang (Owen Liu) is a Chinese graduate student of Shanghai Institutes for International Studies (SIIS), and he is now studying at Johns Hopkins University, Nanjing University Center (HNC) as an exchange student for a certificate project. His major is international politics and relations, and his research focuses on Sino-U.S. relations, international strategy, and East Asian politics and regionalism. He is fluent in English and writing, and has rich experience in studying and working with foreigners. You can find him at his Sina Weibo (Microblog) http://weibo.com/longlivechina.

Sara Nawaz is an M.Phil. student in Development Studies, at Oxford, United Kingdom. Originally from the Washington, D.C. area, with a background in economics, Sara is currently pursuing her Masters of Philosophy in Development Studies at the University of Oxford. She is interested in the intersection of environmental and development, particularly through the lens of food systems and social movements in Latin America. You can find her at www.thegoodfoodgirl.com and @sara_nawaz.

Jeremy Peters is currently pursuing an M.A. in China Studies and International Economics from the Johns Hopkins School of Advanced International Studies, the first year of which he lived and studied in Nanjing, China. He previously spent two years living in Washington, D.C. working for the Woodrow Wilson International Center for Scholars, the Center for Strategic and International Studies, and GreenPoint Group, a boutique-style U.S.-China strategic advisory firm. Jeremy grew up in Charleston, SC. He graduated with a B.A. in Intercultural Studies and Chinese from Wofford College, for which he spent time abroad in Beijing, China and St. Petersburg, Russia.

Shoaib Rahim is a Fulbright Scholar and a graduate of the Master of Engineering Management Program at Duke University. He is currently working and living in his home country of Afghanistan where he runs a consulting firm providing technology consulting and management consulting services to local companies. He also coaches the debate team at the American University of Afghanistan on a voluntary basis and works with other youth groups in Kabul focusing on development issues.

Sumithra Rajendra is a 2006 Fulbright Scholar. She has an M.A. in International Relations from the Maxwell School of Citizenship and Public Affairs, Syracuse University, and a B.S. in Electronics Engineering from Multimedia University, Malaysia. She currently works for the International Finance Corporation and is based in Washington, D.C. An avid intervarsity debater, Sumi was the 2006 Asians Intervarsity Debating Champion. In her free time, she adjudicates speed debate tournaments for young policy professionals at the Center for Strategic and International Studies (CSIS), and serves as a liaison for Young Professionals in Foreign Policy (YPFP).

Benjamin Ross is a writer, artist, musician, gardener, tinkerer, and outdoorsman located in a small town in Northwest Florida. He grew up in a small town in North Alabama, then moved on through various colleges and jobs in small towns across America. His work includes publications in the fields of Underwater Archaeology, Public Land Management, Regional Planning, and Outdoor Recreation Impact Management. He has no place to call his home.

Hamza Safouane is currently working on a mentoring project between Germany and Tunisia to promote female entrepreneurship. He was formerly working as a project manager and research fellow at a Moroccan think tank. He was born and raised in Morocco and is currently living in Germany. He studied at the Maxwell School of Citizenship and Public Affairs, Syracuse University, where he graduated with two M.A. degrees, in Economics and International Relations.

Nick Santos is the founder and Executive Director of Environmental Consumer (http://enviroconsumer.org), a non-profit that develops actionable information and resources for consumers to reduce their impact. Nick also develops GIS-based software and databases to help analyze and understand environmental impacts and indicators in California. He previously worked for climate campaign 1Sky and local environmental nonprofit Sierra Nevada Alliance. His website is http://nicksantos.com and he can be reached at nick@enviroconsumer.org.

R.P. Thead is a writer based in Washington, D.C. He published his first novel, *The Sovereign Soil*, in fall 2012. You can find his other writings and contact him at www.rpthead.com or @RP_Thead.

Kimberly Williams is a Canadian-based medical student and epidemiologist. She grew up in Edmonton and graduated with an M.S.c. in Global Health from the University of Alberta. She is currently the Vice-President of Global Health at the Canadian Federation of Medical Students and a University of Calgary medical student. She is the co-author of a book 12 Stories. Narratives from New Canadians and continues to participate in global health research.

Michael Young (aka Futurome) is a Baltimore-based analytical chemist and hip-hop producer. He grew up in Maryland, and played guitar and saxophone with many different bands, ranging from blues-rock to Ska. Currently, he is working with local hip-hop and pop artists in the DMV area, and specifically helping to usher in a Baltimore-based hip-hop scene. You can find him on Twitter, @futuromemusic.

This book is dedicated to SGT David Allison Jr., whose generous support made this book a reality.

Patrons who also supported this book

Robert Franklin Pulliam

SGT Paul M. Dunaway, USA, Retired

David and Debbie Walther

Kimberly Ly and Bart Nadherny

Dr. and Mrs. Larry B. Thead

John, last name unknown

Introduction

R.P. Thead,
with Sabith Khan
and Deven Walther Thead

Who is the Millennial Generation? A Global Snapshot

There are competing definitions about who constitutes the Millennial Generation. A Google search will return various definitions of this group using age brackets: some definitions say those born between 1980 and 1990 and others say anyone born after 1982. The authors in this book were all born in the more general age range used to define a Millennial: the generation born between the late 1970s through the early 1990s. But the Millennial Generation is more an idea than a category on a census form.

This group of people came of age during a specific and peculiar time in history. We did not grow up with the Cold War. The oldest of us were 12 or 13 years old when the Berlin Wall fell. We did not enter adulthood amid a geopolitical rivalry threatening mutual and global destruction. We did, however, grow up during a relatively peaceful time compared to the World Wars of the first half of the 20th century. This does not mean there has not been other needless violence since the breakup of the Soviet Union. There has been plenty and there still is.

We are a generation of the information revolution. We came of age alongside the Internet. Some of us can remember the first time we got online; we could recognize the sound of a dial-up modem anywhere. But for some of us, broadband Internet was always there in the background and perpetually on. It was a part of life, like the telephone was for our parents' generation. Today, social media plays a large part in how we communicate with each other. Some of us found one another via social media to collaborate on this book, and it is how we plan to tell the world about it.

Who Are We and Where Do We Come From?

Currently about 7 billion people live on this planet. Conservative estimates by the United Nations project this total at over 9 billion by 2050. Most of this population growth will take place in the developing world. For example, by 2050, over 35 percent of the world's population will live in China and India.[i] More than half of the world's 9 billion people, about 6.3 billion, will be living in cities. This is an enormous percentage increase from today, where about 37 percent or over 2.5 billion of the global population lives in urban areas.[ii]

Presently, more than half of the 7 billion people alive are under the age of 30; almost half of the world's population is under the age of 25.[iii] This statistic includes most of this book's contributors, as well as a few senior Millennials. However, youth populations are not spread evenly across the world. For example, in the Middle East and North Africa countries, more than 60 percent of the population is under 25.[iv]

Lack of opportunity is a theme running through many of the essays. The 2008 global financial crisis has not been kind to us. One of the biggest challenges facing the Millennial Generation is unemployment. Like the global youth population, joblessness is not evenly distributed among countries. Knowing the severity of the problem may help readers better understand the opinions and motives of some of the writers and the countries where they live and were raised. There are no global Millennial-specific data sources for unemployment. The International

Labour Organization, a UN agency that deals with labor issues, estimates 75 million unemployed youth, defined as ages 16-24, worldwide. In 2011, the global youth unemployment rate was at 12.6 percent; it was projected to increase to 12.7 percent in 2012. This number is expected to rise still.[v]

Some regions of the world have fared worse than others. In the Arab world, an average 27.5 percent of the total youth population is unemployed. Considering youth percentage of the total population there, this means that a large percentage of the total Middle East and North Africa population is either unemployed or underemployed.[vi] In Europe, EU youth unemployment stood at 22.1 percent at the end of 2011, slightly higher than the Eurozone[vii] youth average of 21.4 percent, and more than double the regional average. Joblessness is worse in some EU countries than others. For example, at the end of 2011 Spain and Greece had youth unemployment rates of 48.9 and 49.3 percent, almost five times the Eurozone average of 10.2 percent.[viii] None of these numbers fully capture the NEETs, or young people "not in employment, education, or training."[ix] The unemployed who have stopped seeking jobs are missing in official statistics.

In the United States, the world's largest national economy, youth unemployment, also defined as ages 16-24, stood at 17.1 percent in July 2012,[x] which is about twice the national average. Total Millennial unemployment, defined at ages 18-29, in the United States is estimated at 9.7 percent.[xi]

Why a Book of Essays?

Most existing work and research regarding this generation has thus far been American-centric. But discussion of the Millennial Generation and its role in the global order should not be limited to the West or to a single country. For a globally-aware and connected generation, a narrow focus on one specific country counters the inclusive nature of our age demographic. Existing U.S.-specific research is the first step to create a body of knowledge that considers the Millennial Generation a unique demographic that requires specified study. Yet the United States population only comprises a small percentage of the total world population and the global Millennial population.

Some of the essays approach issues that concern a specific part of the world, like Hamza Safouane's compelling piece on the Arab Spring and what he calls "Generation 2011," although such reverberations from regional and domestic upheaval are easily felt around the world. Others, like Makda Getachew's contribution on youth unemployment in her home country of Ethiopia, tell a bigger story. As this essay shows, Ethiopia could easily be substituted with another country to approximate the difficulties youth face in other parts of the world. Issues that the Millennial Generation faces and their root causes can be generalized, although they are hardly identical in certain countries and regions. Sumithra Rajendra and Shoaib Rahim, from Malaysia and Afghanistan, respectively, argue that some of these causes can be addressed by fully integrating youth into national and international policy and dialogue, versus considering young people as marginalized stakeholders.

There are too many Millennials to ignore. The pair of essays regarding China, one by Owen Liu, a Chinese national, and another by Jeremy Peters, an American, are written by two people from countries with very different histories and cultures. Still, a unified message emerges: under the surface, the country that most Chinese know and the problems the nation faces differ from what its government would prefer the world to know. However, we want the world to hear our voices about this and other topics that are important to us.

Although this book is not comprehensive in terms of topics or geographical representation, we hope it is an important step to study our Generation or at least let others hear what we have to say. Study of a diverse generation should beget a diverse body of knowledge. The countries, opinions, religions, and viewpoints represented here show competing interests and priorities of our generation. At the same time there appears to be consensus regarding our frustration with the status quo.

We also agreed that no one person should attempt to speak on behalf of such a diverse global demographic. Instead, we decided to speak for ourselves.

i United Nations Department of Economic and Social Affairs (UNDESA). The *2010 Revision* of the *World Population Prospects, May 2011*. Accessed January 5 2013. *http://esa.un.org/wpp/*.

ii United Nations Department of Economic and Social Affairs (UNDESA). *World Urbanization Report – March 2012*. Accessed January 5 2013. *http://esa.un.org/unup/pdf/WUP2011_Highlights.pdf*.

iii UNDESA 2011.

iv International Labour Organization (ILO). "Global Employment Trends for Youth 2012." 2012. *http://www.ilo.org/wcmsp5/groups/public/---dgreports/---dcomm/documents/publication/wcms_180976.pdf*.

v ILO 2012.

vi Ibid.

vii These countries use the Euro as their currency.

viii European Commission (EC). *Unemployment Statistics*. Eurostat. Accessed January 5 2013. *http://epp.eurostat.ec.europa.eu/statistics_explained/index.php/Unemployment_statistics*.

ix ILO 2011.

x Bureau of Labor Statistics (BLS). "Employment and Unemployment Among Youth Summary." 2012. Accessed January 5 2013. *http://www.bls.gov/news.release/youth.nr0.htm*.

xi National Conference on Citizenship. *Millennials Civic Health Index*. 2013. Accessed 12 February 2013. *http://www.ncoc.net/index.php?download=114kcfl1573*.

Part 1

Essays on International Relations and Foreign Policy

Global Youth: Why this Group is More Important than Ever

Shoaib Rahim and Sumithra Rajendra[1]

Youth is a transient period of life, nestled between childhood and adulthood. It is never quite completely detached from the experiences and emotions of childhood. Yet young people experience and affect the next course of evolution in life, which is adulthood. There is a reason why the statement "Youth of today are the leaders of the next generation" is a cliché. Despite the obviousness of this, discussions around youth policy are often done in a vacuum, isolated from its vital linkages to childhood and adulthood. Youth policy is often boxed in and treated as a category of its own, as if the state of "youth" was an entity in itself, frozen in space and time.

The youth issue, much like the gender issue, has always been placed in its own separate and specific category and addressed when necessary. It has been marginalized. It is time that policy makers and influencers fully integrate youth considerations when tackling all development challenges. The often-practiced piecemeal approach to youth issues is no longer sufficient in the unfolding development narrative of today. Now

---

[1] The findings, interpretations, and conclusions expressed in this publication are those of the author(s) and should not be attributed in any manner to The World Bank, its Board of Executive Directors, or the governments they represent.

more than ever we need to pay attention to the voices of youth, involve them in policy discussions, provide them with access to jobs, narrow skill gaps, and offer youth opportunities for active citizen participation.

In our essay, we outline youth-led political movements and social movements throughout the 20th century. We draw comparisons to some and explore reasons youth are involved or uninvolved in their nations' politics. Then, we provide some concrete examples from personal experience: Shoaib in his native Afghanistan and Sumithra from her home in Malaysia. Later, we provide some first-step general policy guidelines to address the full integration of youth into national and international development policy in the future.

The Time is Now

Forty percent of the world population is under the age of 24. That is two out of every five people on the planet. Eighty-five percent of the world's youth live in developing countries, with about 60 percent of them in Asia. The gender distribution among this group is about 50-50. Ten percent of the men and 20 percent of the women in this group are illiterate. About 1.2 billion of them are adolescents just entering their reproductive years.[i]

These numbers tell us that the majority of the world's young live in developing countries. And these numbers are likely to continue to rise due to poor gender rights in most parts of the developing world, where there is a lack of awareness and availability of contraceptives. We can also expect an increase in food scarcity as a result of a growing global population and a failing global food system, as well as continued lack of adequate access to healthcare and education. The list goes on.

Global demographics were discussed in the book's introduction, but the topic is worth revisiting to properly frame this issue and essay.

> According to United Nations projections, the 6.9 billion population number will rise to 9.3 billion by 2050, the equivalent of adding another India and China to the world. That's an

optimistic scenario, one that assumes the worldwide average birthrate, now 2.5 children per woman, will decline to 2.1. If birthrates stay where they are, the population is expected to reach 11 billion by midcentury — akin to adding three Chinas.[ii]

This projected population growth also demonstrates that it will become increasingly difficult for governments and global donor organizations to continue their fragmented approach to youth challenges. The status quo will not be adequate. Current government and international organization policies regarding youth tend to focus on short-term gains, or are fragmented at best. The overreliance on quantifiable indicators by the United Nations Millennium Development Goals is a telling example.

As a result, policies often overlook this large and growing youth demographic that is catalyzing attention where and when it can. History shows that a large youth bulge seen in many developing nations amid a domestic climate of corruption, repression, lack of access and opportunity encourages uprisings, revolts, radical movements, and homegrown resentment. Large-scale social unrest is not always predictable, but it is not difficult to identify common indicators that youth-based movements share. The Harakat al-Shabaab al-Mujahideen (HSM) movement, which literally means "Movement of Striving Youth," is a militant group based in Somalia. The leadership of this youth-based movement appears in propaganda videos to appeal to disaffected Muslim youth and inspire them to join the Islamist struggle.[iii] Such groups feed on apathy, resentment, and general disenchantment among youth growing up in nations where they feel they have no voice or opportunities, and where oppression is common. Why are terrorist and militant groups capitalizing on this global reality while most governments and donor organizations are not?

Currently, a majority of domestic and international development programs directed towards youth focus only on increasing employment with vocational training and improved educational opportunities. We argue that these programs should be expanded towards the development

3

of public and private structures where youth can participate in national dialogue. Global youth need venues where they can provide input to leaders and policymakers regarding the most pressing issues facing their nations.

Listening to the Next Generation: Why is This so Difficult?

Not surprisingly, "about 80 percent of the world's civil conflicts since the 1970s have occurred in countries with young, rapidly growing populations."[iv] A simple statistical analysis representing college campus demonstrations, youth-led uprisings, and civil conflict in a country would correlate directly with the youth bulge. One need only remember the baby boomers in America who led the Vietnam War demonstrations, the youth-led revolt in Tiananmen Square, or the majority of current uprisings sweeping North Africa and the Middle East to find evidence.

The developed world has experienced a declining trend of youth-led demonstrations since the 1970s, a possible indication that the developed world has more structures and institutions designed to systematically capture the youth voice, such as the National Youth Councils adopted by most EU member states.[v] Alternately, factors such as better job prospects, stable political structures, fulfillment of skills and passion, and the ability to marry and start families could support youth.

The world saw powerful youth movements from the beginning of the 20th century through the late 1970s that focused predominantly on fighting colonial rule and tyrannical regimes in the developing world. This includes, for example, the Muslim Brotherhood Movement in Egypt, the anti-colonial movement in India, which had a majority membership of Indian youth, and the Iranian Revolution against the Shah. However, following these movements, global youth experienced a relatively long slumber of political inactivity. A rejuvenation of such movements in the developing world is now seen in the ongoing Arab Spring in the Middle East and North Africa.

Regardless of country and culture, there is a strong need for society's youth to be active participants in the political process, albeit in a constructive and sustainable manner. A vibrant and politically engaged youth serves as the moral compass of society at large, without which the masses will have unchecked and unguided systems of governance and a society in crisis. Greater youth engagement and youth involvement in all aspects of governance is imperative for meaningful and sustainable growth of a society and its economy.

Dictatorships and autocratic regimes prey on political apathy of the masses, particularly of the youth, to maintain power. Phrases such as, "Politics is a dirty business, in which I refuse to participate," "Politics is not for me because I'm a normal person," and "I'm not naïve; I know I'm just one person and I can't make a difference" are common among groups who suffer from political apathy. How can the sleeping masses be awakened? Many would say education is the key; it plays a dominant role in guiding international development policy. But the relationship between education and political involvement is tenuous at best. Educated and highly educated people generally avoid risk, conflict, and controversy. In most cases, societies with such high levels of apathy end up with a small group of noisy rioters burning flags and effigies, upsetting traffic any chance they get. These noisy rioters hijack the narrative and serve as pressure groups for those in power; they lean on the people pulling the strings for short-term political gains. Familiar examples include the Tea Party in the United States and the religious and government-sponsored Basij-e Mostaz'afin in Iran. The fundamental weaknesses of these movements lie in their short sightedness. They are more or less temporary troublemakers with narrowly defined interests.

However, even political apathy cannot be continuously sustained. Suppression coupled with worsening economic conditions are often perfect ingredients to break this malaise and disillusionment. Mohamed Bouazizi, age 26, sacrificed his life by burning himself in public to awaken the Tunisian people and begin a series of uprisings we now refer to as "The Arab Spring." Whether Tunisia, Libya, and Egypt are better off since the Arab Spring began remains to be seen. Certainly when youth came together in these places, they became difficult to ignore. The median age in Tunisia is 30.5 and 24.8 in Libya.[vi]

In Afghanistan, the median age is 18.2 years.[vii] By most estimates, more than 60 percent of the population is below 25 years of age,[viii] a disproportionate share of the national population that surpasses the global average. However, outside of private sector businesses and their youth-targeted advertising, very little is done to acknowledge this reality. The willful ignorance of Afghanistan's increasingly aging ruling class has added to the sense of hopelessness of this young and silent majority. The consequences of the leaders' intentional blind eyes to this youth demographic in Afghanistan are especially dire considering the active recruitment targeting of youth by insurgent groups for their own violent purposes. Ironically, the radical insurgents seem to have caught on to the energy that youth offer and actively provide what young Afghans desire: a sense of purpose. They prey on young peoples' ability to impact their own world. International organizations should inspire youth with a sense of purpose, cause, and empowerment in Afghanistan and other developing countries. We are in no way downplaying the efforts of development agencies and international organizations but suggest that these efforts are too small in reach and do not entirely meet the employment, political, and social needs of Afghan youth.

There are rays of hope. Recently, a socio-political movement calling itself "1400 Afghanistan" was founded as the platform for youth voices in the country.[ix] This group, mostly young professionals with advanced degrees from reputable global universities, has caught the attention of optimists and critics alike. Its name, 1400 Afghanistan, indicates the new century in the Persian calendar, which begins in the year 2020 of the western calendar. Unlike many donor-funded youth associations, this one is independent and home-grown, which makes it unique in the current context. Its grassroots credentials give it credibility and relevance among the Afghan youth.

Muslim-majority Malaysia, an emerging nation with a median age of 27.1,[x] is experiencing a similar trend to Afghanistan. During a recent forum at a prominent local university in Malaysia, Sharifah Zohra, the forum moderator and president of a women's group (Suara Wanita 1 Malaysia) in Malaysia, openly chastised undergraduate K.S. Bawani. This was caught on camera.[xi] Normally, this rude act would have been forgotten and no one would have raised a fuss. Such is the way of life in Malaysia: seniority prevails. As a young person you "must not know better" and are expected to accept all criticisms leveled at you. But things have changed, and Malaysian youth regardless of race and religious affiliations are no longer satisfied with old-school attitudes.

The video of Sharifah chastising Bawani went viral and soon Sharifah was the one facing shame and ridicule in the court of public opinion. The popularity of this particular video can be attributed to several things. First, it is currently an election year in Malaysia so the populace is more sensitive to any policy-related discussion. Second, Malaysians are active social media users with a platform and outlet for their voices. Third, there is a growing youth population in Malaysia that desires a stake in local policies. Unlike previous generations, this generation of Malaysian youth is not satisfied with being told what is good enough for them.

In 1971, the Malaysian government enacted a policy prohibiting students from expressing any "support, sympathy, or opposition" to any political party.[xii] This act sought to stymie student voices. Further, this was a tacit acknowledgement by the government that student voices were unworthy of attention. The motivation behind this act was to prevent support for the opposition party. The current ruling coalition, Barisan Nasional, has been in power since the country gained independence from Britain in 1957. The numerous opposition parties in Malaysia (such as the DAP, PAS, and PKR) are generally small and weak and rarely garner enough support to win a majority of seats in Parliament.

Laws forbidding student organizations, which are stifling to the opposition, are obvious ruling party tactics to maintain the status quo and ignore inconvenient opinions. However, this practice creates a culture that continuously validates the notion that only those who are older are wiser. Technology, especially the proliferation of social media, has been a huge catalyst in continuously challenging this notion. We sometimes ponder reasons underlying ruling class and government dislike for youth. Some of this animosity may stem from the fact that only a few years ago these same youth were only children: helpless, obedient creatures whose developing ideas regarding right and wrong hardly qualified them to comment on the complexities of national government and politics. Changing one's psyche overnight is not easy.

A more relevant explanation could be that we live in a time where the pace of change is far greater than before. Technology changes the way we interact, learn, and mobilize. The demographic most adept at these changes are the youth. They are quickly leaving their slow-paced elders behind, which causes two effects. One, the youth begin to expect more from society, but when reality does not meet expectations it causes greater frustration and negativity. On the other hand, the older age groups who have worked hard to achieve their positions in the world feel threatened by these up-and-coming youngsters. Naturally, the quickest and most convenient solution would be to simply resist change, as we see in many countries.

Still, the status quo does not truly reflect global demographics and the global youth majority. The global average age of Members of Parliament is 53 years, with Arab countries having the highest average age at 55. We live in a world where governments increasingly appear out of touch with the changing dynamics and priorities of the populations they govern. We believe this is a serious cause for concern. To a certain sextent, this vast age gap explains the lip-service that global institutions pay to youth in terms of short-term projects, with almost no emphasis on long-term and sustainable outcomes.

The Youth Bulge is Not Going Away

The world's growing population will continue to grow. As it grows, rapid technological innovation will continue to provide platforms for all individual voices. Youth now can effectively channel their frustrations through multiple online channels including blogs, Twitter, Facebook, Instagram, and other social media outlets. Where traditional cultural norms and values once shunned the very notion of free expression of thought and ideas, particularly in the East where "the young are to be seen not heard", a growing number of youth can now express their thoughts on a global scale. Consider Pakistan's charming Malala Yousafazai Vigils, the 14 year-old who expressed her thoughts about the Tehrik-e-Taliban through a series of blog posts. She wanted to be heard, and she frightened rebels so much with her sharp thoughts that they thought the only way to stifle her was to eliminate her. She survived an attack by gunmen, and is currently recovering abroad in the United Kingdom. Governments need to encourage voices like Malala's and offer effective channels for a thousand more Malalas to flourish without fear of retribution.

Youth will find a way to rally the cries of the unemployed, the disenchanted, and the oppressed through street demonstrations and revolts. They want to be heard and now they have a way of reaching out. The question is, are we listening? A youth bulge does not have to automatically translate into uprisings or create negative outcomes. Additional factors contribute to unrest, such as war, a lack of job opportunities, dissatisfaction with value systems in a country, poverty, lack of food, etc. However, the bulge coupled with these factors can lend to explosions of unrest that would worsen volatile situations.

How Do We Address the Bulge and Youth Issues at Large?

We have a few ideas regarding this:

1. Increase collaboration and partnerships between agencies that are tackling childhood, youth, and adult-focused development challenges. Identify and understand linkages and formulate policies for youth with these policies affecting children and adults in mind and vice-versa.

2. Create spaces for youth to be actively involved in political processes. Youth voices not only need to be heard but also acted upon. Youth need to know that they have a stake in the process, and that they have equal ownership as every citizen in the country. Since youth political movements tend to be located in the center, attention should be given to ensure that active youth participation in the political process occurs at all levels.

3. Focus on integration in the job market, particularly in situations where youth have been exposed to taking up arms, joining radical groups, and participating in criminal activities. Focus should be on restructuring the value hierarchy for youth who have been involved in armed political or criminal activities.

4. Establish a clear link between education and job skills. Education focus must extend beyond the 3Rs (reading, writing, and arithmetic). Provide practical training that is mindful of market demand and provide required skills.

5. Better synergies across youth and gender issues could ensure that awareness and change in perception and attitudes occur at an earlier period in one's life.

The good news is that donor and development agencies have begun to acknowledge that youth is no longer a "component" of policy. On October 2012, the United States Agency for International Development (USAID) launched a policy on youth in development. This policy hopes to "strengthen youth programing, participation and partnership in support of Agency development objectives and mainstream and integrate youth issues and engage young people across Agency initiatives and operations."[xiii] Similarly the United Nations launched a global trust fund on January 25, 2013 that aims to boost youth volunteerism in the hopes of "transforming the energy of the world's young people into tangible global development targets.[xiv] It remains to be seen if these are knee-jerk reactions to the youth bulge or long-term policies that will result in measurable and sustainable success. A key piece of the youth puzzle not being addressed is engagement with local governments to systematically focus on youth issues and integrate them at all levels of local government. We cannot stress this enough: strategic integration is critical to the success of policies aimed at mobilizing, empowering, and providing opportunities for youth.

The global community only stands to lose by ignoring the youth agenda, particularly in more volatile developing nations. As witnessed by the recent Arab Spring, youth will take up arms, revolt, and demonstrate in volatile environments. Whether we care to acknowledge it, this growing demographic of the global population will largely shape population control, gender issues, food policy, water scarcity, and environment issues in the coming years. It is time that we no longer refer to discussions about youth as the "youth issue," but rather focus on it as a major development challenge for the global society at large. Let us start by involving youth in the discussion. It is time for youth to not only be seen but also heard.

---

[i] United Nations Department of Economic and Social Affairs. Youth Social Policy and Development Division, "FAQs." Accessed 1 February 2013. *http://social.un.org/index/Youth/FAQs.aspx.*

[ii] Kenneth R. Weiss, "Runaway population growth often fuels youth-driven uprisings," *Los Angeles Times.* 12 June 2012. Accessed 1 February 2013. *http://www.latimes.com/news/nationworld/world/population/la-fg-population-matters2-20120724-html,0,982753.htmlstory.*

[iii] U.S. House of Representatives, "Al Shabaab: Recruitment and Radicalization within the Muslim American Community and the Threat to the American Homeland." July 27, 2011. Accessed February 1, 2013. *http://homeland.house.gov/hearing/al-shabaab-recruitment-and-radicalization-within-muslim-american-community-and-threat.*

[iv] Weiss, 2012.

[v] European Union. "Europa: Summaries of European Legislation." Communication from the Commission to the Council on European policies concerning youth participation and information [COM(2006) 417 final - Not published in the Official Journal]. Accessed February 1, 2013. *http://europa.eu/legislation_summaries/education_training_youth/youth/c11200_en.htm.*

[vi] CIA Factbook. "Median Age." Accessed February 1, 2013. *https://www.cia.gov/library/publications/the-world-factbook/fields/2177.html.*

[vii] CIA Factbook. "Afghanistan." Accessed February 1, 2013.

http://www.indexmundi.com/afghanistan/demographics_profile.html.
[viii] International Labour Organization, Civil Military Fusion Center. "The Youth Bulge in Afghanistan: Challenges and Opportunities." 2012. Accessed February 1, 2013.
http://apyouthnet.ilo.org/resources/the-youth-bulge-in-afghanistan-challenges-and-opportunities.
[ix] Emma Graham-Harrison. "Young Afghans form new political movement with hopes for the future." *The Guardian.* December 12, 2012. Accessed February 1, 2013. *http://www.guardian.co.uk/world/2012/dec/12/afghanistan-new-political-party.*
[x] CIA Factbook, "Median Age."
[xi] "Listen, listen, listen, listen, listen." YouTube. Accessed February 1, 2013. *http://www.youtube.com/watch?v=CflYB49Z6fo.*
[xii] Liz Gooch. "Malaysian Students Seek Full political rights." *The New York Times.* 23 April 2012. Accessed 1 February 2013.
http://www.nytimes.com/2012/04/23/world/asia/malaysian-students-seek-full-political-rights.html?pagewanted=all
[xiii] United States Agency for International Development (USAID). "Youth in Development Policy." October 2012. Accessed February 1, 2013.
http://transition.usaid.gov/our_work/policy_planning_and_learning/documents/Youth_in_Development_Policy.pdf.
[xiv] UN News Center. "UN trust fund to enhance role of youth volunteers in global development." January 25, 2013. Accessed 1 February 2013.
http://www.un.org/apps/news/story.asp?NewsID=44007#.USK8oDn3Ay4; United Nations Development Programme. "The Global Parliamentary Report." April 2, 2012. Accessed February 1, 2013.
http://www.undp.org/content/undp/en/home/librarypage/democratic-governance/the-global-parliamentary-report/.

The Arab Spring and "Generation 2011": Succeeding Where Others Failed

Hamza Safouane

Modernity is often perceived as a distinct period of time and history that is situated between an archaic premodern era and followed by obscure postmodernity.[i] According to this normative narrative, Western societies, already entangled in their postmodern era, can act as guides into modernity for the rest of the archaic world. Secularization, democracy, and openness to Western progressive values are some of the milestones that delineate the path to achieving a modern society. Yet, this narrative contradicts the argument made by German philosopher Immanuel Kant in his essay, "An Answer to the Question: What is Enlightenment?" Kant explains that enlightenment is the major step to modernity, and that a society becomes enlightened when it transitions to "adulthood" by liberating itself from obedience to another society. That is, modernity is reached when a society uses its own reason to solve its problems and becomes solely responsible for its failures and successes. Conversely, an un-enlightened society has yet to reach modernity because it is still subjugated by the reason of others.

The Arab Spring is a paragon of modernity but surely not the modernity set forth by the West, whereby modernization is tantamount to westernization. The theoretical debate whether the Arab world was impervious to modernity and hence democracy finally found its empirical answer two years ago in Sidi Bouzid, Tunisia, in the periphery of a peripheral country. In December 2010, a twenty-six year old Tunisian street vendor set himself on fire, which caused a massive shock wave across the Arab world. The resulting political and social upheaval toppled some of the most unmovable autocrats in the world. With the Arab Spring, we see empiricism trumping theory as Arab societies have finally caught a glimpse of what their modernity looks like, respective to each nation's peculiar history and culture.

While historically the Arab world has experience with westernized modernity, the Arab Spring bears genuine, but overlooked or ignored, traits of enlightened modernity. For that purpose, I offer a brief discussion of the experience of the Arab societies with westernization. Then, I examine the Arab Spring and the resulting claim of modernity through an exploration of the authors of the Arab Spring national movements. I explore what can be labeled as "Generation 2011", the Arab cohort of the greater Millennial Generation responsible for political change in the Arab Spring. Last, from the perspective of progress toward democracy and modernity, I discuss the Islamist political parties that came to power following Arab Spring elections in several countries with the exception of Algeria.

Dictatorial Modernity and Genuine Modernity

Arab regimes have claimed to represent modernity throughout the post-colonial era. In reality, this claim was an illusion. From the West, Arab states borrowed elements of modern politics and government such as parliamentary government and electoral processes. They also imported western security apparatuses, including secret police and national armies, carefully omitting essential elements of a democratic system such as freedom of speech, free and fair elections, and effective multi-partisanship. Some countries such as Tunisia under President Bourguiba even employed principles pertaining to gender equality and secularism to establish a modern state. Throughout this essay, secularism is defined as a political process aimed at restricting the role of religion in the public sphere. Conversely, secularization is a generic notion that describes the sociological process of religion's progressive withdrawal from the public sphere. While this definition is not satisfactory to describe such a complex process, it must be clearly distinguished from secularism, which refers to a political program.

Most Arab countries tried to marginalize or control religion. Yet secular transformation of society, which is inseparable from the concept of progress in Western societies, has not been similarly experienced in Arab countries. In Europe, secularization was a gradual process shaped and nurtured by socioeconomic and political developments and was supported by an intellectual body of ideas. But the Arab experience has been marked by a perception that secularism was first an alien ideology imposed by colonial rule and then supported domestically by local elites who came to power in the post-colonial period. Thus, the modern Arab experience with secularism developed through a state-imposed, top-down process. However, Arab autocrats used such elements of modernity as justifications so their dictatorial regimes could be excused or tolerated.

Conversely, the Arab Spring bears several aspects of genuine modernity that are often misinterpreted by Western observers. The most important aspect is the process, forcibly engaged by Arab demonstrators, of nation building, that is re-politicization of the public sphere. This point will be discussed later, but it is important to first dispel some commonly held assumptions about modernity that limit the understanding of the Arab Spring national movements. I argue that modernity does not necessarily work in tandem with secularism, moral liberalism, and permeability to Western values. Disposing of such prejudices becomes all the more important following the misleading first months of collective euphoria and optimism regarding the Spring, which at least momentarily challenged the culturalist myth of Arab imperviousness to democracy. The electoral processes that followed brought back long-held skepticism, and disappointment, from many observers regarding the ability of Arab societies to fully embark on the path to democracy. The culturalist myth seemed to persist.

Certainly revolutions take years to play out. The transition from autocratic regimes to democratic societies is a process measured in decades, not in years or months. The United States needed more than a hundred and fifty years after its own revolution to enact the Civil Rights Act of 1964 that ended segregation in public places and banned employment discrimination.

Unfortunately, melancholy and ambivalence regarding the fate of Arab democratization prevail. International apprehension regarding the democratic fate of these countries has focused on the rise to power of Islamist parties, violent episodes of social or religious tensions, attacks on demonstrating women in Egypt, and the latest political developments in Egypt's constitutional drafting process. Western media headlines praising the democratic transformations of the Arab spring were replaced by apprehension of neoauthoritarianism. Seemingly the Arab world is doomed to choose between secular dictatorship or Islamic totalitarianism.[ii]

Such disappointments, unfortunately, restrict the understanding of the societal transformations in the Arab societies by irresponsibly simplifying them to a struggle between secularists and Islamists. This narrow view touts secular political parties as the embodiment of Western values of progressivism and modernity, while the Islamists would represent the refractory element in the Arab world's democratization process. The consequence of this reasoning is to consider the electoral victories of non-secular parties in Tunisia, Morocco, and Egypt, and their likely future success in Yemen, Libya, and Syria as major setbacks rather than appreciate them as the exercise of the right to vote freely for the first time. Under the fallen regimes, we were not permitted this right.

The Victory of Generation 2011: Overtaking the Public Sphere

Modernization does not necessarily involve secularism. Most Arab autocratic regimes strived, often violently, to de-Islamize the public sphere. Secularism in several Arab countries starting from the 1950s succeeded largely because of the indisputable political legitimacy of leaders, such as Nasser in Egypt and Bourguiba in Tunisia. Yet, it was not so much secularization but was rather a political attempt on behalf of these leaders to domesticate religion. For example, in the late 1950s and part of the 1960s, leading university centers for Islamic studies such as Al-Azhar in Egypt, Zaituna in Tunisia, and Al-Qarawiyyin in Morocco became publicized and, as a result, lost their religious autonomy. In Tunisia, about a month after the country's independence from France in 1956, President Bourguiba turned Zaituna into a modern university and cut its links with the mosque. In 1961, a college of Islamic Law and theology was created and became part of the Zaituna University. In Egypt, President Nasser established Al-Azhar in 1961 as a public university, adding several non-religious colleges in the areas of science, medicine, economics, and agriculture. In Morocco, Al-Qarawiyyin became a public university by royal decree. In 1963 it was placed under the supervision of the Moroccan Ministry of Education. The secular institutionalization of these universities is significant because each provided prestigious Islamic education and had been linked to the mosque for more than 1,100 years.

These attempts to contain and domesticate Islam were necessary to build a strong central state. But following the humiliation of Egypt, Jordan, and Syria in the 1967 Six-Day War, the Arab modernizing regimes began to lose their appeal to the public. The religious sphere became progressively more appealing to people and not the state-dominated institutionalized sphere. The return of Islam to the public sphere developed into an illegitimate Islamist opposition, especially in the 1980s, marking the return of the sacred in Arab societies. From that point forward, governments no longer sought to control and marginalize the religious sphere but rather to fiercely fight it. Islamists became public enemies. As the Arab authoritarian regimes monopolized and controlled the public sphere and lost touch with the needs of society, Islamists reached out to a great share of the population and provided social assistance. Islamist opposition was not an outcome of the Arab Spring but has been present for several decades.

The Arab Spring protests were, at first, not political or instruments of political parties with an Islamic referential. The Arab Spring national movements were merely seizing the opportunity to finally topple anachronistic and repressive regimes. There were no religious slogans and the protests did not follow any religious practice.[iii] The first large demonstrations occurred on Fridays after afternoon prayer and were initially called "day of rage," expressing deep weariness with the status quo. There were no population-wide intentions to replace it by a theocracy. Consider the immolation of the young Tunisian street vendor in December 2010. The practice is formally prohibited in Islam, since suicide is haraam, or forbidden, but the self-immolation of Mohamed Bouazizi was an expression of the impossibility to articulate any political opinion in the public sphere.

The 2011 Arab national movements did not politicize religious discourse with sermons in mosques. Instead we witnessed the re-politicization of a population that desired dignity and aspired to be treated as citizens. To achieve these goals, populations took over the public sphere. Additionally, the conquest of this new space was implemented with virtual spaces, heavily using networks, which completely circumvented control of the central state and the mosques. This political conquest shows the genius of the Arab Spring generation or what can be labeled as Generation 2011. This generation managed to achieve what previous generations could not, and did it without creating new parties and without guaranteed freedom of expression.

One important objection to Generation 2011 is a view that it is deeply conservative and neither ready nor willing to engage in a modernizing process of reforming Islam. Such objection is seen in episodes of intense and sometimes violent Arab demonstrations against criticism of or assaults on Islam. This sensitivity of Arab societies regarding Islam creates consternation in the West. As I argue in the next section, this sensitivity is not rooted in a lack of religious maturity or secularization, neither of which were the prime objective of the Arab Spring. Rather, state-building deficiencies are the main culprit. The problem is not religious, but strictly political.

The Next Victory: Beyond Religious Nationalism

The conquest of the public sphere leads to the emergence of the citizen. Not surprisingly, early on, demonstrators called for dignity, human rights, elections, and good governance. Such demands demonstrate the primary concern for citizenship, which had to be earned by challenging the political status quo. Although citizenship should be a given in a defined, sovereign nation, the Arab Spring uprisings exposed a previously unnoticed fact: In many Arab countries, "citizens" do not entrust their identity and honor to the state and its symbols. Rather, the emotions and conscience of Arab populations view the state as changeable, corrupt, and unconcerned with the interests of its people. A population must draw its pride from somewhere else, and the remaining sources to feed one's national ego are affiliations with extra-national entities such as the Arab community and/or Muslim Umma (the community of Muslims) in Arab societies. For decades Arab populations have gained self-esteem in larger, holistic entities[iv] such as pan-Arabism and pan-Islamism.

This is evident when regarding reactions to critiques against Islam in many Arab countries. Consider the recent controversy triggered by the video "Innocence of Islam," which portrayed the Prophet Muhammad in an extremely derogatory manner. The deadly attack on the U.S. Embassy in Benghazi, where U.S. Ambassador John C. Stevens and three U.S. nationals were killed, was allegedly a revenge attack that occurred during the confusion created by the demonstrations against the film. It was, therefore, a terrorist reprisal attack to avenge the killing of high-ranking Al-Qaeda leader Abu-Yahya Al-Libi,[v] and not the deed of angry demonstrators.

Violence against religious minorities continues to occur in some Arab countries. This type of violence is embedded in the cultural, linguistic, religious, and ethnic dynamics of a country, and is not limited to the Arab world. Nevertheless, in the case of "Innocence of Islam," demonstrators who took to the streets in several Arab cities as a reaction to the video did not march in front of churches or synagogues. They did not burn Bibles or lynch priests and rabbis. Instead, protesters marched in front of embassies, mostly American ones, and burned flags. The film insulted a faith and source of hostilities appeared to be religious, but the demonstrations were directed at symbols of American sovereignty. In other words, the riots were not theological.

Angry mobs can easily become irrational but their choice of symbols of American sovereignty as a target is not a casual decision. In general, protesters retaliate against what they perceive being the equivalent of what has been attacked. In a very morbid sense of symmetrical logic, the murder of a high representative of the U.S. State Department by Al-Qaeda's elements would be, in the eyes of that terrorist group, a retribution for the killing of an Al-Qaeda high-ranking official.

Such simple symmetry does not apply to the embassy protests and flag burnings in reaction to an assault on Islam. The Muslim Prophet is, in the collective unconscious of Arabs, the flag of Muslims. Interestingly in Libya rebels promptly waved the Libyan flag that was used prior to Qadhafi's 1969 coup d'état. If the film had been directed at the symbol of an Arab state, perhaps a national army, it would most likely have triggered no reaction. On the other hand, one who threatens to burn the Qur'an will likely trigger demonstrations.

This religious nationalism is not an error in judgment by the demonstrators. It is the consequence of Arab states' failure to constitute liberal nationalism and enable citizenship. By the end of the 20th century most Arab states were developmental failures. Rising poverty, increasing inequality, corruption, and the absence of a public sphere to voice the population's needs and concerns led delegitimized autocratic modernizing states. In such societies, there is no relationship of trust between the state and the population. Therefore, the state cannot be the recipient of national pride and honor. As long as Arab states do not protect the rights of the citizens, Islam will remain a national flag of many demographic and opposition groups. The Arab world needs nation-building, not an Islamic revolution or what is often portrayed in Western media as misplaced over-sensitivity to an American filmmaker's decision to ridicule the Prophet or to a Danish newspaper's publication of caricatures of the Prophet. Secularization, along with any reform of Islam, may happen progressively in tandem with political and socioeconomic developments that involve all actors of civil society, as in the case of Western Europe. The purpose of the Arab Spring is to encourage nations to defend their public goods, national interests, territory, and population. The Spring is about creating a nation and government that grants all of its citizens equal rights, regardless of how secular or morally liberal that society is.

The actors of the Arab Spring are the young men and women of Generation 2011 and the Islamist parties that benefited from it.

Who is Generation 2011?

The characteristics of Generation 2011 make it unequivocally modern compared with its predecessor. This generation is not a barometer of conservatism, progressivism, or any openness to Western values. Rather, the modernity of the Arab Spring generation must be understood as a departure from the previous generation and the bearer of a new worldview. Generation 2011 is part of the greater Millennial Generation, but its geographic location and shared history, especially during the Arab Spring, makes this group unique even among its global peers.

Generation 2011 differs from its parents first in terms of demography. Fertility has dramatically declined across the Arab societies. Since 1950, the Middle East and North Africa (MENA) population has more than quadrupled from 104 million people to 432 million in 2007.[vi] This demographic shift was caused by declining mortality and birth rates, which did not start to drop until the mid-1960s, from seven children in 1960 to an average of three in 2006.[vii] Today, some Arab countries exhibit birth rates comparable or lower than those in OECD countries (Organisation for Economic Cooperation and Development, composed of the major industrialized countries). In 2011 Tunisia had, for instance, one of the lowest fertility rates in North Africa with about 2.02 children per woman, lower than France (2.08) and the United States (2.06). Morocco and Libya were at 2.19 and 2.12 births per woman. Egypt is right below three children per woman (2.94). In the United Arab Emirates, Bahrain, and Qatar, the rates are all below two.[viii]

Another element characterizing Generation 2011 is the rapidly increasing literacy rate across the Arab world. There has been great literacy improvement across the MENA region. In 1980, literacy rates for people aged 15 to 24 (who are now aged 48 to 57) ranged between 30 percent and 60 percent , while the rate in seven other countries was as high as 70 percent to 80 percent. In 1980, only Lebanon, Jordan and Bahrain had a rate higher than 80 percent.[ix]

There is a much different picture concerning literacy rates in the region 30 years later: on average, youth literacy in the Arab world rate is over 80 percent.[x] The improvement is even more impressive when looking at young female literacy rates. In 1980, female literacy rate for the age group 15 to 24 in the Arab world was at 55 percent. Thirty years later, that rate is at 83.6 percent.[xi] More remarkable is the female enrollment in tertiary education (university level). In 2011, the ratio of female to male tertiary enrollment in Arab countries was 1.015. This is a slight advantage for women, which does not take into account greater gaps in several Arab countries. In 2009 in Tunisia, that ratio was at 1.51, meaning that there are more than 150 women for every 100 men enrolled in university. Even Saudi Arabia exhibits a ratio that is above average in the Arab world.

Taken together, this is a situation where young Arabs, male and female, receive, on average, more schooling than their parents did; they will also have fewer children. Renowned French demographer Emmanuel Todd added that the dropping rate of endogamy (first-cousin marriage) in the Arab world, combined with increasing literacy and decreasing fertility rates are the key demographic factors behind the

Arab Spring.[xii] According to Todd, such factors radically changed the authority relationships between men and women, as well as between young people and their parents. The Arab individual, or the precursor of the Arab citizen, began to appear with this generation. This individual is young, urban, has more years of schooling, marries later and outside the family group with smaller age difference with his or her partner, and will have fewer children than his or her parents did. The Arab youth feels less strongly bound to the family group and the patriarchal customs that have dominated traditional family relationships.

Those structural changes within the family circle condition the worldview of the current Arab generation. When looking at some of the first slogans used in Arab Spring, there was no reference to pan-Arabism or pan-Islamism, the usual holistic ideologies that were claimed by former generations. Further, it is not surprising that no single charismatic leader emerged from the Arab Spring with whom protesters can identify, although the West tried to put a face or spokesperson on the Arab revolutions and uprisings. Messrs Morsi, Ghannouchi, and Marzouki will not replace Nasser, Bourguiba, or Qadhafi, all providential men. The Arab Spring is a revolt against patriarchy, in the private family sphere and the public government sphere with the toppling of autocratic regimes. Although it is far too early to determine whether Arab societies will embark further on the path toward democracy, Generation 2011 seems very aware of an essential truth about democracy: power is incarnate in a function, not a person, and hence, remains faceless. This aspect of the Arab Spring might be a first sign of a major anthropological transformation of Arab societies.

Yet, one paradox remains. The youth who represent the majority of the Arab population and played the leading role in the Arab Spring did not gain access to power as a result of the uprisings, whereas the Islamist parties, who had little to do with the revolutions and uprisings, benefited from them. Another legitimate question is why the massive involvement of young women in demonstrations across Arab countries only resulted in a marginal increase in their political representation in some countries.

It seems that the widely accepted prominent role of women as activists remains independent from their presence in parliaments, governments, and other institutional bodies.

Why Did Islamist Parties Win Elections?

As I argued earlier, the Arab Spring enabled the conquest of the public sphere and the re-politicization of the Arab citizen, which occurred outside the influence of any holistic ideology or religion. However, Islamic nationalism remains strong; it can be seen in the controversies triggered by episodes such as the cartoons of the Prophet Muhammad or the movie "Innocence of Islam." In this regard, it is important to bear in mind that Islamist nationalism is a political attitude that is primarily directed at the West's perceived assault against Islam rather than a movement to counter Arab secularists. The question remains: Why did Islamist parties win elections in Tunisia, Egypt and Morocco?

For the past three decades, Islamist movements have been active actors of dissent and their militants have often experienced incarceration, torture, and exile, despite periods of relative tolerance towards them. Islamists managed to set a wide coverage of national territories, both in urban and rural areas. Their proximity to society and their concern for people's daily problems positioned them to compensate for the absence or lack of state support. Islamist parties became more visible and acquired some sense of popular gratitude, which reinforced a self-maintained image of honesty that contrasted with the governments' and mainstream political parties' reputation of being deeply corrupt. Finally, Islamist parties have often exhibited strong internal discipline and democratic processes of electing party officials when secular opposition parties were fragmented.

Islamist parties across the Arab countries are diverse, but one important aspect is commonly shared by the Justice and Development Party (PJD) in Morocco, Ennahda in Tunisia, and the Freedom and Justice Party (affiliated with the Muslim Brotherhood) in Egypt. Before the elections that brought them to power, they were all forces of opposition. But in countries where the political system was locked and often dominated by a single party, and where civil societies were either closely controlled or repressed, Islamist parties represented the most credible alternative.

In spite of their appeal, Islamist parties are far from having full control of the political arena, even in Egypt where their success was greatest in elections. Indeed, these parties face many constraints. People today will not hesitate to take to the streets if they are unhappy with a government. This legacy of the Arab Spring, the strength of public opinion, holds true for countries where the regime has been toppled. This also goes for those, such as Syria, where the end of the status quo is near.

The controversy following Egyptian President Morsi's Revolution Protection Law and the referendum for the Constitution is strong evidence of the difficulty finding a balance between the demands of the Islamist party's constituents and the concerns of those who did not vote in its favor. The recently adopted Egyptian constitution is a good example of the attempt of trying to strike such a delicate balance: it never goes far enough for the Salafist camp as the State will not play the role of arbiter of conservative Islamic values, nor does it venture too far on the liberals' side as the principles of Shari'ah are the main source of legislation. In spite of this compromise, cross-sectional demonstrations greatly undermined the Freedom and Justice Party and the Muslim Brotherhood.

The second constraint for the ruling Islamist parties is their lack of total control over the religious sphere. In Egypt, the Muslim Brotherhood shares power with the Salafis of the Al-Nour party (the Party of the Light) as they came second in the 2011-2012 legislative elections. To keep the Salafis as political allies, President Morsi must at the very least pretend to pursue an Islamization of society. The Egyptian constitutional articles on the principles of Shari'ah as the main source of legislation (Article 4) or the proclaimed duty of the state to preserve "the genuine nature of the Egyptian family and its moral values" (Article 10) are vague but sufficient guarantees for the Salafist party. On the other hand, if the Muslim Brotherhood attempts to exert too much control over the religious sphere, it will likely irritate imams of Al-Azhar University, which has been granted some level of autonomy after the Arab Spring. Indeed, if religion is identified with the state, the unpopularity of the current government could undermine religious institutions, which will either accelerate the secularization of the society or lead to a greater popular appeal of less mainstream religious affiliations such as Salafism.

The third constraint is closely related to the previous one. Islamist parties tend to have a very liberal economic stance. President Morsi's party clearly favors free markets, competition, and deregulation. It is very likely that economic price, as a result of these liberal policies, will be paid by a large share of the population. This will weaken the President and his party.

All these constraints are evidence that President Morsi and the other ruling Islamist parties are merely involved in the game of politics. Indeed, as the Muslim Brotherhood transitioned from an opposition party to a ruling party, it had to accept the autonomy of the political field. The situation is similarly constraining for other Islamist parties in power. For instance in Tunisia, the Ennahda Movement (Renaissance Movement) is facing opposition from the imams against bringing faith institutions under the authority of the state, as well as from strong trade unions who are able to rally large parts of the population to protest against unpopular economic measures. In Morocco, the PJD (ruling Justice and Development Party) has, de facto, no control over religious affairs. Religion is under the full authority of the monarchy.

By becoming political forces, Islamist parties have become reluctant actors of the democratization process. These parties are also part of the Arab Spring path to modernity: they must join the political game and accept the autonomy of the religious arena as free from political or ideological control. Yet this development does not herald the advent of a secular society.

A genuine path of Arab modernization could be that religion becomes part of the political game instead of dictating what politics should be. By remaining not institutionalized (except in Morocco), the religious field encompasses enough diversity to be part of the political arena. Instead of social secularization, there could be a political secularization and, hence, debate over and reform of Islam.

Certainly, adopted constitutions emphasize Muslim identity of the state and society but it is commonly agreed that Shari'ah can only be a source of legislation and reference point rather than the law itself. The politicization of the public sphere and the subjection of religion to politics will probably not prevent society from being conservative, but could possibly give more strength to the notion of individual faith.

The Next Big Test

Moving forward, discussion about the "Arab street" should cease. Emphasis should instead be placed on "Arab opinions," for these are as diversified as the national interests that define each Arab country and society. This may be the greatest achievement of Generation 2011: voicing its interests in the public sphere and expecting newly elected leaders to stand for them and defend them locally and on the international stage. This may also be the greatest challenge ahead. Organizing free and fair democratic elections is a simple task compared to creating a genuine and inclusive political community that represents the general will. On one hand, this requires a political system that is widely accepted by the people. On the other hand, such a political system must be composed of effective and well-organized bureaucracies, institutions, and political parties. There must also be widespread participation in public affairs.

The situation faced by Egyptian President Morsi, is an example of a struggling nation lacking the essential elements of nation building, or the "degree of government."[xiii] Morsi's problem is not legitimacy, as he is Egypt's first democratically elected president. It is his ability to lead that does not inspire confidence by a large part of the Egyptian people. His ability to bring economic and social change is simply not trusted; this is not to mention the degree of corruption that exists at all levels of the Egyptian political system. Legitimacy is easy to obtain. Credibility takes longer to build. Unfortunately, a lack of credibility may oblige a leader who wants to remain in power to take actions that may undermine legitimacy. This is the next big test of Egypt's nascent democracy. It is also a concern of other Arab countries struggling in the wake of their own revolutions.

Yet, cautious optimism regarding the future of the Arab national movements is important. Generation 2011 men and women, educated and less educated, jobless or employed, have all shown great determination in assuming their new roles in the public sphere. Their rallying is spontaneous, civic, peaceful, and above partisan ideologies. It is also leaderless. The pride of Generation 2011 and its newfound dignity will be great assets in its struggles to overcome the numerous roadblocks and uncertainties on the path to building a modern political community proper to each Arab country.

---

[i] Michel Foucault. "Qu'est-ce que les Lumières." *Magazine Littéraire*. May 1984.

[ii] Olivier Roy. "The Transformation of the Arab World." *Journal of Democracy*, July 2012, Vol. 23, Number 3.

[iii] Ibid.

[iv] Ibid.

[v] CNN, "Pro-al Qaeda."

[vi] UN Department of Economic and Social Affairs. "World Population Prospects: The 2006 Revision." Accessed January 15, 2013. *http://www.un.org/esa/population/publications/wpp2006/wpp2006.htm*.

[vii] Roudi-Fahimi and Mary Mederios Kent. "Challenges and Opportunities: Population of Middle East and North Africa," *Population Bulletin*, Vol. 62, No. 2, June 2007.

[viii] CIA Factbook. "Country Comparison: Birth Rate." Accessed January 15, 2013 *https://www.cia.gov/library/publications/the-world-factbook/rankorder/2054rank.html*.

[ix] Hassan R. Hammoud, "Illiteracy in the Arab World." *Literacy for Life*. 2006. UNESCO. *http://unesdoc.unesco.org/images/0014/001462/146282e.pdf*.

[x] UNESCO. "Fact Sheet Adult and youth literacy." September 2012. Accessed January 15, 2013. *http://www.uis.unesco.org/literacy/Documents/fs20-literacy-day-2012-en-v3.pdf*.

xi World Bank. "Literacy rate, youth female ages 15-24." Accessed January 15, 2013. *http://data.worldbank.org/indicator/SE.ADT.1524.LT.FE.ZS/countries/ZQ-1W-1A?display=graph.*

xii Emmanuel Todd. "Allah n'y est pour rien!: Sur les revolutions arabes et quelques autres" (Allah had nothing to do with it!: on Arab revolutions and other ones). *Le Publieur.* June 2011.

xiii Samuel Huntington. *Political Order in Changing Societies.* Yale University Press, 1968.

Pushing Past the Talk: Evaluating the Strengths of Youth as Potential Problem Solvers

Andrew Leon Hanna

There is no greater beauty to me than the unity on display when youth from all over the world come together to discuss common challenges and potential solutions. Despite thousands of miles of separation and different cultures, we are able to come together in one space, whether physically or virtually, in deep respect of one another's dignity and various backgrounds. I have personally had the honor of experiencing this electrifying energy at international conferences and meetings, and in each case was astounded to remind myself that this type of unity is actually very new in the larger context of global history and geopolitics. The Millennial Generation's interconnectivity and ability to see beyond the divisions of our parents, our enthusiasm for social change, and our innovative minds are unprecedented. Moreover, I believe that these generational traits are severely underutilized in a world where too many people remain uneducated, unemployed, hungry, and unsupported.

Oftentimes, talk of youth empowerment and the energy of young people is merely talk. Political leaders and global decision-makers use rhetoric to reach the youth vote or to check off a box of constituencies mentioned in speeches. Currently, there is a growing body of research and ongoing discussions regarding youth empowerment to ensure that youth have a say in decisions that affect them. There is so much talk that, at some point, we really start to become desensitized.

That desensitization, though, is far from an optimum scenario in today's world of complex and interconnected global challenges. Today, over half of the world's population is comprised of youth: that is over 3.5 billion people under the age of 30.[i] Sadly, the International Labour Organization estimates that, globally, 75 million youth are unemployed.[ii] This number would be three times as high if underemployed youth were also counted.[iii] It appears, too, that the larger trend is not a positive one.[iv] We as a society need to ensure that we prepare and empower our young leaders, partnering with them to utilize the Millennials' ingenuity to solve the globe's largest challenges. In beginning to understand how to go about this, we must truly take stock and focus on what I find to be the three major and unique assets that our Millennial Generation brings to the table: interconnectivity, innovation, and energy towards social change.

Unprecedented Interconnectivity and Unity

Today's global youth are interconnected in a way that our predecessors could have never dreamt. With live television, fingertip emailing, rapid social networking, and always decreasing barriers to international travel, there has never been a time like this for youth from all over the world to share ideas with one another and with world leaders. Millennials take this interconnectivity as a given reality of life: it is hard for many of us to believe that a Ghanaian teenager chatting with a friend thousands of miles away in China was absolutely unfathomable not so long ago. Today, that type of connection is considered normal.

This interconnectivity means that state and global leaders have a far greater ability to reach out to youth and, crucially, to gather their ideas and perspectives. New methods of doing this are becoming more effective, from a Google Hangout featuring American vice president Joe Biden discussing gun control policy, to Twitter discussions with policymakers, to the United Nation's new "MYWorld" survey that allows people all over the globe to comment on determining priorities for the post-2015 development goals. Additional work must be done to increase the scope of these projects and we must do more to reach those who are most marginalized, but every step is a step in the right direction. We must ensure that national and global agenda-setters take seriously the feedback gained from these young people's responses. As we will see later, this is in everyone's best interest.

As time passes, greater interconnectivity is matched by a more inclusive generation of young people. The struggles of past generations within and between nations are often not as prevalent among youth as they were among their parents. In the United States and South Africa, two nations recovering from bitter segregation across racial lines, there has been tangible progress towards reconciliation. New conversations not possible a decade ago are taken for granted today. In so many places, Millennials are moving further and further away from the discrimination and divisions of the past. Youth peace-building initiatives, such as Liberian Volunteers for Peace, Seeds of Peace, and the PeaceCorps, exemplify the potential of young people to successfully undertake the critical challenge of creating peace in communities and states. Indeed, the success rate in achieving the Millennium Development Goals in conflict areas is astonishingly lower than in areas not hindered by conflict.[v] There must be unity and healing before social problems can be addressed, and the youth of today are most equipped to be given the reins to lead this healing process.

A Striking Passion for Social Change

There is a capability to unite and connect, but is there a desire to leverage this for real social progress? In short: yes. The Millennial Generation is not short on passion and energy. Like never before, youth around the world are connecting in person and through social media to initiate countercultural changes focused on tackling major issues like unemployment, poverty, lack of quality education, and conflict. Additionally, more and more young people around the world are coming together to show their passion through direct service, frequently stepping up to come to the aid of the people most in need in their communities.

Indications of the Millennial Generation's itch to change the world are clear. There is ample evidence of recent social justice movements ramping up across the globe. 2011 alone saw countless protests for social change in nations around the world. This included 100,000 Chilean students taking control of 300 schools in a call for a revamped education system, Greek youth coming together in Syntagma Square to protest the new austerity package in light of the government bailout, Angolan youth protesting a lack of freedom from autocratic rule, Israeli youth tenting in protest of what they consider the lack of a sufficient welfare state, and much more.[vi] The energy and organizing ability of youth largely channeled the Arab Spring movements across the Middle East, as young people took to Twitter and Facebook to plan live demonstrations that led to the toppling of regimes that were once thought to be permanent mainstays. The Arab world has a shockingly high average youth unemployment rate of close to 30 percent.[vii] This was and is undoubtedly a driving force of the Middle East's fervent reawakening.

Millennials are also setting an unprecedented standard for social involvement through community service. In the United States, today's youth have been consistently lauded for their involvement in service. Statistics in 2005 showed a new height in volunteering levels among youth in the U.S., as 15.5 million teens participated in volunteering efforts to contribute more than 1.3 billion hours of total service to communities across the states. This 55 percent rate among Millennial teens was more than one and half times the 29 percent rate of adult volunteering.[viii]

The response to Hurricane Katrina in New Orleans and the 2010 earthquake in Haiti was outstanding as youth from around the nation flocked to these disaster areas in droves to help support those in immediate need of help. As far back as 1995, the Japanese government was caught off guard by the overwhelming response of youth to assist in the recovery after the Kobe earthquake.[ix] This pattern of young people reaching out to those in need through direct service has been growing and only underscores the generation's passion for civic engagement and tackling social issues.

A Track Record of Innovative Ideas That Work

Our interconnectivity and passion lay the groundwork for the world's youth to be problem-solvers in both local and global communities. The final component that is necessary for youth to be key players in solving community and global challenges is a generation-wide ability to create and execute innovative ideas to tackle these challenges. The Millennial Generation has proven over and over that it has the ingenuity and capability of generating new and original ideas that fit the needs of its communities, and we have also shown the ability to carry them out in cost-effective and efficient ways.

First, a successful and sustainable, socially-focused initiative requires a deep understanding of a problem at hand and of the specific community hosting that issue. Young people may not have decades of experience or advanced education, but we most certainly can tell you what is working in our communities and what could potentially work. This knowledge is critical when designing initiatives to make a long-term, positive impact. We cannot afford to ignore the excellent and innovative ideas that young people have gained from their experiences growing up in their communities.

There are many examples of these successful ideas. We have frequently seen youth innovate to make an impact in unprecedented ways and with few resources. Organizations like Restless Development and Global Changemakers serve as hubs for youth all over the globe who are running community impact initiatives and are creatively addressing large-scale issues. The Youth Empowerment Programme in India, for example, utilizes peer educators to provide life-changing education to over 36,000 young people a year; this same youth-led project is making similar impacts in Nepal, Zimbabwe, and South Africa as well.[x] This example specifically highlights the impact of peer education and mentoring; adolescents place a higher weight on the actions and influences of peers than on any other group of people.[xi] Thus, youth have potentially the greatest ability to impact the lives of other youth; this is but one specific area in which youth must be engaged to create progress.

Other examples of youth taking action successfully can be found through a snapshot of Global Changemakers, which is a network of 750 members from 121 countries. Community Action Projects that these young people have created, using only a relatively small amount of grant money, have reached over 4 million people in more than 70 countries. These life and community-changing initiatives include projects such as HIV/AIDS education programs around the world, an initiative that brings sustainable energy to remote areas of Sri Lanka, an online tool for fighting corruption in schools in the Philippines, education programs for marginalized girls in Jordan, a music school for kids in Haiti, a youth entrepreneurship program in Brazil, and so much more.[xii] Everywhere we look, youth are utilizing their intimate understanding of their communities and their creative ideas to successfully change people's lives in sustainable ways.

Moving Forward with Youth at the Forefront: Investing in Real, World-Changing Solutions

The Millennial Generation brings the qualities of interconnectivity/unity, passion, and innovation to the table in a way that no other group can. These are qualities that are crucial to a global society attempting to tackle deep and pervasive social issues. In a world in which widespread unemployment persists as the global labor force rises towards a projected 3.5 billion people by 2030, we must critically consider the capabilities of youth and invest in them properly so they can lead our world effectively now and in the future[xiii]. Instead of being a burden on society or a marginalized stakeholder group, youth must be seen as an asset towards solving the world's greatest challenges;

governments and organizations must allocate resources and attention accordingly.

The Millennial Generation has shown truly striking unity, passion, and innovation. We have risen to the challenge time and time again, and I believe that we will continue to rise. It is time that we, as a national and global society, entrust responsibility to and empower youth as partners in solving community and global challenges. Indeed, the Millennial Generation is our hope for the future and for today.

---

[i] EuroMonitor International, "Special Report: The World's Youngest Populations." 2012. Accessed January 15, 2013. *http://blog.euromonitor.com/2012/02/special-report-the-worlds-youngest-populations-.html*.

[ii] International Labour Organization. "Global Employment Trends for Youth 2012." 2012. Accessed January 15, 2013. *http://www.ilo.org/wcmsp5/groups/public/---dgreports/---dcomm/documents/publication/wcms_180976.pdf.*

[iii] McKinsey Global Institute. "Education to Employment: Designing a System that Works." 2012. Accessed January 15. 2013. *http://mckinseyonsociety.com/downloads/reports/Education/Education-to-Employment_FINAL.pdf*; McKinsey Global Institute. "The world at work: Jobs, pay, and skills for 3.5 billion people." 2012. Accessed January 15, 2013. *http://www.mckinsey.com/insights/mgi/research/labor_markets/the_world_at_work.*

[iv] ILO, 2012.

[v] United Nations. "The Millennium Development Goals Report 2011." Last modified 2011. Accessed January 15, 2013. *http://www.un.org/millenniumgoals/11_MDG Report_EN.pdf.*

[vi] Jack Shenker. "How youth-led revolts shook elites around the world." *The Guardian*. 2011. Accessed January 15, 2013. *http://www.guardian.co.uk/world/2011/aug/12/youth-led-revolts-shook-world.*

[vii] ILO, 2012.

[viii] Corporation for National and Community Service. "Youth Helping America: Building Active Citizens: The Role of Social Institutions in Teen Volunteering." 2005.

[ix] James Youniss, Susan Bales, et al. "Youth Civic Engagement in the Twenty-First Century." *Journal of Research on Adolescence*. 2002. pp. 121-147.

[x] Restless Development. "Restless Development." Last modified 2013. Accessed January 15, 2013. *http://www.restlessdevelopment.org/where-we-are.*

[xi] B. Simons-Morton and R. Peer Chen, "Parent Influences on School Engagement Among Early Adolescents." *Youth & Society*, 41. 2009. pp. 3-25.

xii Global Changemakers. "British Council Global Changemakers Annual Report 2011-2012." 2012. Accessed January 15, 2013. *http://www.global-changemakers.net/wp-content/uploads/2011/04/Global-Changemakers-Annual-Report-2011.pdf.*
xiii McKinsey Global Institute, 2012. "The world at work."

The Young, the Educated, and the Restless

Makda Getachew

…It is good to be young. You may not have money but you have good health. Even if you are not endowed with great looks, you are intelligent. In case you have not acquired any substantial knowledge, you would have confidence. There might be no love in your life, but your hope will keep you going. If your life lacks happiness, at least you have your burning rage. If you can't take enough of the oppression, you will think of a revolution. If you struggle to stay alive or if you are tired of living, you will commit suicide. Even if no one knows you, you will have a history. Because you are young…

– Sibhat Gebreegzhiabher, Ethiopian writer,
translated from his book *Tikusat*

The late Sibhat's description of the wonders of being young in Ethiopia is moving. His description suggests the countless alternatives available to a young person and points to the joy of being young, despite all of the challenges. I wonder to myself how many youth in Ethiopia and elsewhere in the region will share Sibhat's observation. Are we young people living a fulfilled and meaningful life? Are we, the largest cohort of the population, contributing to positive developments? Are we utilizing our energies, creativities, and skills? I hope to address these questions, among others, in this essay.

In Ethiopia, as elsewhere across Africa and as noted in this book's introduction, the youth population has been growing at a high rate. Young Ethiopians face several challenges to fulfilling their aspirations and dreams to lead decent lives and contribute positively to their communities. However, it is unwise to treat the youth population of the country as a homogenous group; one must remain cognizant of the gender, geographical, social, and economic differences that exist among youth populations in Ethiopia and across the rest of the world. I believe that the most pressing youth development problem is a lack of opportunity to acquire decent jobs. Young Ethiopians who are tired of being paid lip service that they are tomorrow's leaders will tell you that being young is not very easy; youthfulness is far from the romanticized description of Sibhat. They would rather become something today than live on the promise of tomorrow.

Initially, when outlining this essay, I did not consider focusing specifically on Ethiopia. But, I thought it was best to write about concrete issues that really matter to me. Alternatively I decided to discuss problems I encounter rather than write a general and theoretical analysis regarding youth employment problem in Africa, which is an enormous continent and very difficult to generalize. However, I believe the situation in Ethiopia provides a good reflection of the general situation in the region. Here, I will broadly discuss youth unemployment in Ethiopia.

Development interventions often focus on those groups defined with a textbook interpretation of 'vulnerable:' youth lacking basic education; youth who live in remote areas without access to social services; young people who have lost their parents to HIV/AIDS and who have had to leave their schooling to support their siblings; and young girls who face challenges of harmful cultural practices. Indeed, these are all vulnerable young people. Effort should be made to ensure that they do not fall through the cracks and that they are supported. But there are others.

Millennials Speak.

Among youth affected by the issues above, we tend to omit another group of young people when discussing disaffected and vulnerable youth populations: educated Ethiopian youth.[i]

Educated but Jobless, Educated but Deprived

The number of young Ethiopians graduating from higher level (tertiary) public and private education institutions every year is growing. In 2011-2012, the annual growth rate of tertiary education graduates was 13.4 percent.[ii] In the past 10 years alone, the number of public universities in Ethiopia has increased from a little more than 10 to 31. The number is still rising. The private sector has emerged as a player in the growth of higher education following the 1994 nationwide Education and Training Policy, which sought to create a universal and inclusive Ethiopian primary education system. This development has also contributed to the increase in university graduates.[iii] The number of young people receiving higher education as a percentage of the national youth population might still be very low if not for this 1994 initiative. There is no denying that access to higher education has never been better in Ethiopia. This is good news!

Academic development theories attest that a country's human resources are as important as its financial, natural, and infrastructural resources. Thousands of young people enter higher education institutes all over the country with hopes and dreams for a better life, for themselves and for their families. Yet life is not a bed of roses for a majority of these college graduates. Many struggle to find jobs within their field or area of study after graduation. For some, securing a job that is remotely close to their field of study is a luxury. The majority of the lucky minority who have actually found jobs, usually after considerable wait, are employed with a salary that barely supports their basic monthly cost of living, let alone improves their families' lives.

As a result, it is very common for many young workers to continue living with their parents and rely on handouts from friends and families to make it month-to-month. They lose hope as they witness the cost of living increase as their salaries stagnate or increase at a snail's pace. For our parents' generation, a university education really made a difference in one's quality of life. A university graduate could easily afford better clothes, better accommodation, and better food. Across the board, university graduates could expect to live a better life. This is no longer the case. The returns of higher education in terms of quality of life are far from satisfying; they have diminished.

According to the Central Statistics Agency 2011 urban employment survey, the average urban youth (15-29) unemployment rate in Ethiopia is estimated at 30.3 percent for females and 16.5 percent for males, a 23.7 percent average. The unemployment rate for this 15-29 age group is much higher than for other groups in the country. A decent life with a nice house, a nice car, and some savings in the bank is becoming a distant and unrealistic dream for many college graduates.

Why are the Educated Unemployed or Underemployed?

I, like many others in Ethiopia, grew up being told that if I studied hard and went to class regularly and graduated on time, I could expect to live a comfortable, economically-secure life. One can only imagine the disappointment young people face when these promises turn out to be false. The school-to-work transition for many is difficult. In this section, I discuss some of the factors behind the transition that many young Ethiopians face.

Too Many of Us, Too Few Jobs

The first obvious issue is the enormous youth population in Ethiopia. Africa is the youngest continent in the world, with more than 20 percent of its population within the 15-24 age bracket. This number is certain to grow. Ethiopia's youth population is estimated at 23 million.[iv] For a country of around 84 million people, youth make up a large proportion of our population. There are not adequate jobs to accommodate the millions of young Ethiopians entering the job market every year. In Ethiopia, the public sector continues to be the largest employer, while the national private sector is still its infancy. Much of the private sector is comprised of small-sized firms that mostly employ family members. Large manufacturing industries and service providers are now starting to expand, but not at a rate that would allow the private sector to absorb the country's enormous human capital.

Among the bottlenecks to rapid private sector development in the country are pervasive ethnic and patronage politics. Availability of resources and ease of doing business is more favorable for some than others, so the business environment is not a level playing field. While middle-sized enterprises have great potential to create diversified types of jobs, the reality is that these middle-sized firms or enterprises do not receive the support they need to expand and thrive. Instead, they remain on the economic margins while large enterprises benefit from tax breaks and subsidies.

Micro-enterprises receive microfinance support, and in many cases, free factors of production such as land. Large businesses cluster to pool their strength and resources to negotiate with the government for favorable support of issues that protect their operations. Middle-sized enterprises are often regarded as too small to be worthy of policy considerations although they have potential to absorb many young job-seekers. Creating an ideal business environment for middle-sized enterprises to grow to large businesses is important in Ethiopia as it increases the country's foreign direct investment (FDI), foreign exchange, and tax revenue, as well as creating jobs for many young people.

For most social science, natural science, and engineering graduates, the best employment prospects are foreign development organizations operating in the country. As a young person employed by an international development organization in my country, I am grateful for these organizations, but the situation scares me. Logically, these organizations are supposed to drive themselves out of business. As the country continues its development, partly as a result of these organizations' work, the need for the organizations in our country decreases. However, if national employment, at least the urban population, depends on the international public sector, international civil society, and philanthropy sector for employment, one cannot help but ask what employment prospects will look like in the future.

Not What You Know but Who You Know?

Although we cannot claim that everyone who secures a job did so because he or she knew someone who knows someone, it is not an exaggeration that personal relations play a great factor in how quickly and how easily young people secure jobs in this part of the world. Networking is a professionally accepted approach to securing a job, but when personal relationships outweigh qualifications and competence, there is a problem. This implies that those without relatives in institutions where they would like to work, or any institutions that pay a decent salary, will be left on the margins, unemployed. This is nepotism. This public/secret membership in the ruling political party is part of the hidden criteria for joining the civil service. Civil servants should not be made political instruments. This undermines the universal equality of democratic government and the impartiality of our university system. The extent to which politics is intertwined in our education system is alarming. When freshly recruited university lecturers are sent to two weeks of mandatory workshops on implementing government policy, one questions their roles and the impartiality of our education system.

Are the Educated Youth Choosy?

Most analyses and public statements attempting to identify the root causes of educated youth unemployment conclude by highlighting youth's negative perception of manual labor. For example, in Ethiopia, which is currently experiencing an infrastructure development and construction boom, there has been steady job growth in cobblestone manufacture and placement. Government efforts to expand the national network of roads have created numerous jobs for young people who work these cobblestone projects. The jobs pay well and can be secured with minimal training. It is commendable when development efforts utilize labor-intensive technologies to create job opportunities while meeting the country's development targets. However, disappointment and shock were evident in the key note speech at a recent Addis Ababa university graduation ceremony. The Minister of Civil Service instructed the graduates not to wait around for government jobs but to go out and take what jobs were available. These include cobblestone jobs, which he described as a lucrative initiative that is highly supported and incentivized by the government.

The public is divided. While the minister's statement reflects government thinking, it created waves of disappointment among students who questioned the purpose of a three to five-year university education only to lay cobblestones. However, other students responded to the speech by saying that youth should stop looking down on manual labor and instead embrace all jobs that can support one's livelihood.

A graduate could decide to pursue this manual line of work for several reasons. First, the country's employment situation could necessitate this type of employment for graduates who lack a support system and must simply earn a living. An acquaintance of mine left an underpaying job related to his degree in psychology after a few months and instead completed three months of training in mobile phone maintenance. He shelved his psychology degree to get his hands dirty and get ahead.

We should not frown upon these individual choices. But we will remain disappointed if it is the policy and approach of the government to absorb university graduates in manual labor jobs that do not require university degrees. After all, these young people completed three to five years of university education with hopes of specializing in one academic discipline. The young man who studied sociology might have dreamed of working in community organizations dealing with domestic violence. The young lady who graduated as an urban planner may have seen herself working at one of the city administrations assisting planning of the newest residential area. Young people dream and hope: this is what we do and were told to do. And it is difficult, and also incorrect, to tell a generation to dream modestly and lower its expectations.

We are Told to Become Job Creators

The number of jobs available for the number of young people entering the job market is not proportional. As a result, many young people are expected to become job creators instead of job seekers. At every graduation ceremony, from the tertiary institutions that grant master's and Ph.D. degrees to short skills training programs, no graduation ceremony in the country is complete without the famous "Cease becoming job seekers and become job creators" mantra. It is a noble idea but is easier said than done. This rhetoric is being told to young people fresh out of a school setting that does not teach adequate entrepreneurial skills, cultivate an entrepreneurial mindset, or provide applicable and practical real-world skills. On-the-job experience is a prerequisite for a young person to create or engage in a profitable business that will employ him/her and others.

We must question if our university system is conducive for those young people who are truly interested in being entrepreneurial. Good ideas alone will not yield much in real world results without proper training. There should be a support system to help bring these ideas to life. The national finance system should be flexible, and the overall regulatory environment should encourage new businesses rather than killing it by requiring the purchase of sales registration machines. The machines, which cost 7-8 thousand *birr* (Ethiopia's currency), are purchases mandated by the Ethiopian Revenues and Customs Authority. For entrepreneurship to become the major solution for the youth employment challenge that the government currently considers it to be, the purchasing power of the general population must improve too.

The viewpoint that everyone can and should run a business is myopic. The number of microfinance institutes in the country is expanding; they provide young people who wish to open a business a good opportunity for raising start-up capital. However, there is at least some level of political influence on the disbursement of this funding. Young people who consider starting a business should think outside of the box and engage in areas that could enhance booming sectors, such as agriculture and construction.

Employers Expect "Finished Products"

Most private sector companies and public enterprises consider the hiring of young people a costly investment. These businesses are not interested in providing on-the-job training and guidance for ill-prepared employees. This practice marginalizes young people who desperately want to join the workforce and gain some useful experience. Some companies offer unpaid internships, but many young people cannot afford to engage in unpaid work. Transportation costs alone are a barrier to this method of gaining work experience.

The quality of education available, as will be discussed, is below the standard potential employers expect from a university graduate. Considering the employment situation in Ethiopia, employers must act responsibly and as stakeholders in the national economy. Instead of competing for those experienced professionals employed at another company, they should consider hiring talented young people. They should pursue young graduates without formal experience or specific skills but who could be valuable long-term assets. The social impact of one company taking a risk on one young inexperienced graduate would be negligible. Imagine if every business and business owner in Ethiopia provided mentorship, on-the-job training, or some start-up capital to at least two young people. Private companies are profit-seeking at their core, but as members of the same national society we are all responsible for addressing social problems.

Independent Thinkers or Competent Followers?

Although I did not study in Ethiopia for my higher education, my friends and relatives did (and still do), and I had the opportunity to teach at a public university. In the course of writing this article, I also tried to

46

gather insights from young people who recently graduated from higher education institutions, teachers and lecturers in colleges and universities, and people who are responsible for job recruitment. The information I gathered makes me question how much our education approach prepares young people to become solution seekers rather than followers. To what extent does a university education help young people develop independent thinking and analytical skills? And does it equip students with the basic skills expected from a graduate of a certain field?

When I first went to Europe to pursue my undergraduate degree, I had a very difficult first semester at the International University in Bremen, Germany. Although I was top of my class for four consecutive semesters in high school, my first semester in university abroad was very difficult because I was never taught critical thinking in high school. At university, the professor expected us to discuss freely in class, express our opinions, and debate with him openly. We were expected to take opposing stances and deliberate on key issues. We were asked to criticize the authors of our course readings. These tasks were difficult for me because the education I knew was very much focused on memorizing and reproducing knowledge.

My informal consultation with various people suggests that university education in Ethiopia is not very different from high school. There is very little freedom to think and argue in our universities without being grouped into a political, religious, or other interest group. Professors who fear the consequences of being pigeonholed also avoid open debates on sensitive issues. While universities are supposed be places where people may challenge even the existence of God, in Ethiopia, questioning even a minor detail on a certain policy is frowned upon. Our education institutions should instead prepare young people to creatively confront the country's pressing problems, and brainstorm, test, and prototype new ideas. The strong division between academic disciplines fosters competition rather than collaboration, and risks producing students with very narrow areas of expertise and difficulty finding work. In our globalized economy and rapidly changing labor markets, it is quite important for a young person to acquire flexible skills that can be easily adapted to different scenarios and work settings.

The government is cognizant of the mismatch between labor market requirements and job skills acquired in school. A limited number of spaces are available in universities, relative to the number of young people in the country. To make university education worthwhile for the lucky few, as a first step, the government has been emphasizing Technical Vocations Education and Training (TVET). In addition to some implementation problems, the most worrying issue relating to TVET is societal perception. Students who enter TVET institutions are unable to pass the 10th grade national exam, which is part of the university admission process. This statistic creates a mentality of failure among the TVET students and their families. To address these concerns, more could be done to raise awareness about the career potentials of TVET graduates, cultivate interest in TVET fields from an early age, and enhance the relationship between the training institutes and potential employers.

The Plight of Mass Production: Quantity at the Expense of Quality

In the past decade the number of public universities in Ethiopia has grown exponentially along with private higher education institutes. On the face, this growth is very promising and implies that more students in all parts of the country will have access to higher education. But many are concerned by how the focus on quantity is undermining the quality of the education. We understand that a country cannot achieve a very high standard level of education and believe the government's assertion that it is a work in progress. However, enrolling students in higher education institutes without adequate laboratories, libraries, or competent lecturers is worrying because these institutions are mass-producing the next generation of leaders, business people, politicians, civil servants, teachers, judges, doctors, parliamentarians, civil engineers, nurses, and so forth. The quality of our human resource will affect the efficiency of our public offices. It will affect our industries, how much foreign direct investment we can attract, our competiveness, and our productivity. It will also affect our future health, judicial, and education systems. As we focus now on the quality of our education, too much damage may have already been done. The attitudes and motivations of young people could be severely affected, which is difficult to reverse.

Things are made worse by the zero attrition rate policy and loose assessment approaches many of the university and colleges seem to apply. The government's love affair with numbers is very strong and risks overshadowing the quality of human resources institutes are producing. Perhaps underlying the logic behind these approaches is the assumption that everyone, if given a chance, can learn and master a subject. Yet this approach removes youth motivation to work hard in university or life in general. It is assumed that we are all inherently winners. The already relaxed entry requirements for higher education have deteriorated the sense of competition and the generation's values of hard work. The role of international development frameworks, specifically education policies and approaches, must be highlighted. Development frameworks such as the United Nations Millennium Development Goals (MDGs), eight social and economic goals intended to be met by 2015, guide many of the development activities in countries such as Ethiopia. The problem with the MDGs is that all of the indicators, which guide national development indicators, are quantitative and have thus instigated a rush to meet these narrowly-defined, number-oriented targets.

Is Pursuing Higher Education Still Worth it?
Many instructors I have talked to have echoed similar observations about why young people attend university: it is the next step after secondary education. That is, certification papers, not knowledge or skills, are the primary motivator driving many university graduates.

A society that was once a believer of education is now becoming cynical about higher education as graduates struggle to secure employment. The return on education investment, along with the quality of education, is making young Ethiopians question the merit and utility of attending university. An 18 year-old high school senior I spoke with shocked me when he said he does not plan to join any university in the country. Instead, he has begun collecting various computer science and programming-related books. He is convinced that with mentoring he will receive from a willing professional he can acquire the necessary skills by himself, circumventing university. He reached this decision based on the experiences of his senior friends who have already joined university and are disappointed with the quality of education provided. He shared that in his class, there were very bright students who are highly ambitious and determined but are desperately searching for educational opportunities abroad. His story reflects the growing loss of trust in our education system. The children of almost all high-ranking public officials study in institutes outside of the country. Have they too lost faith in the education system?

Jobless Graduates and a Private Sector without Human Resources

The greatest irony is that the emerging private sector in Ethiopia is dissatisfied with the quality of college graduates. A lack of quality human resources is consistently mentioned among its challenges. Yet many educated young people still struggle to find jobs. Why is there not a better link between the private sector and our education institutions? Why are different business sectors not participating in curriculum development? A friend who lectures at a private university college told me that her college attempts to develop its curriculum through stakeholder consultations, partnership building, and inviting representatives from the private sector. However, only few industry actors invited to participate in the formulation are responsive. Thus, the private sector may lack awareness on its role in skills development.

If organized, certain private sector clusters could also indirectly influence the quality of education. For example, a certain sector could help create entrance qualifications and agree to set the minimum human resource standard it expects from graduates of certain fields. All universities and higher education institutes that teach a certain field would need to examine their curriculums to match them with industry requirements and needs. Alternately, the responsibility of certifying a graduate could be undertaken by an external professional association, as is done in many countries. Quality of any product must be judged by its customers, which in this case are potential employers.

A Pleasing Career or One that Pays the Bills?

When I studied in Europe and America I was fascinated by how students are free to make different choices regarding their academic majors, change their choices, and try various things before settling on one. I was amazed how some students took a year off to "find themselves" while traveling the world. That practice is unthinkable where I am from, perhaps due to economic limitations. But the benefit I see in the paths taken by our European and American counterparts is that they eventually find the career path that best suits them and allows them to be most productive. In Ethiopia, efforts should be made to empower teachers and parents to help young people from an early age to identify their talents and interests. When living in a developing country, one cannot pursue all interests since a particular education field might not be available and job prospects might not be promising. However, we must remember that a decent livelihood is not only decent pay but shows young people doing what they are inspired to do. Young people do not have adequate information about different educational fields and work in their chosen fields. This deficit calls for good career guidance in secondary schools.

Conclusion and Solutions

All of us, individuals, government bodies, civil society, and private sector, should not ignore the challenges young Ethiopians face in acquiring decent jobs. Some young people like me who have been fortunate enough to secure relatively good jobs should remain concerned about our fellow youth who have not been so lucky. The ramifications of the youth employment challenges go beyond individual troubles.

As for solutions, below are some ideas for consideration:

1. The disconnect between policymakers and the aspirations of the public, especially youth, has to be bridged. We need a political and economic framework that invests in human capital development and gainfully engages young people to channel their energy and talents towards socioeconomic development. This does not necessarily mean recruiting young people to be party members. The views, concerns, and needs of young workers should be represented in worker organizations and trade unions.

2. Young people must nurture the value of working together. For example, youth who own businesses in the same area of production could cooperate to supply their products to local and international buyers who require supplies in bulk. The value chains that youth cooperatives participate in should not just be linked to government-incentivized sectors but also be associated with booming economic sectors.

3. The government should carefully consider active labour market policies that support young people. For example, it could create incentives for employers to hire young people. But for active labor market policies with minimized side effects to really work, enhanced coordination is needed between the various government bodies whose mandate areas directly or indirectly concern youth. These include the Ministry of Labour and Social Affairs, the Ministry of Youth and Women, Customs and Revenue Authority, Ministry of Trade, etc. The cost of these

interventions might be significant, but the cost of high and long-term youth unemployment will be higher.

4. There needs to be space for active policy dialogue. The solutions for every problem need not come from the government. We need think tanks and active, conscious, and independent civil society organizations that provide their views and assessments on draft policies and strategies. The government might not like opposing views, but opening the space for policy dialogue will be to its benefit. Discourse and dissent refines and polishes policies. Blindly copying and pasting models from other countries will not work.

5. NGOs and other development organizations, as well as government organs and education institutes, must think how they can assist young people who lack social capital to acquire sought-after workplace skills and experience. We should also assist those from disadvantaged backgrounds access unpaid internships that might be relevant for the career they want to pursue but which are not available for financial reasons.

6. We all need to become entrepreneurial. The country badly needs young people, regardless whom they work for, who attentively observe their environments, identify problems, analyze situations, and seek solutions. The soft skills necessary for success must be integrated in our formal and informal education structures.

7. The youth population and society in general must regain its social commitment. We have to be concerned with what is happening in our societies. The media can play an important role in this.

8. The private sector and public enterprises should each play a significant role in tackling youth unemployment challenges. Corporate social responsibility should be embraced and these sectors should play an active part in curriculum development. Organizations should also be willing to provide on-the-job training.

Studies have shown that difficult working conditions or unemployment at an early age increase the likelihood of subsequent unemployment. Unemployment in the first year of one's career sets a tone for life. Early unemployment diminishes future employability and earning because the attitudes and behaviors established at a young age tend to persist. Economically, high youth unemployment and underemployment result in smaller tax revenue. It also means that the youth, who constitute the largest population cohort in our country, have less to spend on products and services and little or no saving for investment. Young people have no incentive to save.

An acquaintance with a degree in marketing who works for an international organization as an assistant once shared the reason why she does not save. She said she could save a certain amount of her salary with the hope of putting a down payment on a house or purchasing a car. However, the rate of price increase of such assets, the rate at which the value of our currency declines, and the very slow rate of salary increase implies that by the time she had saved enough money to buy the car she wanted, the price of it would have doubled. Perhaps this is why Addis Ababa and other major cities burst with coffee places, night clubs, restaurants, and high-end boutiques that are always crowded with loyal young customers.

Moreover, youth unemployment and underemployment is a waste of potential human resources and talent. It also means that investment in education and training is wasted, especially since educated youth struggle to find decent work. The potential consequences of tension between an increasing output of educated and trained young people and the limited absorptive capacities of labor markets has been illustrated by the wave of discontent that swept North Africa during the Arab Spring. The revolutions have shown how economic and political upheaval result from neglect of youth unemployment if no proper corrective policy and program level measures are taken.

We should not, however, blame only the government and expect it to solve these problems. As individuals we should identify and take ownership of these problems and do our share to contribute solutions. Investment in youth, especially in youth employment, by all of us is an investment in society as a whole. Youth employment can have multiplier effects throughout the society and economy by shifting young people from social dependency to self-sufficiency.

---

i During the process of writing this article, I had very informative and dynamic discussions, in person and by email, with Yabets Sileshi, Anteneh Dagnachew, Osman Nigus, Gezahegn Dugassa, Yordanos Seifu, Sisay Asfaw, Mekdela Mekuria, Segen Yainshet, Adam Aberra, Ayenew Haileselassie, Gifti Jihad, and Fitsum Zewudu. I am very grateful for the insights of these vibrant youth and young adults.

ii Ethiopia Ministry of Education. Education Statistics Annual Abstract 2011 2012.

iii MOE, 2012.

iv United Nations Department of Economic and Social Affairs. 2010. The 2010 Revision of the World Population Prospects, May 2011. Accessed 10 January 2013. *http://esa.un.org/wpp/*.

The Future of the Sino-U.S. Relationship: A Chinese Millennial Perspective

Owen Liu

In early November 2012, I attended a joint concert held by the Military Band of the People's Liberation Army of China and the United States Army Band, "Pershing's Own," in Nanjing. This shared performance was part of a military-to-military exchange project between China and the United States. The visit of "Pershing's Own" to Beijing, Shanghai, and Nanjing was in response to the PLA Military Band visit to America one year before. Numerous high-level officials, including officials from the Ministry of Foreign Affairs of the People's Republic of China and the U.S. Consul-General in Shanghai also attended the concert. Both bands played extraordinary performances. I enjoyed the concert and it also gave me time to reflect on the greater picture of the two countries' bilateral relationship in the coming century.

On the surface, I saw a bright future for the Sino-U.S. relationship in the smiling faces of the artists and officials of both countries. However, Sino-U.S. relations may not be as ideal as seen from the surface. The Sino-U.S. relationship and the countries' interactions have increasingly become a dynamic factor in changing the Asia-Pacific security structure. Both countries are looking for ways to cooperate with one another while staying on the alert for the other's hostility. I believe that the biggest problem in our bilateral relations is what has been referred to as

56

"Strategic Distrust."

Many problems between the United States and China, which include issue areas such as Taiwan independence, the South China Sea, economic and trade frictions, and tensions on the Korean Peninsula, can be regarded as extensions of the mutual distrust. As Wang Jisi and Kenneth Lieberthal, Sino-U.S. relations experts (one from each country) argued in a recent joint report, the issue of mutual distrust of long-term intentions, this "strategic distrust," has become a central concern and element of the U.S.-China relationship. Although Beijing and Washington each seek to build a constructive partnership for the long-run, their bilateral history and current diplomatic activities have not, however, produced trust regarding long-term intentions on either side. I argue this mutual distrust is becoming more serious.

Strategic Distrust: Sources and Origins

There are several fundamental sources of growing strategic distrust between the United States and China. They include: the different political traditions of the two nations, conflicting value systems and cultures, and an insufficient comprehension and appreciation of each other's policymaking processes, which also includes relations between the government and other domestic entities.

The first highlights structural and deep-rooted elements that are not likely to be subject to major change. Political traditions in a country are often the product of that nation's history; this cannot be changed. It is more realistic for Washington and Beijing to address the second and third sources of strategic distrust.

The two nations should focus on improving their understanding of one another's domestic situations and work together more effectively in international endeavors in bilateral and multilateral situations. Often mutual reassurance does not play out domestically, as is often seen in U.S. politicians' public statements regarding Chinese behavior and its true intentions.

Additionally, a structural contradiction between China and the U.S.

has been growing over the last decade or more. This kind of trend may continue due to China's rise and America's so-called "pivot" to this region, a term used by the Obama administration for its new strategic response to China's rise in the Asia-Pacific region. China and America face a difficult security dilemma as their security purposes and interests become increasingly intertwined and complex.

The existing Sino-U.S. relationship has evolved from being "strategic competitors" at the beginning of President George W. Bush's first presidential term to being "responsible stakeholders" at the start of Bush's second term. But there are still hidden dangers. China and the U.S. are attempting to take "concrete actions to steadily build a partnership to address common challenges" at the official level.[i] So far, Beijing and Washington have established more than 60 distinct bilateral channels to strengthen communication and deepen mutual understanding. However, the countries' "mutual distrust" continues to grow despite these efforts. Distrust is corrosive and creates a vicious cycle, producing attitudes and actions that contribute to greater distrust. Distrust also prevents leaders on each side from being confident that they truly understand the thinking of leaders on the other side regarding the future U.S.-China relationship. Distrust is a path, and it appears that their relationship is becoming dependent on a path paved with this "mutual distrust".

Chinese leaders may privately acknowledge that China has benefited from the regional peace and stability that the U.S. military presence offers in the Pacific. But Beijing remains deeply suspicious about longer-term U.S. intentions toward China and its military plans in the region. From China's perspective, the U.S. military presence along its periphery, its longstanding policy and support towards Taiwan, and its promotion of democracy and human rights are all potential threats. Also, some U.S. observers suspect that China's strategic ambition is to push the United States out of East Asia and some of the Pacific, and become the dominant regional hegemon akin to the Sino-centric order of China's imperial period. Chinese leaders deny such an ambition and attempt to reassure U.S. audiences in public and private that they do not seek to evict or supplant the United States in the region, militarily or politically. Nevertheless, suspicions about China's real beliefs and intentions persist. Mutual distrust remains.

The Four Problem Areas

From my American studies on Sino-U.S. relations, I have encountered many American scholars who argue that China's rise may negatively affect America's powerful geopolitical and economic position in the world. Four points are commonly made in this argument.

First, the mutual distrust between China and the U.S. has the potential to generate problems and strategic miscalculation on many major issues. These miscalculations include issues related to both China's and America's core and important interests in this region, such as Taiwan.

From the perspective of Beijing, leaders in Zhongnanhai, the Forbidden City garden that is the headquarters of the Communist Party of China, have no illusions that the People's Liberation Army is a match for the U.S. military. They know they cannot compete with decades of research, experience, and world-leading military spending of the U.S. in the near term. China does seek niche capabilities to exploit U.S. vulnerabilities to deter, complicate, and delay, if not defeat, a U.S. or other foreign intervention in the Taiwan scenario.

Beijing also seeks more broadly to prevent the United States and its allies from containing China's economic and military development through military action or by shaping China's military modernization strategy. Operational capabilities developed in this modernization process may have broader applications to assert Chinese territorial claims and other future interests beyond the Taiwan Strait. However, decision-makers in the White House treat Asia as the most important region in the world for future American interests; American leaders are especially sensitive to Chinese actions that suggest the People's Republic may be assuming a more hegemonic approach to the region.

Second, China's support of some American-defined "rogue regimes" such as North Korea and Iran may prevent America from managing the instability in these countries and also undermine the relations between America and its regional allies.

For example, China's top priority on the Korean Peninsula is to ensure overall stability along its Korean periphery. China shares a large border with North Korea; instability there is not in China's short or long-term interests. China's preference for stability and security on its periphery has therefore influenced Beijing's handling of the North Korean nuclear weapons issue. China has consistently demanded that the North Korean nuclear impasse be solved peacefully through dialogue. Beijing has gone so far as to assume the role of host and broker during the Six Party talks in an effort to find common ground between the United States and North Korea and the other members of the Six, which will promote progress toward a final agreement. While frustrated by the North's nuclear weapons policy and desirous of a resolution leading to a non-nuclear peninsula, Beijing will likely be content with the status quo impasse as long as stability on the peninsula is maintained.[ii] It will be more difficult for America to carry out its own policy that intends to force North Korea to give up its possession and use of nuclear technology.

Third, China's territorial disputes with its neighbors might create head-on conflict with America's interests in the region, as evidenced by recent flare-ups between China and Japan. Finally, the cooperation and mutually strategic tacit support between China and Russia on regional hotspot security issues, which are sometimes not limited to East Asia, may produce some American concern. It could create the prospect of a "New Cold War" between two different blocs: U.S. and its allies versus China and Russia. This behavior is evident in Russian and Chinese behavior on the UN Security Council. Policymaking elites in Washington have surely noticed the debate among Chinese scholars regarding the possibility and feasibility of constructing a more formal alliance between Beijing and Moscow. I believe such discussion may cause discomfort and anxiety. Although neither Beijing nor Moscow officials have spoken openly about this, the reality that Beijing and Moscow are growing closer may create American uncertainty regarding its status as the leading power in Asia-Pacific region.

The Tragedy of Pessimism

China's rise is the most important factor shaping its regional structure and even the global security structure. It also has a unique role in shaping America's larger geopolitical strategy, forcing it to adjust its security strategy and policies in East Asia and the Pacific. Washington will need to be prepared psychologically for the impact China's rise may have on the United States' relative power and influence in East Asia and beyond. While China is unlikely to openly challenge U.S. preeminence in political, economic, or military power for the foreseeable future, the rise of China's relative international power and influence may present an economic challenge to the United States. This may also alter U.S. strategic relationships with friends and allies in the region, and even globally, as those nations accommodate China's rise.

The security game between Beijing and Washington will largely determine the direction and trend of the security structure in the Asia-Pacific. The Sino-U.S. relationship is and will continue to be the most important and dynamic force in re-shaping the East Asian security order.

Pessimists regarding the bilateral relationship warn that the most dangerous scenario the United States might face in the early 21st century is if China becomes a potential hegemon in Northeast Asia. John Mearsheimer, a Chicago University professor who is often labeled an "offensive realist" in international relations studies, once worried that a wealthy China would not be a status quo power but an aggressive state determined to achieve regional hegemony.[iii] This is not because a rich China would have wicked motives, but because the best way for any state to maximize its prospects for survival is to become a hegemon in its region of the world. From other academic perspectives, conflict, even large scale war, between these two countries is inevitable as it is the

61

natural law of balance of power. That is, the existing hegemon, in this case the United States, will undertake every possible means to maintain its status while the emerging power seeks to reshape the regional and even world order according to its own will. The conflict will begin at the regional level as every emerging power rises from its own region. These are very narrow readings that attempt to squeeze a complex relationship into convenient theories based on historical narratives.

I do not fully agree with Mearsheimer's assumptions for several reasons. First, China is really concerned in the short and medium-term about its internal affairs, especially the political stability and legitimacy of the Communist Party regime. China has major problems at home. In fact, Beijing has not been preparing for serious conflict with the United States or its allies in the Asia-Pacific. China's behavior model is quite different from the Soviet Union's, as Mearsheimer and other scholars attempt to draw parallels between the Sino-U.S. relationship and the bipolar world of the Cold War. Beijing's priority is to meet domestic requirements, economically and socially, and maintain the stability of this regime. Therefore, China is not a challenger or rival to the United States and the U.S.-led regional security order in the short and medium-term since China is not capable or willing to do so. As a result, the new U.S. policy, the "rebalance" or "pivot" strategy, unnecessarily compounds Beijing's insecurities and will only feed China's aggression, undermine regional stability, and decrease the possibility of advanced cooperation between Beijing and Washington.

Second, pessimists may ignore the preeminent advantage of U.S.-led security and economic regimes. The United States is a "structural power," that can maintain its influence through adjusting alliance arrangements and the rules of global institutions while its "hard power" (traditional military strength) is in relative decline. Hence, I believe American observers often overestimate Beijing's power and ambitions towards its region and the world. Actually, compared to the United States, China's military capabilities fall short in the quantity and quality of its nuclear weapons arsenal, battleship quality and quantity, fighter aircraft, and so on.

China cannot match America. It has almost no formal allies that it can rely on in case of open conflict, while America has many reliable and responsible friends in the Asia-Pacific, including Japan, the key to America's regional security network. Instead, China has several hostile peripheral neighbors that share numerous territorial disputes, while the United States is able to act as a neutral force and sustain its own prestige. Therefore, instead of inflating estimates of Chinese power and turning to a policy of containment, the United States should recognize China's underlying weakness and focus on its own enduring strengths. The correct China policy would be to assuage, not exploit, Beijing's anxieties, while protecting U.S. interests in the region. China should also take feasible actions to improve its transparency in a number of fields, including its military modernization. This important first step would show China's real intentions of its rise while playing down anxieties from America and China's peripheral countries.

Finally, I believe that both Beijing and Washington are capable of working together to create a "new type of relations between great powers," as President Hu Jintao proposed in the opening speech of the 4th China-U.S. Strategic and Economic Dialogue in May 2012. China is not the Soviet Union; the world as it exists today is not defined by the adversarial nature of the Cold War. As interdependence and bilateral relations between China and the U.S. grow and mature, both Beijing and Washington should have more courage, confidence, and wisdom to build a novel relationship. This new relationship should benefit from peace, security, and prosperity in Asia-Pacific. The approach to realize a new type of bilateral relationship for the 21st century should be one of "balance" between Beijing and Washington: balance of power, balance of interests, and balance of trust. To start, the greatest effort should be paid to addressing the issue of strategic distrust in economics and trade, military affairs, cybersecurity, and multilateral dialogues.

Conclusion

The November 2012 joint concert performed by the Military Band of the People's Liberation Army of China and the United States Army Band, "Pershing's Own," in Nanjing, was an amazing effort, and it gives me hope and confidence for the relationship between my country and the United States for the coming century. However, it is important that their bilateral relationship be more than a public performance and mere rhetoric. It is critical for both sides to truly engage on every issue and seek solutions rather than just listen to one another perform symphony music.

Strategic distrust can be just a bump in the road. It is not impossible to meaningfully address its sources. The United States and China will remain the two most consequential countries in the world over the coming decades. The nature of their relationship will have a profound impact on the citizens of both countries, on the Asia-Pacific region, and indeed on the world. Strategic distrust will inevitably impose very high costs on all concerned if it continues to grow at its current pace. Leaders on both sides should very carefully consider how to manage U.S.-China relations to maximize cooperation and minimize tensions and conflict, despite each side's deep distrust of the other's long-term intentions.

A responsible, strategic approach toward China must include preparation of U.S. domestic, foreign, and defense policies to deter and deflect Chinese actions that are contrary to U.S. interests. However, the United States must realize its overriding stake in pursuing a strategy that effectively integrates China into the existing global economic and security systems in a way that reinforces the American people's long-term security, prosperity, and peace. Additionally, China needs a comprehensive thinking towards its America policy and regional strategy that will ensure its domestic economic, political, and social success. China requires domestic stability so that its rise and development in the region are more acceptable. But domestic stability is not enough in the long-term. Stability must also mean a reduction of hostilities and fear from other countries. I believe that China and America, two great nations, will discover a new, mutually-beneficial path to achieve such goals and make the world more secure and prosperous now and for the future.

---

[i] U.S.-China Joint Statement. November 17, 2009. *http://www.whitehouse.gov/the-press-office/us-china-joint-statement.*

[ii] The Center for Strategic and International Studies (CSIS) and the Peterson Institute for International Economics (PIIE). "China: The Balance Sheet: What the World Needs to Know Now About the Emerging Superpower." *Public Affairs*, 2006. p.147.

[iii] John J. Mearsheimer. *The Tragedy of Great Power Politics.* New York, Norton, 2001. p. 402.

Riches, Wrinkles, and Rallies: Societal Changes Shaping China's Future

Jeremy Peters

I arrived in China in 2008. As an American and member of the Millennial Generation, I was thoroughly unprepared for the debunking of my previous notions of a communist dystopia blanketed in pollution. Since then, during my graduate studies in China and while working on China issues, I have learned an important lesson: broad generalizations about the country as a whole are not accurate. Provinces vary substantially, in food, clothing styles, local dialects, and even in languages. From the cosmopolitan inhabitants of Shanghai, to the entrepreneurs of Wenzhou, to the warm and friendly people of Sichuan, stereotypes about China's regions abound. This is a very diverse nation.

However, one evident trend across China is rapid change as a result of increasing openness to the outside world and improving economic development. Per capita disposable income, a reliable indicator of this trend, more than doubled between 1990 and 2000, more than tripled between 2000 and 2010, and is projected to continue rising in the coming decades.[i] Improved mobility, health, education, and purchasing power will no doubt change Chinese citizens' societal circumstances for the better. But economic development has and will continue to produce several side effects that must be addressed in the future.

China's changing social dynamics, positive and negative, can be best categorized in three major components: new or widening societal divisions, demographic shifts, and changes in social consciousness. First, the rich/poor and urban/rural divisions are more pronounced than ever. Second, in the coming decades, Chinese policymakers will need to address the demands of a rising middle class, an aging labor force, and a lopsided sex ratio caused by the one-child policy. Third, rapid spread and proliferation of the Internet is educating more Chinese citizens about domestic and international affairs. Their increased social awareness correlates with both a rise in internal social unrest and increased vocal nationalism. While many of these dynamics exist globally and in other nations, they are unique to China in the pace and scale they develop. There is a heightened need for prompt and comprehensive policy responses.

Societal Divisions

One of many social divisions in China that are immediately apparent is the disparity between the rich and poor. There is widespread social inequality, although economic development has increased standards of living across the board: according to the World Bank, in 2011, China's GDP per capita at purchasing power parity (PPP, a measure used to approximate the relative value between currencies) was $8,400; China's middle class continues to grow in size and prosperity every year.[ii] However, one can hardly ignore leading government officials who drive sleek, foreign-made cars and send their children to elite private schools in the West. They live in luxury apartments while millions of migrant laborers work in cities for near-poverty wages and without access to social services. The country's Gini coefficient (a measure of income inequality, with a coefficient of 0 being perfectly equal and 1 being perfectly unequal) has been rising almost continuously since the early 1980s.

It has been estimated that inequality has already reached alarmingly high levels: while an index of over 0.5 is considered "extremely severe,"[iii] one recent household survey estimated the Chinese Gini to be as high as

.61.[iv] As of this writing, the government has not published the official Gini coefficient for over 10 years and has yet to implement effective measures to curb the widening income gap. There are barriers to addressing this issue such as players with a vested interest in maintaining the status quo. For example, the rising influence of special interest groups and the high level of representation afforded to managers of state-owned enterprises may prevent income inequality from being seriously addressed for some time.

Additionally, one cannot discuss inequality without focusing on regional disparities in income and wealth. Historically, provinces along China's Eastern coast have long held vastly more wealth than their inland counterparts. Currently, foreign direct investment is heavily concentrated in the coastal regions and incomes in these provinces are significantly higher. City-dwellers also earn substantially more than their rural counterparts; the flawed *hukou* (户口) system of residential registration divides the population into *nongmin* (农民 ; peasant) and *feinongmin* (非农民 ; non-peasant). This system provides urbanites with superior healthcare, schooling, and social services such as job loss insurance, while migrant workers and rural residents fall behind. It assumed that the rural population is able to rely on land as its own social safety net. However, income inequality is slightly lower in urban than rural areas.[v]

China hopes that in the coming decades massive urbanization may help bridge this rural-urban gap in social services and income and reduce overall inequality. The current urbanization process is happening rapidly in almost all of China's provinces and will play a dominant role in the overall continuity and sustainability of economic growth.[vi] The key questions that Chinese policymakers must address now include how to improve the quality of life for rural residents and migrant workers, prevent unfair land acquisitions that fuel social unrest, and ensure that growing and developing cities run on sustainable, clean forms of energy.

Demographic Shifts

Shifting demographics will inevitably change how different generations relate to one another. China's "one child policy," instated in 1979, has ensured that its demographic landscape will soon look like that Western countries and Japan. That is, China will have increasing numbers of elderly and retired while the working-age population decreases. Although there are still plenty of individuals who need to be absorbed into the national work force, the working age population has already begun to shrink.[vii] Chinese children have a traditional obligation to support their parents in old age with a national culture and history marked by filial piety. However, unlike Japan and the West, "China will grow old before it gets rich,"[viii] and the burden of caring and providing for the elderly will fall upon a generation lacking the necessary financial resources to assume this task. This trend is already evident in many families where only children, particularly sons, face immense pressure to succeed.

This success includes an expectation of home ownership as a prerequisite to marriage while supporting two parents and four grandparents; if a male marries this burden doubles. Wives are commonly expected to work but women still earn less on average than men. This is similar to the situation in Western countries although the income gap in China is widening.[ix] Additionally, this aging trend means that domestic consumption must increase as a percent of GDP as the elderly require more care. Chinese workers will have to transition into more value-added industries in order to maintain steady increases in income required to finance such expenditures as increased and additional health care and other assisted living costs.

Another of the many unintended consequences of China's one-child policy is a significant gender gap in the younger generations. Traditional Chinese culture values sons over daughters and many couples choose to abort, abandon, or not register daughters. In 2000, 120 males were born for every 100 females; in 2010 this number had only slightly improved to

118 males per 100 females[x]. It is difficult to determine what social problems will arise in a society with many more men than women. However, Chinese culture strongly disparages the unmarried and views childbearing as a family duty; men who do not marry are called *guang gun* or "bare branches," single women in their 30s are *sheng nü* or "leftover women." There will likely be high levels of openly expressed dissatisfaction with the dating pool. Although the government has prohibited doctors from revealing the sex of a fetus to parents, this policy is easily circumvented via bribes. Official campaigns to improve perceptions of having a daughter have enjoyed moderate success. The role of women in society is improving: more are enrolling in college and more are getting better jobs. However, most continue to expect husbands to have more important jobs. Institutional factors such as the male-female wage gap and the consistently all-male Politburo both remain obstacles to changing hearts and minds.

China's rapidly expanding middle class is another factor that will have significant political and economic implications in the next decades. The actual number of people that can claim membership in China's "middle class" varies depending on one's definition: McKinsey Global Institute defines it as those with PPP incomes between $13,500 and $53,900; the Chinese Academy of Social Sciences defines it as assets from $18,100 to $36,200; and China's National Bureau of Statistics defines it as incomes from $7,250 to $62,500. It is difficult to calculate valid demographic statistics with so many competing classifications of middle-class. In her book *The Chinese Dream: The Rise of the World's Largest Middle Class and What It Means to You*, Helen Wang defines the middle class as college-educated individuals with incomes between $10,000 and $60,000, and estimates that this increasing demographic was above 300 million in 2010.[xi]

Brookings Institution expert Cheng Li has written extensively on attitudes of the Chinese middle class, noting that these citizens are more likely to be dissatisfied with sub-par government performance and will be more demanding of politicians than their lower or upper class counterparts.[xii] Moreover, spending habits of the middle class will likely change as policymakers attempt to transition the country from an investment-led model to one driven by consumption. The growing number of consumers has already made China the world's largest market for automobiles, luxury goods, art, antiques, and many other quality items. The views and lifestyles of this consumer base will heavily influence China's politicians' priorities and abilities to achieve certain goals. Eventually, these politicians will have to listen and become more responsive to the middle class as its collective voice becomes louder and their vested interests more intertwined with the economic success of the country.

Increasing Social Consciousness

More Chinese citizens are developing an awareness of their domestic politics and the country's international affairs. The story they hear is increasingly not filtered through the lens of the official party line. Over the next several years China will see rapidly increasing levels of Internet access and information, growing in tandem with the middle class. In China, the number of Internet users or "netizens" has increased from 58 million a decade ago[xiii] to over 500 million today;[xiv] their numbers and ability to access information will continue to improve. Online shopping on sites such as Taobao and Amazon.cn are increasingly popular, in part because these sites have tailored their offerings to Chinese tastes with options such as same-day delivery, cash payment on delivery, and discounts on various Chinese holidays. The Internet, while often censored, provides unprecedented levels of information to these new users, creates new forums for public discussion, and serves as a window to the outside world. This increased access to unbiased information is a national trend. It will no doubt increase standards of living and have a positive impact on China's human capital.

One prominent example of increased Internet access as more Chinese citizens become part of the Internet society and global online community is the growth of Sina Weibo, China's micro-blogging service that is very similar to Twitter. Sina Weibo is a somewhat free outlet for self-expression as it is relatively uncensored by the government. It also serves as a source for news that previously would go unpublished by state-controlled media. In 2012, several protests erupted in the cities of Dalian, Ningbo, and Shifang as news spread about the planned construction of plants that were potentially hazardous to both the environment and public health. Each organized protest used social media to plan and rally the protestors.[xv]

As of this writing, Western social media such as Facebook and Twitter continue to be blocked. Chinese services such as Weibo, Renren (a Facebook counterpart), and QQ (an instant messaging program) are currently self-regulated due to an implicit understanding that allows them relative independence as companies. However, government censorship efforts have tended to focus more on efforts to organize mass protests or gatherings than on general anti-government speech. In the West, several sites have sprung up in recent years to monitor public opinion as expressed on Chinese micro-blogs. The opinions expressed on these platforms have significance for policymakers, business leaders, and general China watchers alike.

Also as a result of increased social awareness, Chinese domestic policymakers will continue to grapple with rising levels of social unrest in the years to come. China's "mass incidents," which include riots, strikes, and other forms of protest, grow almost exponentially every year. They numbered more than 180,000 in 2010. These protests are, in general, not necessarily anti-government or anti-party in nature. But they successfully draw attention to specific instances of environmental degradation, official corruption, forced land acquisition, or other such policies. Mass incidents are considered potentially destabilizing if handled poorly. Hu Jintao's (president of the People's Republic of China, March 2003–March 2013) pet term "harmonious society" (和谐社会) was likely meant to address the issue of social unrest, yet the last full year of his presidency saw the highest number of mass incidents on record. Official responses to social unrest vary, but too often the government attempts to simply cover up the incident that incited or caused protests rather than handle the issue causing discontent.

There are some areas of common agreement between the government and the public. In particular, perceived mistreatment of China at the hands of other nations is common ground in an increasingly strained government-citizen relationship. Fierce nationalism is hardly a new social dynamic in China; it has been present for centuries. Occasionally, it has taken on a violent character, such as during the Boxer Rebellion, anti-Soviet protests at the height of Sino-Soviet tensions, and anti-American protests after the 1999 accidental bombing of the Chinese embassy in Belgrade. However, the sitting government intentionally stokes this nationalism with an education system that emphasizes periods of foreign domination while providing only fleeting acknowledgement to foreign aid or suffering inflicted by government policy. This includes forgiving portrayals of the disastrous Great Leap Forward and the Cultural Revolution; the 1989 Tiananmen Square demonstrations are noticeably absent from official history curriculum. Slogans such as "never forget national humiliation" (勿忘国耻) are commonly known by Chinese citizens.

During my time in China, I have seen this nationalism take on an intensely malevolent character. For example, smoldering nationalism manifested during a dispute between China and Japan over an island chain known in China as the Diaoyu islands and in Japan as the Senkakus. Banners and signs were plastered across the country on the sides of buildings, and even at grocery store entrances, proclaiming that "The Diaoyus are China's." (钓鱼岛是中国的); purchases of Japanese-made products decreased dramatically during this time. At one point, a Chinese citizen was nearly beaten to death by a protesting crowd for driving a Toyota.[xvi] If such a violent response can erupt over five uninhabited islands with a smaller surface area than Guam, one can only imagine the outrage if other disputes do not go China's way and these nationalistic fires are aggressively fed.

Conclusion

When I first arrived in China, I was overwhelmed by the largesse of its modern cities and the efficiency of millions of people moving about every day on a massive and expanding public transportation system. The country's physical artifacts and structures are a reminder of its rich culture and history that pre-date many Western nations. I could not believe how, in a country with over one billion mouths to feed, food and water could be so cheap compared to the cost of living in the United States, a country with about one-third of the Chinese population. China, from this cursory glance, appeared to be doing everything right. My first impression of the country's expedient accomplishments was one of admiration. It made me question whether the West would be left behind if it was not made aware of whatever magic formula for growth China has discovered.

Over time it became clear to me that China does not have everything right. Beyond Western rhetoric of a totalitarian behemoth destined to overtake the United States, it is important to realize that China still faces many challenges at home. Many of these challenges will be exacerbated in the coming years rather than solved by economic development. Societal divisions are increasingly widening and destabilizing, demographic shifts are exerting stress and testing the limits of the current model, and growing social awareness means that the Chinese people will expect their government to be responsive and produce quality results. While some in the West may use these challenges to criticize a system it ideologically opposes, it is important to realize that both the U.S. and China each have daunting internal questions to grapple with in the 21st century. I believe we all stand to benefit through understanding and cooperation. China has a long way to go in terms of economic and human development. Economic growth is only part of China's rise. Without seriously addressing some of the domestic issues discussed in this essay, it can expect its path to global power to be quite bumpy.

i Annalyn Censky. "China's Middle-Class Boom." "CNN Money," June 26, 2012. *http://money.cnn.com/2012/06/26/news/economy/china-middle-class/index.htm.*
ii The World Bank. "Data: GDP per capita, PPP (current international $)." Accessed January 13, 2013. *http://data.worldbank.org/indicator/NY.GDP.PCAP.PP.CD.*
iii Xuyan Fang and Lea Yu. "Government Refuses to Release Gini Coefficient." *Caixin.* January 18, 2012. *http://english.caixin.com/2012-01-18/100349814.html.*
iv "Inequality in China: To Each, Not According to His Needs." *The Economist.* December 15, 2012. *http://www.economist.com/news/finance-and-economics/21568423-new-survey-illuminates-extent-chinese-income-inequality-each-not.*
v OECD. "China in Focus: Lessons and Challenges." OECD, Paris.
vi Jonathan Woetzel, et al. "Preparing for China's Urban Billion." McKinsey Global Institute. 2009.
vii William Kazer and Yajun Zhang. "A Raft of Surprises from China Stats Chief." *Wall Street Journal: China Real Time Report.* January 18, 2013. *http://blogs.wsj.com/chinarealtime/2013/01/18/a-raft-of-revelations-from-chinas-statistics-chief/?mod=WSJBlog&utm_source=Sinocism Newsletter&utm_campaign=a9597eebad-Sinocism_01_22_13&utm_medium=email.*
viii Frederik Balfour. "China's 'Demographic Tsunami.'" *Businessweek.* January 5, 2012. *http://www.businessweek.com/magazine/chinas-demographic-tsunami-01052012.html.*
ix Biwei Su and Almas Heshmati. "Analysis of Gender Wage Differential in China's Urban Labor Market," Discussion Paper No. 6252. Institute for the Study of Labor. December 2011.
x Tania Branigan. "China's Great Gender Crisis." *The Guardian.* November 2, 2011. *http://www.guardian.co.uk/world/2011/nov/02/chinas-great-gender-crisis*
xi Helen Wang. "Defining the Chinese Middle Class." *Forbes.* November 24, 2010. *http://www.forbes.com/sites/helenwang/2010/11/24/defining-the-chinese-middle-class/.*
xii Cheng Li. "China in Transition". *Brookings Institution.* September 19 2011. *http://www.brookings.edu/research/interviews/2011/09/19-china-li*
xiii "China's Netizens Top 58 Million, Next Only to the U.S." *People's Daily Online.* December 19, 2002. *http://english.peopledaily.com.cn/200212/18/eng20021218_108703.shtml.*
xiv Yixuan Zhang. "Number of netizens reaches 500 million in China." *People's Daily Online.* January 13, 2012. *http://english.peopledaily.com.cn/90882/7704757.html.*
xv Christina Larson. "Protests in China Get a Boost from Social Media." *Businessweek.* October 29, 2012. *http://www.businessweek.com/articles/2012-10-29/protests-in-china-get-a-boost-from-social-media#p2.*
xvi Amy Qin and Edward Wong. "Smashed Skull Serves as Grim Symbol Seething Patriotism." *The New York Times*, October 11, 2012. *http://www.nytimes.com/2012/10/11/world/asia/xian-beating-becomes-symbol-of-nationalism-gone-awry.html?_r=0*

Which Way Forward?
The Role of International Organizations in World Politics
Jillienne Haglund

The past few decades have witnessed an unprecedented expansion in the activities of international organizations and the influence of international treaties. From the United Nations Convention on the Law of the Sea Treaty to successful attempts to phase out ozone-depleting substances under the Montreal Protocol, we can observe various successful efforts to address international issues using a multilateral process. The international public sector plays an important role in our current global order.

Specifically, the past 60 years has seen increased legalization of human rights; countries increasingly look to international law to address human rights concerns. This was evidenced in the adoption of the non-binding United Nations Universal Declaration of Human Rights (UDHR) in 1948. The UDHR was the first international declaration of the human rights to which all human beings are entitled. UDHR's adoption was a precursor for the adoption of the International Covenant on Civil and Political Rights (ICCPR) and the International Covenant on Economic, Social, and Cultural Rights (ICESCR), both of which entered into force in 1976.

Today various treaties address specific human rights (i.e., The Convention against Torture, CAT), specific groups of people (i.e.,

Convention on the Elimination of All Forms of Discrimination Against Women, CEDAW, Convention on the Rights of a Child, CRC), and specific regions of the world (i.e., Inter-American Convention on Human Rights, IACHR, European Convention on Human Rights, ECHR). The proliferation of international legal rules established through international treaties as a means to address human rights violations has become the avenue for oppressed groups and individuals to legitimately present their human rights concerns.

The growth of legalization as the primary tool to address human rights abuses presumes that countries uphold the treaties they ratify in the domestic sphere. Despite this growth in legalization as a tool to address human rights violations, we often observe a lack of respect for and noncompliance with ratified international treaties. We also observe the anomaly of compliance by countries that have not ratified international treaties, particularly international human rights treaties. Scholars find varying effects of treaties on the behavior of countries. For example, among many scholars studying compliance with human rights treaties, Hill finds empirical evidence that ratification of the CAT and ICCPR usually result in worse human rights practices while ratification of CEDAW typically results in improved human rights practices. If international law and legalization have such varying effects on respect for human rights, is legalization then the best solution to improve respect for human rights internationally?[i]

In this essay, I will examine the role of international organizations on policy outcomes. Specifically, I assess the role of international human rights treaties in addressing human rights abuses. International human rights treaties present a particularly interesting case to analyze because these treaties typically do not result in the same types of reciprocal material benefits likely to ensure compliance with other types of treaties (i.e., economic or conflict-related treaties). As a result, human rights treaties present a particularly difficult case for observing compliance with international law.

International Law: The Basics

A useful place to start in answering this question is to address the context where international law operates. When I began studying compliance with international law, I assumed that international law should work much like national law: individuals or countries are aware of the consequences of the failure to abide by laws, and when a court finds them guilty, they must pay those consequences. For example, when an individual commits a murder, he or she understands that if he or she is caught, a prison term is likely. However, international legal commitments often lack "teeth," because very few, if any, international enforcement mechanisms are employed when countries violate their international commitments.

Scholars in international relations argue that the reason international law operates as such is because all countries exist in a single international system characterized by anarchy. In other words, countries operate in an environment without central authority or anything akin to a federal government in the international system. There is no one to legally enforce the "rules." As a result, countries are sovereign, giving them the ultimate authority to govern themselves. The lack of enforcement authority afforded to international legal agreements is particularly pertinent to international human rights treaties, mainly because very few material benefits are associated with fulfilling treaty requirements. *Economic* treaties are often self-enforcing because countries may receive mutual trade or other economic benefits for upholding the terms of the treaty. Both parties have an incentive to make good on their commitments.

With respect to *human rights*, countries can violate the treaty at little cost, except for the potential damage posed to the violating countries' international reputation. Given this lack of incentive to respect rights guaranteed in ratified human rights treaties, how can we ensure the advancement of human rights through international legal rules? In other words, do increased legalization and growth of international legal rules have influence on the decisions of countries to respect human rights?

Compliance with Human Rights Agreements

It is helpful to explore some of the common explanations offered regarding the decisions of countries to comply with or uphold the treaties they have signed. One early explanation for why countries might fail to respect the treaties they have ratified lies in what has been termed "managerial issues." This explanation presumes that countries intend to comply with the treaties they sign; however, various management or technical issues not foreseen by countries might inhibit compliance.[ii] Management problems include ambiguity in the language of the treaty and capacity limitations on the ability of the country to implement the treaty, among numerous others. For example, the language in Article 2 of the ICESCR states that a country should take steps "to the maximum of its available resources…to achieving progressively the full realization of rights" in the treaty. The lack of clarity regarding what constitutes the "maximum of a state's available resources," and the lack of clear-cut timetables regarding acceptable progress to fully achieve the rights in the treaty (or, ambiguity in the language of the treaty and potential capacity limitations), make it difficult to judge whether countries are meeting the terms of the treaty or to assess compliance with the treaty.

A second common explanation regarding compliance concerns the types of countries that ratify treaties.[iii] This argument basically presumes that countries only ratify treaties that are "cheap" or pose very little cost to them. Simply put, countries only ratify treaties with which they are already in compliance, which requires little or no change in human rights behavior upon ratification. For example, countries likely to ratify the Convention Against Torture are those that engage in relatively little torture, such as Sweden or Switzerland.

While neither of these explanations is wrong, neither fully explains compliance. In fact, there are several anomalies left to be explained. For example, sometimes countries insincerely ratify treaties or ratify treaties they did not follow in the past and have little intention of following (i.e., Burundi, Cambodia) and sometimes countries choose not to ratify treaties with which they already comply (i.e., the United States has not ratified CEDAW despite a history of relatively high respect for women's rights).[iv] What, then, best explains compliance? Where should scholars, policymakers, and activists focus their efforts in advancing human rights through international legalization?

I think the best answer is in the realm of domestic politics. Domestic politics as embodied in domestic political institutions or more specifically, liberal democratic institutions, and domestic mobilization, show the most promise in explaining compliance with international legal rules. Domestic political institutions include the national system of rules, statutes, judicial decisions, or norms, and include institutions such as electoral rules, branches of government, and constitutional guarantees such as freedom of speech. Domestic mobilization refers to the extent that citizens organize and join groups to demand some type of social or political change.[v] The domestic legal and political sphere compensate for the lack of enforcement mechanisms in the international realm. As a result, if the unparalleled growth in legalization of international human rights is to have any influence on the advancement of human rights, human rights advocates and activists must shift their focus to reform in the domestic political sphere.

The Role of Domestic Politics in Compliance

Initially, scholars examining the role of domestic politics in compliance with international legal commitments concentrated their focus on the influence of the type of political system, such as democracy, dictatorship, etc. The empirical evidence has provided substantiated support for the important relationship between democracy and respect for human rights; democracies are more likely to respect human rights as well as fulfill their treaty commitments. However, it wasn't long after the important role of democracy was established that scholars began asking what about a democratic political system leads to better respect for human rights or higher compliance with international legal obligations? Disaggregating the specific mechanisms at work in this relationship, I believe, provides the strongest way forward to ensure that all of the efforts of the international community to enhance respect for human rights through legalization have not been in vain.

Some of the most innovative advancements in the study of compliance with international human rights treaties examine the role of domestic political institutions. For example, the role of elections and electoral systems in explaining treaty compliance has demonstrated great promise.[vi] The importance of elections hinges on accountability. In countries where individuals and groups are able to hold their elected officials accountable through free and fair elections, voters can remove those elected officials who are responsible for human rights abuses or fail to uphold international human rights legal commitments. The threat of being removed from office pressures elected officials into honoring their international treaty commitments. Of course, this is rooted in the assumption that voters value respect for human rights. Further, the role of electoral systems is also being examined, specifically, whether plurality systems (electoral systems where the single winner is the candidate with the most votes) or proportional representation systems (electoral systems where the number of seats won by a party or group of candidates is proportionate to the number of votes received) guarantee better respect for human rights.

Others are focusing on whether the size of the electoral district (the number of representatives elected from a given district to a legislature) has an influence on human rights. For example, in countries where voters have greater access to their elected officials or feel a stronger personal connection to their representatives, elected officials are more likely to be held accountable for the failure to abide by treaties and will advocate respect for rights.[vii] Some scholars find empirical evidence for the importance of elections in explaining compliance with international human rights treaties, but there is ample room for further examination of the influence of electoral rules on compliance.

Moving beyond electoral rules, national courts are another promising avenue for human rights advocates to enhance the influence of international human rights legalization in ensuring respect for rights.[viii]

As stated above, international human rights treaties have few, if any, *international* enforcement mechanisms. If there is no international enforcement mechanism capable of adequately punishing government agents for human rights abuses, this task must be undertaken in the domestic sphere. In the realm of domestic politics, the national court is primarily responsible for enforcing the law and as a result, the primary mechanism to enforce international treaties must be the national courts.

National courts must be willing and able to prosecute and punish the individuals and government agents responsible for human rights abuses. Scholars find that countries are more likely to honor their international legal obligations if domestic legal enforcement is strong and effective. Where domestic legal enforcement is weak, however, countries are less likely to honor human rights treaty commitments. Interestingly, officials in countries with strong domestic legal enforcement mechanisms understand there is an increased likelihood of enforcement of international treaties in national courts and as a result are less likely to ratify treaties in the first place.[ix]

Strong domestic enforcement mechanisms are evidenced through separation of powers; where the national court is largely independent of the other branches of government, it is more likely to enforce international legal obligations. This is particularly important when the violators of international treaties are members of other branches of government because the national court may have to make legal decisions that are unpopular with members of other branches. For example, when state agents under executive branch control, such as police or prison guards, engage in torture or other human rights violations, an independent national court will hold those individuals responsible. Further, an independent national court is also better equipped to hold the executive branch responsible for delegating a policy of torture to its agents.

In addition to electoral rules and the national court, freedom of speech and freedom of the press are other particularly important domestic institutions for generating compliance with international human rights legal obligations. Freedom of speech provides individuals with opportunities to bring allegations of torture to light within the state and hold officials accountable. In countries with restrictions on speech, state agents responsible for human rights abuses generally need not be concerned that disclosure of their use of torture, political imprisonment, or other types of rights violations will result in accountability.[x] This is why many dictatorships, which place large restrictions on freedom of speech, also engage in relatively higher levels of torture.[xi] Freedom of the press is also particularly important as it enhances the ability of individuals and groups to publicize and publish human rights violations committed by the state. By bringing these violations to light in the domestic sphere, individuals become increasingly aware of the rights violations being committed by state agents within the country and are more likely to pressure elected officials into policy reform as a result. Where freedom of the press is restricted or largely state controlled, it is unlikely that human rights violations will be brought to light and voters will likely remain unaware of the extent of these violations.

Further, where freedom of speech and press are largely unrestricted, elected officials, including members of the executive and legislative branches, find it in their interest to establish mechanisms to prevent or stop human rights abuses, particularly through repression in the form of physical integrity rights violations: torture, disappearance, political imprisonment, and extrajudicial killing, or unsanctioned killing by government authorities. In countries where human rights violations can be more easily observed as a result of freedom of speech and the press, elected officials understand they are more likely to be held accountable for lack of compliance with international human rights law. As a result, they may find it in their interest to send signals to their domestic audience, their constituents, of their commitment to human rights.

For example, elected officials may establish governmental institutions to limit the ability of state agents to engage in human rights violations. One such institution growing in popularity is the National Human Rights Institution (NHRI). NHRIs are established within countries cross-nationally and are national government-run institutions charged with promoting international treaties on the national level.[xii] These institutions include National Human Rights Commissions and Ombudsman, and they are important monitoring and investigatory bodies.

They engage in activities including on-site visits to places of detention where human rights violations may be occurring, assisting in human rights training for state agents, assisting in the drafting of legislation, and investigating alleged human rights violations, among other tasks.[xiii] These institutions are becoming increasingly popular means to hold governments accountable for rights violations. Furthermore, their adoption is likely to be used as a signal of commitment to international legal obligations especially when elected officials know they are likely to be held accountable as indicated by the freedom guaranteed in speech and press.

Finally, an active domestic civil society, including actors such as human rights non-governmental organizations, legal experts, and pro-rights advocates, is important in generating compliance with international legal commitments associated with human rights. Most of the arguments above presume that the public is willing and able to pressure its elected officials into compliance. Domestic groups will place a high value on rights when there is a good chance they will succeed in achieving their demands or aims.[xiv] International human rights treaties are particularly important in this regard because they increase the likelihood that pro-rights advocates will succeed by providing legal legitimacy to rights claims made in the domestic sphere. Simmons (2009) argues that a ratified international treaty "precommits the government to be receptive to rights demands."[xv] Further, domestic mobilization efforts are more likely to succeed when the domestic institutions I have noted above, including elections, powerful national courts, freedom of speech and the press, and numerous others, are present.

Examples

To illustrate the importance of domestic politics in ensuring compliance with international human rights law, consider human rights violations perpetrated by state agents in Nepal during the armed conflict of 1996-2006. The Supreme Court in Nepal has made various attempts to bring to justice perpetrators of human rights abuses committed during the armed conflict, but a lack of judicial power has plagued the court with repeated failures. For example, Colonel Raju Basnet, commander of the Bhairabnath Battalion in 2003 when systematic forced disappearances and torture were perpetrated with impunity, was promoted to Nepal's ministerial cabinet in 2012. Investigations conducted by the United Nations as well as the National Human Rights Commission of Nepal connect Colonel Basnet with these human rights violations. In June 2007, the Supreme Court of Nepal ordered an independent investigation and prosecution of these crimes, including an investigation of Colonel Basnet. This order, and others like it, has largely been ignored by the Nepalese government.[xvi]

A lack of domestic judicial power (independence and effectiveness of the national court) inherently prevents the domestic judiciary from ensuring that other government perpetrators of human rights abuses are held accountable. In its list of recommendations to the government of Nepal, Amnesty International states that the government must "respect court orders calling on the police to investigate human rights violations and crimes under international law."[xvii] For this and other recommendations made by Amnesty International to be achieved, the domestic judiciary must become independent and effective.

As another example of the importance of domestic politics for ensuring compliance with international law, consider the Inter-American Court of Human Rights (IACtHR) case, *Laoyza Tamayo v. Peru*, in which Professor Loayza Tamayo was held in incommunicado detention, tortured, and sentenced to prison for terrorism due to her association with the Shining Path insurgent group in Peru. The IACtHR found Peru in violation of the American Convention on Human Rights and ordered the victim to be released.[xviii] Loayza Tamayo was released by the government of Peru within a month of the IACtHR decision, largely because the case was able to garner "widespread popular support and media attention."[xix] This example illustrates that freedom of speech and press and a vibrant domestic civil society play a crucial role in the decisions of countries to comply with international law.

Conclusion

In this essay I have argued that the increased emphasis on legalization and legal mechanisms in improving respect for human rights is promising. Additionally, I argue that focusing solely on international enforcement mechanisms is likely to result in low levels of compliance with international legal obligations associated with human rights. How, then, can we guarantee higher levels of compliance?

I believe that the best avenue forward is to focus on the role of domestic politics in enforcement of international treaties. Scholars are beginning to move beyond explanations focused on broad political system types such as democracy and dictatorship, and into the realm of the specific domestic institutions that work in generating compliance. These domestic institutions provide incentives for domestic actors to engage in compliance. Only by focusing on the particular domestic institutions and combinations of domestic institutions at work in the compliance decision-making process can we begin to make policy recommendations and reform suggestions likely to influence state respect for rights. However, the ability to generate policy reform depends on academics, policymakers, and activists working together and engaging one another, rather than speaking past one another. Even within academia, scholars often talk past one another and not to one another in discussions of compliance.

In the field of political science, the study of international treaties and international legal obligations often falls into the realm of international relations scholars, while the study of domestic politics falls largely into the realm of comparative politics scholars. As a result, these groups of scholars often do not engage one another, while they should be working together. Further, there is often even less engagement between academia and the policy sphere. The failure to engage produces incoherent and incomplete research programs as well as few good policy solutions for advancing human rights. For us to build cumulative knowledge regarding compliance with international human rights treaties and respect for human rights, academics, policymakers, and activists must begin to pool their knowledge, observations, and experiences. If the increased legalization of human rights is to influence respect for rights, these individuals must be willing to work together to generate policy reforms likely to enhance compliance with international human rights treaties in the domestic sphere.

I think our generation of scholars, academics, activists, and policymakers is beginning to understand the necessity of working together to accomplish the advancement of human rights through legalization. I am currently working on my dissertation, which addresses the role of domestic institutions in the effectiveness of supranational human rights courts, specifically the Inter-American and European Courts of Human Rights. Upon completion of my Ph.D., I hope to remain in academia, but develop and cultivate relationships with those working in the policy world, making empirically-driven policy prescriptions and recommendations. Through discussions with others in the policy, academic, and activist spheres, I am optimistic that we have common goals in mind and that we can begin to work together through these legal institutions to influence policy outcomes.

We are discovering that international cooperation through international organizations is not the lofty goal once posited by international relations experts, but is something achievable under the right domestic political conditions. By better understanding the role that domestic politics play in the enforcement of international treaties, we can begin to work toward the domestic reform efforts essential for international legalization to play the influential role for which it was originally intended. This may seem a backwards step in the process toward improving respect for human rights or other policy outcomes, as I argue that domestic political reforms, particularly improving democratic governance and the strength of liberal democratic institutions, is an initial necessary condition for ensuring compliance with international law. However, I believe that our generation understands the need to go to great lengths by procuring domestic reforms to achieve greater and deeper cooperation internationally down the line.

These processes may be lengthy, but in looking to the future, our generation understands the value in solving problems through long-term solutions. We have observed our fair share of failures related to the role of international law in generating policy change, most recently evidenced in the unsuccessful climate change negotiations and the failure to meet targeted deadlines as set by the Kyoto Protocol. These failures have greatly influenced our understanding of world politics and are the reason we understand the need to step back and determine which way forward is likely to be most effective for international organizations to influence policy outcomes, even if the best way forward focuses on long-term processes, the benefits of which may only be observed by future generations.

---

[i] Daniel W. Jr. Hill. "Estimating the Effects of Human Rights Treaties on State Behavior." *Journal of Politics* 72(4), 2010. pp.1161-1174.

[ii] Abram Chayes and Antonia Handler Chayes. "On Compliance." *International Organization* 47(2), 1993. pp. 175–205.

[iii] George W. Downs, David M. Rocke and Peter N. Barsoom. "Is the Good News about Compliance Good News about Cooperation?" *International Organization* 50(3), 1996. pp. 379–406.

[iv] Beth A. Simmons. *Mobilizing for Human Rights: International Law in Domestic Politics.* New York, Cambridge University Press, 2009.

[v] Ibid, p. 136.

[vi] David L. Richards. "Perilous Proxy: Human Rights and the Presence of National Elections." *Social Science Quarterly* 80.4, 1999. pp. 648-665; Steven C. Poe, C. Neal Tate, and Linda Camp Keith. "Repression of the Human Right to Personal Integrity Revisited: A Global Cross-National Study Covering the Years 1976-1993." *International Studies Quarterly* 43(2), 1999. pp. 291-313; David L. Cingranelli and Mikhail Filippov. "Electoral Rules and Incentives to Protect

Human Rights." *Journal of Politics* 72(1), 2010. pp. 243–257.

vii Cingranelli and Fillipov, 2010.

viii Linda Camp Keith. "Judicial Independence and Human Rights Protection Around the World." *Judicature* 85(4), 2000. pp. 195–200; Oona A. Hathaway. "Why Do Countries Commit to Human Rights Treaties?" *Journal of Conflict Resolution* 51(4), 2007. pp. 588–621; Emilia J. Powell and Jeffrey K. Staton. "Domestic Judicial Institutions and Human Rights Treaty Violation." *International Studies Quarterly* 53(1), 2009.

ix Staton and Powell, 2009, pp. 149–174.

x Courtenay Ryals Conrad and Will H. Moore. "What Stops the Torture?" *American Journal of Political Science* 54(2), 2010. pp. 459–476.

xi James Raymond Vreeland. "Political Institutions and Human Rights: Why Dictatorships Enter into the United Nations Convention Against Torture." *International Organization* 62(1), 2008. pp. 65–101.

xii Richard Carver. "A New Answer to an Old Question: National Human Rights Institutions and the Domestication of International Law." *Human Rights Law Review* 10(1), 2010. pp. 1–32.

xiii Anne Smith. "The Unique Position of National Human Rights Institutions: A Mixed Blessing?" *Human Rights Quarterly* 28(4): 2006. pp. 904-946; Carver, 2010.

xiv Simmons, 2009.

xv Ibid., p. 144.

xvi Amnesty International. "Nepal: The Search for Justice." ASA 31/001/2013. Retrieved January 14, 2013. *http://www.amnesty.org/en/library/asset/ASA31/001/2013/en/11443e06-3609-4811-87a3-c35eb315f5d1/asa310012013en.pdf.* p. 10,

xvii Ibid, p. 18.

xviii James L. Cavallaro and Stephanie Erin Brewer. "Reevaluating Regional Human Rights Litigation in the Twenty-first Century: The Case of the Inter-American Court." *American Journal of International Law* 102(4), 2008. pp. 768–827; Loayza Tamayo v. Peru, Inter-Am. Ct. H.R. (ser. C) No. 33. September 17, 1997.

xix Cavallaro and Brewer, 2008, p. 789.

Is it Time to Re-Imagine
U.S. Foreign Policy in the Middle East?

Sabith Khan

2012 was a turbulent for the United States: it was an election year, four mass shootings occurred, and superstorm Sandy ravaged the East Coast. In terms of domestic and foreign policy, 2012 was a significant game-changing year, and pivotal regarding the country's changing relationship with the Middle East. I believe this is just the beginning of a long series of changes that can re-configure the relationship of the U.S. with the region. In the past, the United States has had dubious relationships with dictators such as Egypt's Hosni Mubarak and others who have reppressed their people. Current changes signal a window of opportunity to re-engage with the region in a manner that is not only beneficial for its own interest, but also reinforces the U.S as a moral power, capable of leadership in a turbulent world.

"Post-American World"
The world as we know it is changing, and we are witnessing what Fareed Zakaria, former *Newsweek* editor and current CNN host covering international issues, has called a "post-American world."[i]

The U.S administration is fundamentally re-assessing its involvement in the Middle East and will begin scaling down its operations in the region, if the Iraq withdrawal is any indication. While this scale-down is not meant to be defeatist or a negative connotation of the American legacy, the economic and social power-dynamics are changing globally. Consider, for example, the recent economic rise of the so-called BRIC countries (Brazil, India, China, and Russia) and the concurrent rise of Asia. A gradual global realignment in the economic sphere is happening.[ii]

This essay attempts to answer the following questions:

1. What are the implications of the recent moves to "democratize" societies in Tunisia, Egypt, and Libya?
2. What are the implications of these changes to the Israel-U.S. relationship?
3. How will the U.S. deal with the rise of political Islam in the region?

I will look at possible changes likely to occur in the near future and focus on a few key countries while analyzing how and why these changes may take place. In general, I argue that there is a case to be made for less U.S. involvement in the region.

Hot Spots in the Middle East

Iran, Palestine, Egypt, and Syria all captured international news headlines in 2012. Events are taking place in other Middle East countries that can potentially help the U.S. re-imagine its role in the region. While each Middle Eastern country is unique and must be dealt with individually, some lessons of engagement/disengagement are applicable across the region. First, we will look at some facts, and a brief historical background of the U.S engagement in the region, since we cannot delve fully into the decade's long engagement.

Facts on the Ground, as of 2012:

- The U.S. has over 400 military bases in the region, with an estimated 700-1000 globally.[iii]

- Civil war in Syria continues to rage (as of March 2013).

- Israel remains the United States' strongest "ally" in the region.

- A "democratic wave" is sweeping the Arab world, with Tunisia, Egypt, and Libya all in the beginning stages of democratic rule.

- Palestine gains observer status in the United Nations (meaning it is a non-voting member, but has a much more visible role than before).

- U.S. forces are drawing down from Iraq and its "Global War on Terror" is being scaled down in Afghanistan too.

- Tensions in Pakistan persist, with U.S. clandestine drone attacks continuing to kill civilians, creating animosity between Pakistanis and Americans.

"The Times, They are a-Changin"

As Bob Dylan sang in the 1960s, a time of widespread social unrest in the United States and globally, the times truly are changing in the Middle East. Without overindulging in punditry and make sweeping predictions about the future, it is safe to say that the future relationship of the United States and the region will not be the same as it is today.

The relationship with the Middle East will definitely move beyond one based on hydrocarbons and the insatiable U.S. demand for the region's oil. Consider the recent Arab Spring democratic movements across the Arab world, with a visible shift in economic power away from the U.S. Coupled with an enormous demographic shift taking place in the Arab world, where more than half the population is 25 years or younger, we are looking at a very significant shift in population demands, desires/aspirations, and rhetoric.

As Council on Foreign Relations Middle East expert Robert A. Malley stated,

...a lot...is very familiar...A Palestinian bid for an elevation of their status at the UN. An Egyptian president, who, on the one hand, acts in ways that are viewed as quite constructive by the United States when it comes to the relations between Israelis and Palestinians, and on the other hand, takes steps at home that are quite inconsistent with our view of democratic governance. We've seen all of that before. But the difference is that it's taking place in a radically transformed environment where the protagonists have changed identities and worldviews.[iv]

With Islamists in power in Egypt and Hamas more powerful than it was during its last war with Israel in 2008-2009, the United States is trying to make sense of a region that is no longer the one it knew.

But How Will the Arab Street React?

The Arab street, commonly used to mean the common Arab public, has had its share of complaints and sense of wrongdoing by America. The key complaint against the U.S. has consistently been the issue of occupation in Iraq and Palestine, both unsolved and intractable issues. Several opinion polls in the past have shown this sense of being wronged and a consistent negative public opinion of the U.S. in the region.[v] With President Obama's election in 2008 and his subsequent speech in Cairo regarding democratic change in the region, there was a glimmer of hope and newfound optimism in parts of the Arab world. This positivity has not been consistent, however. Feelings appear to be shifting, however slightly.

A recent study by Zogby International, a Washington D.C.-based polling firm, showed that the Arab street has a renewed faith in the Obama administration, with an increase in positivity toward the president and his work. This is certainly good news, considering that the Arab world seemed to have lost all hope and faith in the United States throughout much of the 21st century. An article in *The National*, an Abu

Millennials Speak.

Dhabi-based newspaper, stated,

> In a survey of Arab opinion last month, Zogby Research
> Services found that favorability ratings regarding the United
> States had spiked in most Arab countries. More significantly,
> there were strong majorities in several countries that responded
> that the United States was making a positive contribution to
> peace and stability in the Arab world.[vi]

The article mentions that Iraq, the Palestinian territories, and Tunisia
were surveyed, in addition to the countries that Zogby polls usually
target: Morocco, Egypt, Lebanon, Jordan, Saudi Arabia, and the UAE.
"What the 2012 poll made clear was that the decline in U.S. standing had
been arrested. In Saudi Arabia, for example, favorability ratings were at
an all-time high of 62 percent, while in Jordan and the UAE, positive
attitudes had climbed back to 2009 levels."

There is more to be positive about: "In Egypt, U.S. ratings were still
a low 10 percent. That, however, was double the rating that Egyptians
had given the United States in 2011, although nowhere near the 30
percent level after Mr. Obama delivered his "new beginnings" speech at
the University of Cairo in 2009. In Lebanon and Morocco, attitudes held
steady."[vii]

Moving Beyond "Democracy Promotion" in the Region

While both Bush administrations (George W. and George H.W.)
pursued democracy in the region, "Orientalists" such as Bernard Lewis
called for a very aggressive foreign policy. Lewis is a controversial
Orientalist, whom among other things is credited for coining the term
"clash of civilizations," a theory that posits that the conflicts of the
future will be between "civilizations" rather than nation-states. Samuel
Huntington borrowed the term and wrote his now-famous 1996 book
The Clash of Civilizations and Remaking of the World Order.[viii] Since the U.S.
economy remains stubbornly sluggish, there is very little public support

or appetite for any additional foreign intervention, with the exception of Libya, in the region. Absolutely no one is hungry for large-scale spending sprees in foreign countries while the administration has its hands full with its economy. The U.S. is still trying to figure out how to pay for the 10 years of simultaneous occupation and nation-building in Iraq and Afghanistan. Current strategic thinking about democracy promotion has evolved in the U.S. administration, seen by comparing policies from the first half of the Obama presidency to those of the George W. Bush presidency.

As Michael Hirsh stated in a *Washington Monthly* article "Bernard Lewis Revisited:" "In a new book, provocatively titled *The Case for Islamo-Christian Civilization*, one of those critics, Columbia scholar Richard Bulliet, argues that Lewis has been getting his 'master narrative' about the Islamic world wrong since his early epiphanic days in Turkey -- and he's still getting it wrong today.'"[ix] Bulliet's "clash of civilization" theory is slowly and surely being de-bunked by home-grown democracy movements. The theory has been criticized because it simplifies the complex dynamics between cultures and civilizations and also boxes entire continents into categories of simple terms, ignoring the vast internal differences between them.

The challenge of securing oil flow, maintaining "order" as Huntington so famously wrote in his 1968 book *Political Order in Changing Societies*, and ensuring that the Arab world perceives the U.S. in friendly terms are the key challenges facing the U.S. government.

Enter Soft Power and the Power of Diplomacy

The post-Iraq debacle seems to be the opportune time to deploy "soft-power" or the ability to influence others through culture or other "soft" means rather than "hard" military power, a term made famous by Joseph Nye, international relations scholar and former chairman of the U.S. National Intelligence Council under President Bill Clinton. There is an increased understanding among policy makers and administration officials that military power alone can only go so far in promoting foreign policy objectives. Eventually, diminishing returns arise from the application of only military muscle. Instead what is needed is a constructivist approach to foreign policy that deploys diplomacy to solve problems. In other words, soft power is needed and a move away from the militarily hawkish foreign policy that was the norm for eight years during the George W. Bush era..

A recent National Public Radio article quotes Nye, who said, "In the 21st century, the Iraq War caused a big drop in American soft power. That's because many people in other countries saw the United States as being too aggressive."[x] But, in 2008, when the subprime mortgage crisis hit, U.S. economic power declined too. Before the financial crisis, "there was the idea that Americans really knew how to run an economic system," Nye said. After the financial crisis, the world began to question the U.S. ability to keep its domestic economic house in order. But considering the seemingly unsolvable issues that the European economies are having with economic growth, and economic contraction, combined with an enormous slow-down in Chinese growth, things aren't looking as bad in the United States. "If you compare us [the U.S.] with Europe's economic system, we're doing pretty well," Nye said. "The dollar is still the safe haven."

This prediction seems about right, as there is a growing awareness that the way forward is not to invade countries and spend trillions of dollars on military activity, but to take some of that money and instead invest it in infrastructure, healthcare, and education, as outlined in President Obama's campaign for re-election.[xi] A strategic shift toward the deployment of soft power in the Middle East will be an important first step for the re-alignment of U.S. policy in the region and its move away from forced democracy promotion.

What to Watch for in the Next Four Years
While all is not well in the Middle East, there remains hope. One can hope that the newly formed democracies of Libya, Egypt, and Tunisia will mature and civil society will flourish in each country and across the

region. Places like Syria need examples to look to whenever they begin to rebuild their war-torn country. Several thorny issues must be addressed while the processes of "normalization" and "democratization" continue in these countries:

1.   Israel, the Arab world, and the U.S

As Shimon Peres, the ninth and current President of Israel said in an interview, compromise is needed to build peace in the region.[xii] Since the 1993 Oslo Peace Accords signed between Israel and the Palestine Liberation Organization (PLO), with U.S. President Bill Clinton as facilitator, and the collapse of the peace process, there has not been a sustained vision for peace. With the U.S. and Israel not accepting Hamas as the legitimate ruler of Gaza and not including them in the negotiations, the prospects for peace seem slim.

2.   Rise of Political Islam in the Middle East

The victory of Hamas in Gaza and the rise of the Muslim Brotherhood in Egypt appear at the heart of the dilemma regarding political Islam and the U.S. The United States will continue to promote democracy, but as in both these cases, sometimes democracy produces governments that run counter to U.S. interests.

"We could recognize Hamas, if they recognize us and stop terror," Shimon Peres said in an Al-Jazeera interview. While this is a fine sentiment, the rise of Islamist parties in the region has been extremely problematic for Washington and is democracy gone awry of U.S. interests. The future belongs to the young; they don't want hatred and suspicion. Until policymakers in Washington accept this reality and find new ways to handle and cope with them, there is bound to be misunderstanding and talking past one another regarding political Islam and democratization in the Middle East.

3.   Re-visiting Dependency Theory

Egypt and Israel (apart from Jordan), among other countries in the

Middle East and North Africa (MENA) region receive U.S. aid, a fact that complicates the entire relationship. While the aid gives the U.S. some leverage in each recipient's domestic affairs, it can be argued that this relationship has also created an element of dependency. Dependence is a conditioning situation in which the economies of one group of countries are conditioned by the development and expansion of others (U.S. and Mexico, for example), a theory made famous in the 1960s by scholar Theotonion Dos Santos and former Brazilian President Fernando Henrique Cardoso.

It has been argued that dependence of poorer, peripheral countries on other rich, core countries cannot be overcome without a qualitative change in internal political and economic structures and external relations between and among them. Both Dos Santos and Cardoso claimed that most poor and developing countries started as colonies of core countries and that although the developing countries gradually became independent, their economies remain on the periphery of the global economy, thus maintaining their dependence on the core. One can see how this notion is relevant for understanding just how inextricably tied the U.S. is to the Middle East and perhaps the rest of the world. The U.S. remains the most important "core country" as the largest economy in the world. This condition in itself can be problematic, once the size and composition of this this global "core country" begins to change.

Conclusion

Does a changing world call for greater U.S. involvement? Should the U.S. step up and help restart peace talks between Israel and Palestine, push for greater dialogue with the hard-liners in the Middle East, and boost its imports with all of the countries in the region?

While these are all complicated questions, with each requiring more individual analysis, the short answer is somewhere in between a yes and a no. I believe that each situation and country should be examined, every issue and option should be weighed, and a pragmatic rather than ideological approach should be taken, resulting in a clean break with past policy and strategy in the region.

As we have looked at the changing economic and cultural sphere of U.S. influence in the Middle East, it has become clear that the world as we know it is changing. So too should America's role.

Change should be natural for all geopolitical roles, leaders, and strategies. However, as demonstrated by Janet Abu Lughod, a well-known academic who has written extensively about the Middle East and its relationship with the "West," as core states become peripheral and peripheral states become core states, change, veering off a set path, is also an extremely painful process for everyone involved.

I am a child of the "liberalization" process in India. During this process I witnessed, in a short span, tremendous changes, both good and bad, that middle-class growth brought to my home country. And, having lived in the U.A.E. for over two years, I saw the booms and bust in India's economy. I believe my perspective is also slightly clearer about the political and economic challenges that each country and region face. As someone with a great affinity for the Middle East, I would like to see a more stable, peaceful, and prosperous region, which is not only a desired good, but also a necessity, for pragmatic reasons. There cannot be prosperity without peace.

I am not advocating a total re-examination of U.S. foreign policy, which is not realistically possible en masse. A more nuanced approach to engaging with certain regions is feasible, and in this case, with the Middle East, as well as setting priorities in terms of foreign affairs and strategic diplomacy. No one can undo the mistakes of the past but one can certainly learn from them and make corrections before the world becomes dependent on a different diplomatic path. I imagine a different U.S.-Middle East relationship. It is time Washington reimagines it, too. In that new diplomatic path lies the prospect for positive U.S. relations with the rest of the world, and the Middle East.

ⁱ Fareed Zakaria. "What Does A 'Post-American World' Look Like?" National

Public Radio. June 30, 2011. Accessed November 10 2012.
http://www.npr.org/2011/06/30/137522219/what-does-a-post-american-world-look-like.

ii Zakaria, 2011; Mahbubani, 2012.

iii Richard Johnson. "Graphic: Mapping a Superpower-sized Military." *National Post.* October 28, 2011. Accessed November 10 2012.
http://news.nationalpost.com/2011/10/28/graphic-mapping-a-superpower-sized-military/.

iv Council on Foreign Relations. "U.S. Challenges in a Changed Middle East." November 30, 2012. Accessed November 10 2012. *http://www.cfr.org/middle-east/us-challenges-changed-middle-east/p29577.*

v Shibley Telhami. "The 2011 Arab Public Opinion Poll." The Brookings Institution. November 21, 2011. Accessed November 10, 2012.
http://www.brookings.edu/research/reports/2011/11/21-arab-public-opinion-telhami.

vi James Zogby. "Obama Gets a Second Chance in Arab Public Opinion." *The National.* December 30, 2012. Accessed 10 January 2013.
http://www.thenational.ae/thenationalconversation/comment/obama-gets-a-second-chance-in-arab-public-opinion; Arab American Institute. "Arab Opinion Polls." 2012. Accessed December 10, 2012. *http://www.aaiusa.org/pages/opinion-polls/.*

vii Ibid.

viii Samuel Huntington. *The Clash of Civilizations and Remaking of the World Order.* Simon & Schuster, 1996.

ix Michael Hirsh. "Bernard Lewis Revisited." *The Washington Monthly.* November 2004. Accessed November 10, 2012.
http://www.washingtonmonthly.com/features/2004/0411.hirsh.html.

x Marilyn Geewax. "Can U.S. Still Lead In Economic And 'Soft' Power?" National Public Radio. October 22, 2012. Accessed November 10, 2012.
http://www.npr.org/2012/10/22/163387838/can-u-s-still-lead-in-economic-and-soft-power.

xi Angie Drobnic Holan. "A Scorecard on President Obama's Campaign Promises." September 4, 2012. Accessed November 10, 2012.
http://www.politifact.com/ohio/article/2012/sep/04/scorecard-president-obamas-campaign-promises/.

xii Al Jazeera. "Shimon Peres: 'Self-victimising Palestinians.'" December 30, 2012. Accessed January 10, 2013.
http://www.aljazeera.com/programmes/frostinterview/2012/12/2012122610132412135.html.

Part 2

Essays on Popular Culture

The New Economics of Digital Content

R.P. *Thead*

It is 2013. If you are reading this collection of essays there is a very good chance that you are reading it in an electronic format on one of the many eBook readers or tablet computers available on the market. If you are reading this in paperback, there is an even better chance that you purchased it from an online retailer, probably Amazon.com. And if you are reading this several years from now, the likelihood of both is even more so. Our entire world is changing. You can see it in the essays written by the forward-thinking people who have made this book possible.

This essay will examine developments in the publishing industry and draw comparisons to the music industry, highlighting the mistakes of the latter and forming 21st century business scenarios for the former. I make several broad predictions regarding the future of the publishing industry and the effects of these developments on how we produce and consume information. I argue that the ease of self-publishing books, especially the advent and spread of inexpensive eBook readers such as Amazon's Kindle and Barnes and Noble's Nook, in addition to inexpensive tablet computers, have large democratizing effects on the book and publishing industry, albeit at the sacrifice of that industry's profits. But, by creating a true free market for digital content (bonanza or free-for-all might be more suitable terms), much of this content, which is copyrighted, intellectual property, is losing its value.

As a result, this lost value is being shifted to different points along what I call the "digital content chain." That is, as a result of a large supply of content, value has shifted from the content itself to the production and consumption of the content and its ability to drive online advertising. I argue that in order to stay current with this new distribution of value, the publishing industry needs a serious rethink regarding the pricing of eBooks. Additionally, I make predictions regarding the future profitability of the publishing industry and the livelihood of brick-and-mortar retail bookstores.

What Constitutes a Book?

What is a book? In the good old days, if you wanted to break into the writing world as a published author, you could write an 80,000-100,000 word manuscript (about 300 pages) and start knocking on publishing house doors in an attempt to have a one take a chance on you and your book. If you were lucky, and as a first-time writer found either a big publishing house or a smaller outfit willing to take a chance on your book, you could probably hope to get your book published and for sale in bookstores in one to two years. And, if you were even luckier, you could keep 5-10 percent of the profits. And if you were lottery-winning lucky, the publisher would invest in the promotion and marketing of the book so that people would know it existed and maybe buy a copy.

But to get as far as becoming a complete failure as an author, you had to have someone tell you, "Yes, this is a book. The words that make up the story that you wrote is a book that can be read because we say that it is a book." The publishers could do this because this was the only way to get your book published. Alternative options in the good old days, after being rejected by publishing houses, included going through what is called a vanity press. This process means fronting money for production and printing to have a large run of your book printed, usually many hundreds if not thousands of copies, then selling them one at a time by yourself. That is a lot of risk for a product that usually fails, but it is a different world.

Enter Amazon.com

Amazon.com has revolutionized the retail market, especially books.
Amazon began primarily as an online bookstore and has grown into a
supersized online shopping mall with unbeatable prices and cheap (and
often free) shipping. In some large metropolitan areas this includes
same-day shipping. As a result of its growth, the search feature on
Amazon's website constitutes one of the biggest search engines on the
whole Internet. Thus, products listed for sale on Amazon.com are
available for purchase by hundreds of millions of people in the United
States and billions globally.

Perhaps you stumbled across this book while searching Amazon for
something about the millennial generation or global demographic shifts.
But there is a very good chance you did not buy this book in a
bookstore. Most traditional retail bookstores despise Amazon, and for
good reason. They simply cannot compete with the online retailer's
prices and selection. Instead of adapting and attempting to truly
compete with Amazon, many traditional retailers have taken punitive
measures against it. Most bookstores will not carry paperback books that
have been produced and published using Amazon's online self
publishing site, Createspace. I know this from experience.

With Createspace, anyone can upload any written work, slap a cover
on it, give it a title and a price, call it a paperback book, and list it on
Amazon.com and begin making royalties percentages on it that are
unheard-of in the traditional publishing industry. And, just as easy, that
same person can put the same book up for sale as a Kindle eBook and
make up to 70 percent royalties on it, which is completely unfathomable
from a traditional publisher, depending on the price. With recent
advances in print-on-demand technology for paperbacks, it is now
economically viable for Amazon to print books as they are ordered,
cutting enormous printing and stocking overhead out of the profit
equation.

Advances in self-publishing have resulted in many poorly-written and
poorly produced self-published books. But, these self-published books

can sell at or below prices offered at retail bookstores and still turn a profit for Amazon and possibly for the author. As a result, most bookstores will not carry books self-published with Amazon's Createspace. By bookstores I refer to the large chains and the small independently-owned stores. Their defiance has a lot to do with wholesale issues; middlemen involved in the book business have to get a cut, and they do not like that Amazon bypasses them. Further, most bookstores will not even take these self-published books to sell on consignment, which is a very low-risk method of trying out new retail items.

Pretending something does not exist is not a long-term business strategy, although ignoring a pressing problem and hoping that it will just go away is a very American way of doing things.

Future of the Publishing Industry

I predict that in five years or less, maybe one-half of the independent bookstores will still be open, and one in ten of the large retailers' brick and mortar stores, such as Borders, Books-A-Million, and Barnes and Noble, will still be open for business. More independent stores will stay open because of customer loyalty. No matter how big eBooks become, physical books, including used books, will maintain a niche market; they also carry a certain aesthetic value that digital files do not.

The large retailers will not be able to handle the large overhead costs for what is a quickly dwindling profit. Why is this? First, stocking books in a large retail store is expensive, and the retail stores cannot compete with the selection of an online retailer. Amazon does not have these problems. With a sophisticated logistics and warehouse system in the United States, the company is able to quickly deliver almost any book ever written. And delivery is only getting faster since the company has begun same-day delivery is certain urban areas. Second, the overhead for a brick and mortar retail store is higher in terms of property rent, electrical, insurance, municipal codes, shoplifting, and other elements. Last, the publishing industry refuses to truly adapt to the times and fully embrace the increasingly popular and inexpensive eBook readers.

In general, I am talking about "trade books" written and marketed for a general audience. This does not include textbooks, which although are still sold in physical, hardback, and paperback formats, are gaining popularity in digital formats as well.[i]

The fundamentals of the book publishing industry have hardly changed in the last century. The publishers are capable of reaching larger, global audiences with more books about more topics, but in general, nothing else has changed. The companies still value and price the products they are selling as if nothing else in the market is different, especially eBooks. And, like book retailers, publishers have taken punitive and anti-competitive measures in a futile attempt to maintain the status quo. For example, in 2012 the United States Department of Justice accused Apple and the publishers of colluding with one another when setting prices for eBooks.[ii] Collusion is considered an anti-competitive business practice in many economies, for good reason, because it is cheating. And cheating is a sign of desperation. Apple and the publishers lost the Department of Justice case.

The traditional publishers, reeling from their collusion suit, went after Amazon in a lawsuit for predatory pricing practices of eBooks.[iii] Amazon was cleared by the Department of Justice. This seems a bit irrational since the publishers need Amazon for sales, a reliance that is likely to increase. I do understand that the publishers' complaint was rational: Amazon was and still is setting eBook prices lower than the publishers prefer, but this is a result of a larger supply of new titles and Amazon's large market share.

With increased competition from self-publishers and Amazon's commitment to low prices, more books are available but they are selling for less money. As it turns out, books and other digital content follow similar supply and demand rules as other price-elastic items for sale. Somehow the publishing industry missed this or thought that it could cheat.

The "Digital Content Chain"

Amazon and its Kindle have effectually devalued the content consumed by Kindle and other tablet computer owners. Content includes the things we consume on our devices (tablets, smartphones, Kindles, iPads): music, videos, pictures, news, and books. Content has not become valueless, but the value of copyrighted material has shifted from its ownership to other points along "digital content chain".

I define the digital content chain with three major components: production (creation) of the content, the distribution of it, and the consumption of content, along with the ability of that content's consumption to drive online advertising and marketing. This chain also includes the ownership of the content: copyrights and intellectual property rights that allow an artist, author, or musician to legally call their creations theirs. Content ownership is present in each part of the chain, but it is the part of the chain that I argue is being devalued. I will explain each part of this digital content chain.

By production, I mean the people involved in the creation of the content: studio engineers, cover and design artists, proofreaders/copyeditors, etc. They are the creative professionals who assist in making an idea reality. Content distribution includes people involved in the promotion, advertising, marketing, and sale of the content (including retail websites). Consumption means whichever device you primarily use to consume content, such as Apple's iPad or Amazon's Kindle. The value added in consumption of this content is its ability to drive advertising and encourage a consumer to buy other products.

Amazon has almost every step of this content chain covered. Consider books. Amazon has production such as Createspace, where you can pay their professionals for services like cover design and editing, in addition to their own traditional publishing house; distribution on the Amazon.com website, and consumption among Kindle readers and tablets; the ability to consume content on one of these readers drives consumers to purchase them.

However, there is still some value in content ownership. Books, music, and movies are still for sale and people still buy them. Intellectual property rights have played and continue to play an important role in a competitive and vibrant capitalist economy. Creators, inventors, and innovators need assurance that what they create is theirs. Some of the things that current intellectual property rights exist to protect, such as books and music, are not worth as much as they used to be. Technological innovation has shifted the value of the content to other points of the digital content chain and away from the content itself. This does not mean that the strength of intellectual property can or should be eroded moving forward. If anything, new and additional steps should be taken to protect devalued content. This essay will not, however, focus on the current state or future of intellectual property rights in the United States or globally.

Businesses that have realized this, or do not have a vested interest in the status quo regarding content value, are doing well. As you will see, Amazon follows and benefits from a similar strategy employed by Apple's iTunes store in the 2000s when they swooped in to profit from the music industry's inability or unwillingness to adapt to a changing marketplace.

Lessons Learned from the Music Industry: Re-Valuing Digital Content

At the end of the 1990s the big music companies attempted to squash Napster, their first formidable rival. Granted, between 1999 and 2001 this competitor was facilitating the stealing of the products the music industry sells. But the file-sharing site's popularity should have been a sign that the music industry had things wrong at the time. Instead of embracing the new way to transmit music and implementing it into their existing business model, the music industry did its best to push what was perceived as a fad to disappear so they could return to selling $20 CDs.

As a result, in 2003 Apple stepped in with its online iTunes Store and its new digital music distribution technology. Apple also invented a new way to consume the music in the form of the iPod, fully embracing the content distribution and consumption parts of my "digital content chain." One could argue that through Mac computers and Final Cut software suite they have the production part of the chain covered, too. Apple also offered new consumer price options in the form of individual songs for sale or, compared to the retail price for a full-length compact disc, album-length products at a discounted, re-valued price.

Apple's iTunes Store was selling the music for less than the music industry has traditionally priced its products. The large distribution of the iTunes Store made it possible for Apple to sell volumes of music with little brick-and-mortar overhead. This gave the music industry's 20th century business model a wake-up call. The iTunes store did not bode well for the brick-and-mortar music stores. Between 1999 and 2009, the music industry declined in sales by more than half.[iv] And, in 2009, Virgin Records closed all of their megastores. In 2004, the year after the iTunes Store was launched, it had sold about 200 million songs; by 2011 it had sold about 15 billion songs.[v] What went wrong with the music industry and what could they have done? A mixture of things.

Doing Business Differently

As I mentioned, the music industry made no attempt to embrace the methods of online distribution that they were fighting with Napster and that Apple took on. I guess the music industry thought they could just "sue it away." But people were stealing music at the rate they were, and still are, for other reasons.

I believe that one of the reasons people stole so much music using Napster and still do with other file sharing sites and bittorrent was a combination of three things. One, people could. With the spread of high-speed Internet service, Napster made downloading, or pirating, music easy and even fun. Two, when Napster came along, there was no such thing as the iTunes Store or even the Amazon Music Store. If you wanted to download mp3s, you went to Napster. And three, the music industry sold a product that was and is inherently over-valued. The success of the Apple iTunes Store and its innovative pricing options evidences this. We witnessed a popping of the music bubble in the first decade of the 2000s. The industry was selling an intrinsically over-valued product and the market reacted. Will the publishing industry suffer a similar fate?

What Can the Publishers Do?

As a first step, the publishers need to realize that the books they sell, especially eBooks, are not worth as much as they used to be. They need to modify industry-standard pricing before their bubble bursts, too.

As a writer and self-published author, I price eBooks lower than a paperback for several reasons. First, I can make more money from a self published eBook than a paperback, even if the retail price of the eBook is 50 percent lower than the paperback due to Amazon's royalty agreements with the authors it distributes. The royalty for eBooks priced over $2.99 is 70 percent. Second, a digital copy of something, speaking from the standpoint of a consumer, does not intrinsically have the same value compared to a physical copy of something. If I make higher royalty percentages and higher total royalties for a digital download as compared to a paperback, and that digital copy costs less than half of the paperback, it would make rational economic sense that I price the eBook the same as the paperback to make more money. The content is the same but in a different format.

But it is easier to share (steal) a digital copy of a book with not just one, but many other people, compared to a physical copy. And, perhaps illegally downloading digital files does not feel as much like stealing as walking out of a store with a CD or book. So, as a seller I have an incentive to price the digital copy lower in hopes that potential customers will see the value of the digital copy compared to the physical copy and purchase it instead of "borrowing" it from a friend or file-sharing site. The industry fails to grasp this second point as I will explain.

Look at some of the Big Six (Big Five) Publishing titles on Amazon and you will notice that the eBooks are priced very close to paperbacks. For example, Jonathan Franzen's 2010 bestseller *Freedom* is available on Amazon in multiple formats. A new paperback sells for about (USD) $10.50; the eBook is priced at $9.99. The overhead for the latter is almost nothing compared with the paperback, thus the profit margins are greater. Yet, the retail prices for both formats are about the same. A quick Google search of the terms "Franzen," "Freedom," and "bittorrent" show some other, less-expensive download options. Stealing a digital copy is just as much work as buying a copy from Amazon. I in no way advocate for stealing content or condone the practice. But I do know there are less intellectual property-respectful content consumers out there than I am. Does the publishing industry know this as well?

The First Steps
The publishing world is already changing. Two companies, Random House and Penguin, of what was called the Big Six Publishers, merged towards the end of 2012 in an attempt to reposition themselves in a rapidly changing publishing market.[vi] If the publishing industry continues to operate like it is still 1950 while profits dwindle, it will fail. As a result, there will be more mergers.

If the publishers take a lesson from the music industry and across the board decide to revalue books, especially eBooks, then perhaps the companies will be both relevant and viable, and profitable without having to cheat in the 21st century. They either do not realize this point or are just ignoring it. They are already losing profits, hence the mergers. To compensate for these lost profits, publishers will need to streamline themselves to compete. This means unloading staff that perform the types of tasks that more and more authors can do for themselves, such as cover design. Powerful and inexpensive computers coupled with easy-to-use software and broadband Internet connections have made it possible to perform these tasks. Publishers need to begin moving themselves out of some of the production part of the digital content chain and focus instead on marketing, promotion, and distribution. The publishing industry will continue to have a comparative advantage with editing. They are too late to the game to get in on the consumption end and produce their own tablets/eReaders.

Thanks to social media, authors are now able to do several tasks that were previously publishing house territory: marketing and promotion. And it can be done for free, although at a smaller scale. I believe that the large publishing houses will increasingly cherry-pick self-published success stories and strike distribution and marketing deals with those authors. But unless this is done as more of a partnership and not from the standpoint of self-appointed industry hegemon, it will not be a successful venture. The publishers will continue to have profitability when it comes to some of the modern-day book-selling titans, such as Stephen King, John Grisham, Danielle Steele, and Agatha Christie. The publishers can operate at scale with these bestselling powerhouses and make large profits. But eventually the publishers will be dealing with a new generation of writers who enjoy the freedom, speed, and profit margins that come with self-publishing.

It's a Brave New Digital World

With the rise and rapid proliferation of social media, the way that consumers discover new books and all other content has changed. Authors no longer need a publisher to tell them what is and is not a book, and the consumer does not need this filter either. The marketing and promotion services that traditional publishers provide will become less relevant as the number of bookstores in the United States and world shrinks and eBooks continue to gain a larger share of the book market. Some jobs in the book and publishing industry are already no longer necessary. This especially means cutting out some of the middlemen, including literary agents. It is one thing for a publisher to pass on a book and tell you that they cannot make money off of it after investing in it. It is quite another for a middleman to tell you that they are not interested in "representing" a writer or a book project.

These changes in the publishing industry have produced some unintended consequences. For one, these changes have further democratized writing and publishing. Blogs and social media have opened up the sharing of information at a rate and scale that no one could have predicted at the turn of the 21st century.

The publishing industry has been quite resistant to change, much like the firearm and fossil fuel industries in the United States. Without serious rethinking and revaluing of the products they produce and sell, the publishing industry will be right behind the music industry on the Long Road to Lost Profits. The Autobahn, it is not.

Currently, no hard data exist on the impact of eBook piracy on the publishing industry. Piracy does not appear to be of great concern to the publishers[vii]. The eReader and eBook trend is somewhat recent so this may change. It is easier to "consume" 1,000 files of pirated music than 1,000 pirated eBooks. Although books and music might be protected under similar intellectual property laws, the differences in time needed and the manner that books and music are consumed make the two somewhat incomparable. As an author, I am unconcerned about piracy of my work (if anyone wants a free copy of anything email me at r.p.thead@gmail.com). The more people I reach the better.

Conclusion

This book you are reading would probably not have happened had I gone, hat-and-essays-in-hand, begging for an agent to look at the manuscript. I hope this essay does not seem to be an advertisement for Amazon.com. It is hard to talk about changes in the publishing industry without talking about Amazon.

I can assure you this is not a hidden promotion for the company. But without Amazon, it is likely this manuscript would have wiled its relevancy away in a slush pile or in the spam folders of some agent's email inbox. Or, had it been picked up by any publisher, the extended production of the book as more and more people got a piece of it would have rendered some of the essays obsolete by the time the book was released. The other authors and I did not need someone to tell us that what we have is a book. We just need people like you to buy it. Or download it illegally. All we care is that you read it.

The marketplace is going to determine the success and relevancy of this book. With the types of publishing capabilities offered to virtually everyone by places like Amazon's Createspace, writers and producers of digital content have only the market to contend with if they decide to forgo traditional publishers, producers, and distributors whose business models are mired in the mid-20th century.

And if a business or industry is unwilling or unable to adapt to a changing market, it will fail.

---

i Julie Bosman and Jeremy W. Peters. "In E-Books, Publishers Have Rivals: News Sites." *New York Times*. September 18, 2011. Accessed January 8, 2013. *http://www.nytimes.com/2011/09/19/business/media/in-e-books-publishing-houses-have-a-rival-in-news-sites.html?pagewanted=all&_r=0*

ii United States Department of Justice. "United States v. Apple, Inc." Accessed December 15, 2012. *http://www.justice.gov/atr/cases/applebooks.html*.

iii Alison Frankel. "DOJ e-books filing: Amazon probed, cleared for predatory pricing." Thomson Reuters. July 23, 2012. Accessed January 7, 2013. *http://newsandinsight.thomsonreuters.com/New York/News/2012/07_-_July/DOJ_e books_filing__Amazon_probed,_cleared_for_predatory_pricing/*.

iv David Goldman. "Music's lost decade: Sales cut in half." "CNNMoney." February 2, 2010. Accessed December 10, 2012. *http://money.cnn.com/2010/02/02/news/companies/napster_music_industry/*.

v Digital Music News. "Apple Has Now Sold 15 Billion iTunes Songs..." 06 June 2011. Accessed 8 January 2013. http://www.digitalmusicnews.com/stories/060611itunes15.

vi Eric Pfanner and Amy Chozick. "Random House and Penguin Merger Creates Global Giant." *New York Times*. October 29, 2012. Accessed January 9, 2013. *http://www.nytimes.com/2012/10/30/business/global/random-house-and-penguin-to-be-combined.html?pagewanted=all&_r=0*.

vii *The Guardian*. "Who's afraid of digital book piracy?" February 18, 2010. Accessed January, 8 2013. *http://www.guardian.co.uk/books/booksblog/2010/feb/18/digital-book-piracy-copyright*

Making it in the 21st Century Music Industry

Michael Young

The music industry needs a serious redesign. As part of the Millennial Generation, I believe we are the people to do it. After all, we are the developers and pacesetters of the industry's current state. The status quo, however, does not fully leverage 21st century technology or reflect purchasing trends. In the late 1990s, beginning with the file-sharing service Napster, we played a large role in fundamentally changing the way that people listen to, discover, and acquire new music. Despite Metallica's complaints I believe the changes were for the better. For those unfamiliar, Metallica sued Napster for 100 million dollars for copyright infringement, drawing the ire of many users due to Metallica's financial success. As a result, the generation has also changed not only the meaning of breaking out or "making it" as an artist or band, but also the path that leads to that success.

Major record labels and other large music industry stakeholders have dragged their feet in adjusting to a constantly changing market and rapid technological advances. They have a vested interest in the status quo, which is why despite the innovation and development of new digital music delivery programs, things still "feel" very static across the industry. Large government and corporations loathe rapid change. Abandoning vested interests and investments is expensive and amortization is not cheap. However, smaller music labels and independent music entrepreneurs can respond more quickly to these changes and leverage innovation. With the information revolution, the explosion of the Internet, and the advent of social media, in the near future we might witness the untimely death of the music industry hegemons: large record labels. I argue this will require a complete refocus on how musicians attempt to make it in the music business. In the process, I briefly discuss the history of the music industry and what it took and meant to make it. Additionally, I provide a quick case study of the industry's marketing prowess and relate my own experience as a musician in the Baltimore, Maryland area. Then I consider some popular online music streaming services and what role they will play in the future of the music industry.

The Music Industry in the 20th Century

For much of the latter half of the 20th century, general music industry practice involved large record labels providing lavish record contracts to bands and artists who could make the labels lots of money through millions of album sales, followed by large-scale tours that often spanned the globe. This was business-as-usual for the hugely popular and highly successful artists and acts. They were the industry cash cows. But, always looking for the next big thing, the labels also took chances on smaller, sometimes unknown groups whose financial success was a gamble for the label. The percentage of bands and artists who have albums certified Gold (500,000 sold) or Platinum (1 million sold) is roughly 5 percent. Therefore, if you lined up 20 bands or acts signed to a label, one band would actually make a profit for the label's investment, which includes the money paid for studio time, marketing, advertising, and distribution. The other 19 acts are financial liabilities.

From the 1960s until approximately 1999, the success rate of performers was completely removed from the success of the record label. That is, even if an album completely flopped, the label could usually recoup most of the costs incurred from recording, producing, and releasing that album and still break even on that act or particular record. Royalties paid to artists and musicians are small, even for the large groups. This means that while the musicians more or less fail, the label moves on. Eventually those musicians might collect a few dollars in royalties every year (split among the entire band). Big music labels like EMI and BMG only needed 5 percent success rate financially; that one record that sold millions of copies could usually cover losses on the other 19 failures, and then some. And that hit record usually ensured the release of at least one or two albums from the same successful band, which was usually guaranteed to enjoy a similar success rate.

It is hard to imagine another industry that can get away with a successful investment rate of only 5 percent and still make money. And, these are "failed products" that are taken to market. They make it out of research and development: talent scouting. This failure rate is unheard-of in other industries. If a pharmaceutical company releases 20 drugs and hopes that one would work, the many people getting rich would be involved in class action lawsuits against the drug company. But in the music industry, 5 percent success was the norm until right around 1999 when Napster entered the scene.

The music industry's failure and success rates are similar now but recouping the cost of albums that fail is becoming much more difficult for record labels. Why is this? For starters, there have been changes in buying behavior. Consumers who at one point would have paid $15-20 for a complete album on a physical format to get one or two songs they liked now have additional options to get just those songs. They may buy that one song on Amazon or iTunes, stream it on a music website or program, or, just steal the whole album using file sharing software such as bittorrent. In less than 20 years, the entire music industry landscape has changed, not for better or worse than 20 years ago, just different.

Fiona Apple: A Case Study

Some Millennials, especially those at the upper end of the generation's age spectrum, enjoy waxing nostalgic about music videos. We also enjoy complaining about the dearth of music video programming on MTV relative to the 1990s and before.

Of course music videos were really just slick marketing tools that targeted the demographic most likely to buy the product they were advertising. It turns out that if you put Fiona Apple in underwear and have her walk around a weird and dark house taking pictures of other half-naked girls while she sings the latest single off of her new album, then that album has a good chance of selling a lot of copies, which in Fiona's case, was about 3 million. I cannot name more than two Fiona Apple songs, but as an impressionable 14 year-old, I can tell you that I sure as hell remember that music video. Selling 3 million copies of an album as a raspy jazz singer when grunge was at its peak is impressive. It is a marketing miracle. But marketing is, in essence, what major record labels do.

In the 1990s and to a lesser extent in the 1980s, music labels were willing to produce high-budget music videos for acts like Fiona Apple and play them on MTV, VH1, and similar stations for two reasons. One, the labels had a roster of similarly-branded artists they could play and cross-promote to create trends in consumer tastes. Two, except for radio, video was the most effective way to sell new music and artists. Viewers could not yet choose, on-demand, what they wanted to watch and listen to without buying it. We had to watch and listen to what was played for us.

I remember the day I discovered that I could record songs off the radio onto blank cassettes; it was one of the happiest days of my teenage years. I remember sitting in my bedroom with my finger on the record button as songs would come to an end, poised to press record it if a song I liked came on, hoping that the DJ would not talk over the song as it began. With this strange, inelegant method, I was introduced to piracy. Way back in the 1990s, if I wanted to listen to a specific artist or song, I had to go to the record store and pay 15 dollars for their album or vote for a specific song on MTV's Total Request Live (TRL). I could try and request it via a radio station, depending on how lucky I was feeling. That was then. Now, I do not even have to purchase a song or complete album if I want to hear a specific track. I can bypass the Apple iTunes Store and Amazon.com and head over to YouTube and stream most of the artists' entire catalogue for free. How has the music industry responded to this devaluing of their product, aside from pursuing copyright violators in court? How can they still make money in a changed marketplace?

In the good old days, this was the path to rock stardom: if you had a good product and you wanted to sell it, the industry was buying. All you needed was a creative sound, time to practice, money needed for time in a local studio to record a demo, and a press kit. This was the basic formula for a shot at landing some version of a record deal. The label would take over from there: they would finance the production of your record in a state of the art recording studio staffed by industry professionals, promote your music through radio play of your single, make a music video to market your image, then repeat this process as many times as they could. The labels were willing to take this risk on relatively unknown artists and bands (95 percent failed, remember). It was not unknown for the Fiona Apples of the world to have their shot at stardom.

Now, most major labels will not touch a band until they have established a nationwide fan base and have several low-budget albums worth of material that the label can use to attract new fans. But how does an artist or band build that initial fan base? How do you get started as a musician?

Do it Yourself (DIY) Music and Who's Making Money

The modern musician is a renaissance man or woman. To be successful, he or she has to be driven, adept at marketing and promotion, and possess the stock to endlessly network using social media. The latter is very similar to walking a tightrope as there is a fine line between targeted self-promotion and spamming your friends. This musician must also be financially literate and capable of balancing a budget. Then there is the music end of things. A modern musician must have a place to record, perform live regularly, and this musician must perpetually create and release new material. In the 21st century, a musician must be able to operate and market himself as if he is a small business. The music is the easy part.

This is the economics of the modern music industry: everyone wants to position himself to "make it" by the traditional industry definitions. Everyone wants the money, big house, and fleet of cars, and everyone else is looking to charge them money to help them do that. Countless individuals make money off of the dreams of countless musicians. With advances in recording technology, especially the use of computers in the process, it is easy to get started without the help of trained or experienced recording professionals. But, quality will suffer, and anyone serious in their desires will reach a certain point where they will want to outsource tasks to professionals. For some, time is the deciding factor to pay someone to record or produce your work. Unless one is very fortunate, odds are someone trying to making it as a musician is working at least a part-time job. Division and specialization of labor are important in any industry. As far as I am concerned, as a musician, that professional who people pay might as well be me.

I have produced music for emcees and aspiring rap artists in Baltimore and the Washington, D.C. metro-area. My role for these artists is determining what style of hip-hop they want to make (old school, dirty south, etc.), then guiding them through my creative process. I then create the instrumentals they will use, which involves an in-person meeting to discuss hard and soft deadlines, my expectations for them, their expectations for me, and signing contracts to protect both parties. Often, I have already made music that they want to purchase from me; other times I will do a project completely from scratch, which costs significantly more, but the music is usually catered to the artist. They then select the beats that they want to use, compose lyrics to these beats, and record them. Afterward, they send the vocals to me and I mix them, master the project, and send them the finished product. They are free to sell it or give it away but I retain exclusive rights to the instrumentals, and I am free to re-sell that music to other artists. That is, if an artist wants to pay an exclusive fee to retain the full copyrights to that instrumental, no one else can use it (but it costs 50 times what I charge to just "lease" the beat).

The artists I have worked with are drawn to the romanticism of taking their one shot and hoping to make it big. While there is money to be made in the production of the music, is there a responsibility to tell the artists that their chances of recouping their investments, far from making it, are almost nonexistent? Some of the emcees I have worked with were not talented, and many did not really possess the drive necessary to advance in a saturated industry that perpetuates a false narrative where artists with million-dollar sweetheart deals were just guys who worked hard and got heard. The reality that most musicians will face is much different.

I will pay half of next month's rent with money I am earning from producing a mixtape for a mediocre rapper, and I am happy to do it. Financially, there is no incentive for me to tell him that he is not good enough. This is not my responsibility. The carrot of success as a musician is shrinking and people like me just help to dangle it as the record labels make the stick longer and longer. But, the industry's carrot is shrinking, too. As the DIY music industry grows it allows room for people like me to capitalize on others. Value is being shifted from the music itself to the production of it by people like me.

This is just one interpretation of what I do, as a musician. I will not pretend that that my intentions are entirely charitable, but at the same time I am doing what little I can to help the city of Baltimore, which has been starving for a vibrant hip hop scene. The city needs some musical identity. I want to help it achieve it. Some artists here (hip hop or otherwise) are creating enormous catalogs of material long before they even see anything that resembles a record contract from any label, major or independent. None of them have "made it."

What Does it Mean to "Make It"?

Consider this scenario: After releasing two complete albums and giving them away online and at shows, a label takes notice of an artist and decides to sign him to a modest record contract. The terms of the contract involve a single album to test the waters together. The digital records are made available on iTunes and Amazon. But before inking the deal, the artist has already done everything that traditionally, the record company used to do: record a catalog of music, build a fan base and generate buzz, attempt to get songs on (college) radio, and make music videos. Yet, the record deal only offers the artist 10 percent on wholesale album sales and they charge the artist for services that the artist used to do for himself and now has experience and skills in. Bootstrapping one's way into a music career has become the norm. Some refer to it as "paying one's dues." But where and what is the return on this investment for both parties? Is a traditional record deal considered "making it"?

There are bands enjoying popular and modest financial success on the independent circuit right now. These artists have gained the respect of critics, writers, and listeners, but they still probably share a one-bedroom apartment or live in their parents' basements. Some of their critics and album reviewers probably bring home a bigger paycheck than they are. Popular music blogs are becoming the new gatekeepers to music industry success. Mentions and coverage by some are almost replacing the sought-after 'record deals' of decades past. But online buzz can disappear just as quickly as it appears, much faster than a recording contract can be dissolved. That is good for listeners who seek out music, people like myself who constantly crave new music. As soon as one band stalls or buzz dies down, there are usually thousands waiting to take their place. As a result, 'making it' as a musician has been redefined. The music industry as a whole, including independent and major labels, in addition to self-promoted and released artists, has become somewhat more democratic than in the past. More decisions are made by consumers; fewer decisions are made for them. This can be bad for the artist but is good for businessmen like me who are ready to help new acts produce the next big thing.

The Future of the Music Industry and How We Hear Music

There is a healthy amount of irony in the way that the Millennial Generation, especially the oldest cohort, consumes music: we come from what is probably the last generation with a radio culture that actually mattered. We got to truly experience multiple new genres of music simultaneously converging over the airwaves. As a mode of transmitting new music and introducing unknown artists, radio is dead. File sharing and streaming may have completed what the video could not and killed radio, but the formative years had already been set for many of us. The role of radio was large for many in our generation whose lives were steeped in music. Personally, it played a large role in forming my identity; I used spent my summer mornings in middle and high school listening to alternative rock radio stations for hours at a time, and sometimes all day. I think most of us have forgotten what it is like to do this and truly discover a band on our own: hearing something new and having to stop what you are doing, becoming entranced by a song or artist. I know our generation is ready for music to be a big part of our lives again, but the way that music plays a role in those lives will be different.

Spotify, an online music streaming service, has promised to be the next big thing that permanently changes the music industry. The person primarily responsible for Spotify making its way to the U.S. from the U.K. is, rightfully, the same person responsible for Napster. Pricing for Spotify is tiered, but for as little as $10 each month, you can listen to as much music as you want as often as you want with no limits, including mobile streaming on smartphones. Programs like Spotify are needed to keep up with the current supply of new music. Demand for new music exists, but the music industry is incapable of supplying it using its 20th century business model. People crave new music but only in the past few years have we reached a point technology-wise that allows us to conveniently discover it.

There is also room, I believe, for a more literal interpretation of DIY music, which I envision as self-uploaded content to a program like

Spotify. I believe that, in general, musicians do want more control over their music, but most are afraid that the money they invest to create complete albums, or even EPs, won't be recouped. Or, worse, no one will listen to the music. I think a major refocus in the music industry will come from the stripped down, inexpensive cost of recording in the near future. Artists can now get open source recording software, plug their guitars, basses, and even drums, into their computer's sound card, and record entire albums. The cost to perform this is negligible relative to time and money spent in a professional studio, and as time goes on, the quality of output will only increase.

Spotify could even capitalize on this by providing in-house or third party mixing/mastering engineers that could take an artist's tracked out songs, and turn them into a studio quality album that users would be able to listen to without having to pay for anything. The only thing a consumer would risk is his time. Spotify could even incentivize this by adding deals to its pricing; e.g., if you listen to 10 percent new artists in a given month, you get 10 percent off your bill for that month. Artists, in turn, could promote themselves on Spotify by making on-screen banners, or purchasing credits where plays of their albums count as double or even triple discounts, almost like a coupon. Website-specific credit and digital currency are both gaining popularity across several platforms.

If someone invented a way for these artists to record and upload their music cheaply, and provided true avenues for marketing and self-promotion on an established platform, it would change the music industry forever. If someone could do this, and the quality output from third party engineers was above-average, it would give up-and-coming artists no incentive to sign with major labels that are only looking to use that artist to make money for themselves and have no interest in fair compensation.

We are moving towards the universal availability of all music. Granted, this will be for a monthly fee, but it is more attractive than the à la carte system that has dominated the music industry for over half a century. The technology to make this a reality currently exists, but the price, literal and figurative, that the music industry must pay to make this change is enormous. At times, I question the necessity for the current music industry. Aside from a conflated sense of fame and for many, the false promise of money, which is quickly dwindling, they offer very little. The old school music industry's value lies in its ability to promote and market through traditional media, at-scale. Without large-scale access to major media outlets and the resources needed to nationally market a product, most music "stars" would be just another track on YouTube. Branding takes time and effort. But social media is changing this, too.

It is certainly an exciting time to be a music fan. Many industries are changing drastically as a result of the Internet, the scope of which we are only just beginning to see and understand, and music is on the receiving end of perhaps the largest shift. Never has there been more access to music, more free access to people and companies who review music, more ways to play and store music, more ways to buy music, more ways to discover music, and more ways to share music. I personally look forward to seeing what the next 5, 10, and 20 years produce for everyone involved in trying to make sure that other people hear musicians, and the result of their dedication, talent, and passion, as well as everyone who has helped them along their path to understated fortune and fame.

The Artist, Incorporated.
The Creative Culture of the Millennial Generation

Rachel Kerwin

As a child, I loved art and thought there could be nothing better than painting all day. It was no surprise that I became an artist. These days, whenever I sit in my studio and tell visitors, "Yes, this is my full-time job," their shock reminds me what an improbable path this is because of our cultural perceptions about art, artists, and what they do. This path seems unlikely because we do not adequately educate young people how to pursue their dreams, and nearly impossible because of the barriers to entry into the vague and mysterious "art world," along with the new realities of the Great Recession into which our generation is graduating. Yet in the United States, descriptions of Millennials as the "DIY Generation" and as "creative entrepreneurs" have become commonplace with sites like Etsy and Kickstarter now bringing in millions for self-employed artists and independent projects. Rather than run from the life of the "starving artist," our generation is taking up its mantra by bringing it out of the isolation of the studio and putting it into the marketplace.

In this essay, I give a personal account of the experience of becoming a full-time artist as a Millennial. I reflect on the ways that our culture and our school systems in the U.S. leave young people unprepared to go their own way. Additionally, I discuss the common criticism of Millennial Generation feelings of entitlement.

Educating an Artist

Why is it so shocking that someone should grow up and make art for a living? In part, centuries of art history have given us stories of artists (some true, some embellished) that shape our stereotypes today. By the time I was 8 years old, I had heard of Van Gogh, a brilliant young man who was talented but unappreciated in his time. Driven by his need to make art, Vincent spent all of his money on paints and was left starving and sick. Then he got into a fight with his girlfriend and cut off his ear …or something to that effect. To a practical 2nd grader, this sounded way too dramatic. The image of the starving artist was cemented and I figured I would make other plans for my future. I still loved art and was lucky enough to have encouraging and supportive teachers. This image of a man who had every opportunity in life but ended up destitute and penniless because of his love of art stayed with me. The lives of many famous artists are dramatized after death, but the image we have of Van Gogh neatly sums up many of the caricatures drawn for "creative" types: messy, strange, manic, irreverent, loner, freak, genius.

Perhaps these stereotypes draw many young people to the arts in the first place, and perhaps many artists purposefully appropriate them to add to their own allure. One clear aspect of all of these attributes is that they isolate the artist. That isolation is ramped up by the "dead artist as genius" narrative that overemphasizes just how unique, untouchable, and unlike you and me these artists really were. Since so much of this retelling is tied up in art history, learning about art becomes an allegorical reading of lives of the artists, convincing people they have to be born with some unique talent to draw, or sing, or dance when in reality, these are all skills that can be learned like any other. Everyone has skills that come to them more naturally, but this idealized view of artistic talent undermines both the confidence of would-be artists as well as the understanding that making art, like any other endeavor, requires hard work, practice, and perseverance. What artists actually do is not a miracle of inspiration but the unbelievably terrifying work of carrying inspiration from a fantasy to reality. Often, it is also the simultaneous business of being self-employed, an independent contractor, or an entrepreneur. The reality of the lives of would-be artists, freelancers, and inventors is that they are left largely to survive alone no matter their degree of education. This is due in large part to the gap between doing well in school and doing well in the real world. The immense structuring of my life as a high school student certainly taught me the value of hard work, but the unrelenting focus of standardized testing and "college prep" did not prepare me for the complete lack of structure in my life after college. In the U.S., does our school system do a disservice to young adults by teaching them how to meet expectations rather than how to define their own goals and forge their own paths?

Amazingly, I felt the pressure of expectations before I even started school. The night before my first day of kindergarten, I lay awake, way past my bedtime, terrified of what the morning would bring. The only thing I really knew about school was that they would test you. So I pulled out my little yellow notepad from under the bed and started recounting everything I had learned. I had already started reading, knew the alphabet and a good bunch of numbers, and could spell out a handful of words. I fastidiously copied these into my notepad, studying for a test that no one assigned me. The next day, when faced with nothing more than a half-day of naps and singing on carpet squares, I recalibrated my expectations. I used to joke that after that first day of kindergarten, I never worried about school again. Of course that is not entirely true, because like most Millennials, I took on the insane accumulation of languages, sports, "extra-curriculars," and prepping for standardized tests to challenge myself and look good for the all-important college admissions process.

There has been a lot of talk about how this atmosphere of loaded-up schedules and "helicopter parenting" (so-called because of the tendency

129

of some parents to "hover" over their children) can ramp up competition and stress in teenagers.[i] Most people view stress as a bad thing, but according to a recent *New York Times* article by Po Bronson and Ashley Merryman, my experience may fit into a larger framework of how genetics affects our reactions to different kinds of stress. A number of research studies have recently begun to look at the COMT gene and how its two variations might affect how we react in times of stress. For some, the COMT enzymes remove dopamine from the brain quickly, and others, more slowly. Our brains react well with a small surge of dopamine, so in a calm state, kids with slow-acting enzymes maintain a productive level of dopamine that keeps them alert and focused while the pre-frontal cortex just does not function as well for those with the fast-acting enzymes. Under stress, though, the positions are reversed as dopamine can flood the brains of those with slow-acting enzymes. This dynamic, says David Goldman, a geneticist at the National Institutes of Health, can explain why some kids are more prone to be "worriers," while others become "warriors." As Bronson and Merryman stated,

> Understanding their propensity to become stressed and how to deal with it can help children compete. Stress turns out to be far more complicated than we have assumed, and far more under our control than we imagine. Unlike long-term stress, short-term stress can actually help people perform, and viewing it that way changes its effect. Even for those genetically predisposed to anxiety, the antidote isn't necessarily less competition—it is more competition. It just needs to be the right kind.[ii]

Pushed by their parents and their surroundings to take on ever-larger academic workloads and extra-curriculars, Millennials like me have generated reams of data for the study of these dynamics.

As a culture, we have pushed the standardized test as a measure of intelligence, aptitude, and school effectiveness, but I believe the "right kind" of stress for many kids is in performing, whether in science fairs, school plays, or showing and explaining their artwork. In times of economic turmoil, arts advocates constantly need to defend the practicality and necessity of art education as funding becomes tight. As so many parents, teachers, and administrators question the efficacy of our schools and practices like "teaching to the test," the arts can offer skills that more closely mirror adult life than the SAT ever could. Public speaking, social skills, complex problem-solving, and judging qualitative relationships are just some of the demands of creating and performing. Standing up to those demands teaches kids to express themselves and not just guess at answers with a No. 2 pencil.

I do believe testing is a useful tool. Looking back at the ways I excelled under that pressure, how I almost needed more stress to perform well, I can see how I developed "warrior" traits that continue to help me today. Yet once I began to see school as just a number of hoops to jump through to get into a good college, it became difficult to enjoy it as anything more. I was still ambitious and full of curiosity, but by the time I was in high school, grades were little more than an entry to be crossed off a checklist. By contrast, art remained fresh and exciting because it was neither something I had to do nor something I was expected to do well. It was a challenge that continued to engage me because it allowed me to choose my subject matter, focus on what interested me, and decide how to express that in my work. In short, it allowed me a measure of freedom to make my own decisions.

Regardless of my cynicism about high school, there was one greener pasture for which I held out unabashed hope: college. The ultimate goal of my high school career was admission to a "good college," where I would learn how to succeed in whatever field I chose. Two paths lay before me: arts and "smarts." It was not hard to see which was the more socially valued. In the glittering future presented to me by guidance counselors, where I mingled with the educated, cultured, and successful, making art seemed more of a parlor trick than a career choice. In the end, I took the path that allowed me to keep my options open. I applied to the art program at Cornell University. I remember the bewildered smiles of otherwise proud adults when they heard of my intention to study art at an Ivy League school. That I continued to see myself as an art major in spite of "better" options seemed antithetical to them, and maybe even to myself. I obsessed about the logic behind those knowing smiles. Was it derision, as I so often assumed? Did they think I got in the easy way? That I would drop it after a couple of years? That it will never amount to anything? The rigors of high school left me feeling that I still had something to prove.

"Entitled" or Engaged?

My college experience lived up to so many of my expectations. Cornell exposed me to new ideas and new people. I made great friends. Learning to think critically about the world and myself led me to understand what I really wanted to do and who I wanted to be. More than ever, I wanted to be an artist. I had felt that art school would have limited my access to other subject matter and left me intellectually bored, but choosing a liberal arts college meant that I was surrounded by fields for which an entire team of advisors, mentors, professors, and alumni were available to help one network, find jobs, and give next steps. Why should art be so different, so isolated? At the end of my senior year, with the intimidating prospect of starting my adult life ahead of me, my friends and I looked for answers from the sources around us.

Unlike what I assumed in high school, no one was there telling me how to be a successful artist. Looking back, perhaps it is impossible that anyone could have or should have told me how to live my life, but what I wanted seemed simple to me at the time. As an art major who had studied under other artists whom I respected, I thought that I could be in no better position to find out how to make my passion into a profession. When asked, though, the answers either seemed too vague to understand or too specific to individual experience to be applied to mine. I had asked one professor if he thought working in a gallery was a good way to learn the business of selling art and get the lay of the land in New York City. He told me I should skip all that and work for Pearl

Paint to get a discount on supplies. Somehow, this did not satisfy me. Since I was part of our Art Majors Organization, we asked career services to come to our meeting and help guide us in the direction of gainful employment.

While we did not expect them to tell us the secret to becoming rich and famous; if our professors could not enlighten us, we doubted that career services would, but we did expect that they might at least have a few resources like art-related job listings, helpful tips for our portfolios and resumes, or connections such as an alumni directory to help us open some doors. Even though our school had all of those things, particularly for other departments, they seemed at a loss. The piece of advice I remember is they had heard that many artists wait tables to make ends meet. I was incredulous. Were we really the first students to ask them these questions?

Maybe we were. Even though Generation X, predecessors to the Millennial Generation, also faced the predicament of graduating into a recession, Gen-Xers began by mistrusting authority, rejecting rules, and avoiding the corrupting power of corporate America. They played in their grunge bands and used their job at Kinko's to make their 'zines. I was taught to believe that making art was, by its very nature, subversive. I was taught to believe that as an artist I should be subversive. For GenX, either their pet projects took off or they fizzled, leaving them to march predictably and dutifully into secure employment. There we met them in the form of our teachers, parents, and other respectable adults.

This was the experience that I was being told to emulate, but I was not subversive; I was sincere. I wanted to be an artist because I found meaning in art and I saw no reason why that could not be a realistic, acceptable, and, perhaps, even a mainstream choice. As Ron Alsop has noted, "[Millennials have] been used to achieving a lot and getting rewarded … They expected that if they did the right thing [and] went to college, they would get the payoff of a good job."[iii] The stable career path, really the only "good job" for us, was to teach. Unfortunately, I could not have wanted anything less. I wanted the option of being an artist to be a real choice and I saw no reason why I could not pursue it the way I would pursue any other career.

What You Want and What You Get

Our demands, when compared to the resignation of GenX, have won us the criticism of being "entitled," which I guess is better than being called a slacker. Beyond my sense of injustice at having to start at the bottom in spite of doing all the "right things" was a sense that the adults around me fundamentally misunderstood what the life of an artist entailed outside the stereotype of scraping by. I had no problem working hard. I had taken every job I could from high school through college, but I knew that doing so just to stay afloat wasted my time and energy in the service of someone else's goals, and usually at less than a living wage. I had been told to follow my dreams and to pursue the life I wanted. I was taught that a great education was the ticket to my success, and I willingly took on student loan debt to achieve my goals. As a recent graduate, I expected real tools to cope with the difficulties ahead, rather than empty platitudes about grit and determination.

In addition to generational differences between artists, many academics believe that art must be divorced from the market to remain pure. As an undergraduate, I appreciated this bubble. The freedom to explore ideas and techniques without the pressure of a full time job is one of the greatest benefits of the traditional, four-year college education. That time does not come without cost, however, and if a student has not learned some skills to navigate the marketplace by the time they graduate, their choices are extremely limited. Artists pay dearly to apply for fiercely competitive residencies or competitions with funding from generous donors. We work other jobs to support ourselves, which greatly limits the time we have to make art, or we go back to school. Often it is some combination of all of these. So many graduates return to school, even taking student loan debt in excess of the $20,000 or more they already have, because it is the only way forward they can see. They seek out graduate school as a haven from the real world, a respite that really does help many artists, especially if they can get someone to fund it. For others, that debt is crushing, and many artists come out with an M.F.A. and no better tools for running the business of their art than when they started, in addition to crushing debt. Because of this cycle, some critics have accused the academic system of breeding dependence rather than teaching self-sustaining practices to young adults. I do not believe this is intentional on the part of our professors and universities, but I do think that students need to be more aware of what they hope to gain from higher education and more proactive in making sure they get what they are paying for.

Millennials in the World

After graduating, I moved to New York. I did my time scraping by, as I had been taught, with my first job out of school, working at a car detailing shop on Queens Boulevard making custom lettering and decals. The pure novelty of it was worth the 45 minute commute. After applying to every gallery desk sitter job I could find and coming up short, I snagged an entry-level position at a design firm in SoHo. I was a glorified receptionist, but soon made my way into an account manager position and felt like I was moving up in the world. Secretly, I hoped for job in a creative field that would satisfy me, because it was so much easier to succeed when I was given direction. As employers are now discovering, our generation thrives under coaching and mentorship. I had wonderful colleagues, I learned a lot, and gained so much confidence by doing a job for which I was well-rewarded.

Still, that old feeling of jumping through hoops had come back. I had continued to pursue painting on the side, but it moved so unbelievably slowly. I spent nearly all my free time in my studio and when I did not, I was wracked with guilt. I lived in constant fear that I was not doing enough. I knew what would happen to a good majority of my peers: without a viable way to make a living from their art, they would get full-time jobs as I had done, and their pursuit of art, now crammed into nights and weekends and occasional days off, would become a hobby. I knew that story and I did not want it to be mine. So I left.

I was not alone, of course. I remember reading articles about the surge of inventors who pursued long-neglected ideas after losing their jobs. To some extent, the difficulty of finding employment and the absence of huge perks and salaries spurred these entrepreneurs to strike out on their own. In my case, it helped that Charlottesville, Virginia, where I moved to be closer to my future husband, was a college town with a healthy art scene. The opportunity to lower my cost of living, while having a studio and exhibition opportunities, was already an improvement over the circumstances of many struggling New York artists. Even with lower rent, though, a graduate student and an artist were not raking it in. The irony was not lost on me when I took a job to help support us by, you guessed it, waiting tables.

I did not regret my decision, but I worried a lot if it was the right one. I searched for artists whose lives I wanted to mimic, looking everywhere for a road map. In recounting their stories, famous artists either glossed over their humble beginnings or romanticized their bohemian lifestyles. Neither gave me much direction. I tried to reconnect to the :art world" by reading show reviews and the art news. My biggest frustration was that everything seemed encoded. Reviews were political minefields, artist statements were a jargon jungle, and interviews were an exercise in name-dropping. Not unlike my studies in art history, I found it difficult to connect with the lives of contemporary artists. I could not relate, because in reality, there was no "art world" to relate to, so much as a conglomeration of art tribes with varying levels of influence. I did not know where I fit in, in part, because I had done so pitifully little to create a tribe of my own and after getting so good at meeting the expectations of others, I no longer knew what I wanted from an art career. I was so used to getting assurance from others that I could not define success for myself. Nonetheless, I moved forward by following the advice of a former professor to "Just make as much art as you can." I have yet to discover my vision of success, but with time, I become less afraid to dive in and make mistakes. I had been raised to do everything "right," but there was not a lot of emphasis on what to do if I got it wrong. Angela Duckworth and her colleagues have discovered that "grit," the ability to get back up when you fall down, is a greater predictor of success than intelligence. But can grit be taught? Duckworth believes so and one of the goals of her research is to determine "which experiences...we [can] give kids to get them in the direction of more grit and not less."[iv]

True Grit, or Tough Luck?

One of the big concerns about the Millennial Generation, that we are coddled and feel entitled to rewards we have not earned, insinuates that we have little grit and are unprepared for the Great Recession. We do not yet know how this economic uncertainty will shape our generation, but Millennials seem show a lot more resilience than we have been given credit for.

As for me, I moved from Charlottesville to Washington, D.C., piecing together a few more stop gap jobs and saving up some money along the way to pursue that childhood dream of painting all day. As I looked for direction this time around, on Google, the only place a Millennial looks, one of the biggest differences was that the resources I found: how-tos for the self-employed, "right-brain" business plans, pricing guides, selling guides, shipping guides, etc. were all in abundance as soon as I stopped looking for ways to be a part of the art world and looked instead for ways to be part of the art market. Artists have been some of the slowest to take advantage of the Internet, as many either did not have the know-how or fretted that options like selling work through a website would look amateur, as opposed to a traditional gallery.

Much of that has been wiped away with the Millennial obsession with access and engagement. Our generation's fluidity with privacy comes with its own issues, but the barriers between art and audience have never been lower. Artists can engage with would-be fans by allowing a peek behind the curtain, whether through works in progress or interactions that show them to be real people with real lives. It allows artists to sell work and build a collector base without the help or cost of gallery representation.

TED talks, Twitter, and Facebook are pushing art institutions to keep up with the interest that individual artists can generate for themselves. At the same time, we have seen an explosion in craft and design, often merging their boundaries with art. This blending has opened up websites liked Etsy, initially intended for the craft community, to artists. Websites that sell reproductions at affordable prices like 20x200, Exhibition A, and Artspace have followed, engaging our generation by making art more affordable and less intimidating than a gallery. The craving for direction in this new market is clear from the cottage industry of "business coaches" and financial advisors who cater to "creatives" that has sprung up over the last four years, filling the gap between the MFA and the MBA. It remains to be seen if these developments will fundamentally change the stereotype of the "starving artist," either through the lives and incomes of individual artists or how we value them as a society. But Millennials are ensuring that isolation is a choice by using the power of the Internet to make a space for art in the mainstream.

---

[i] Bonnie Rochman. "Hover No More: Helicopter Parents May Breed Depression and Incompetence in Their Children." *Time Health & Family*. February 22, 2013. Accessed February 27, 2013. *http://healthland.time.com/2013/02/22/hover-no-more-helicopter-parents-may-breed-depression-and-incompetence-in-their-children/*.

[ii] Bronson, Po and Ashley Merryman. "Why Can Some Kids Handle Pressure While Others Fall Apart?" New York Times Magazine 6 Feb. 2013: n. page. Accessed 27 February 2013. http://www.nytimes.com/2013/02/10/magazine/why-can-some-kids-handle-pressure-while-others-fall-apart.html?pagewanted=all&_r=0

[iii] Sam Weller and Melissa Conrad. "Millennials Will Be Okay." *TimeOut Chicago*. November 30, 2011, n. pag. Accessed February 27, 2013. *http://timeoutchicago.com/arts-culture/15034497/millennials-will-be-okay*.

[iv] Emily Hanford. "Angela Duckworth and the Research on 'Grit.'" *American RadioWorks*. American Public Media, n.d. Accessed February 27. 2013. *http://americanradioworks.publicradio.org/features/tomorrows-college/grit/angela-duckworth-grit.html*.

No Aliens in the Basement: Popular Culture's Take on State Secrets Versus Reality

Anonymous and Patriotic

We all like a good juicy secret. Big or small. Real or fictional. Secrets are just plain fun. I don't care how you get your fix. Maybe you scuttlebutt around the water cooler. Maybe you turn to Tom Clancy, John Grisham, Dan Brown, or Jack Bauer. Whatever, no judgment here. It is totally normal to want to have a few more pieces of the puzzle than everyone else. Being more in the know comes with a confidence that one can do and go where others cannot. That is why so many of us jump at the opportunity to be in on a secret: secrets can make us feel special, and bigger secrets make us feel more special.

In my opinion, that's what lends Washington, D.C. and the surrounding area its potent mystique: the place seems to be just oozing with secrets. Take a look around. Old marble buildings with cavernous rooms adorned with gothic images and strange symbols. Helicopters and motorcades whisking shadowy figures away to closed door meetings. Enormous secure facilities like the Pentagon or NSA or CIA tightly guarded by miles of razor wire and forces of armed guards larger than most small towns. It is understood that a lot of important stuff happens in this town that everyday folks just do not have access to. Moving and shaking is happening to steer the fate of the free world, and we are not invited to the meeting. Washington, D.C. inspires the notion that there is something grand and sweeping right beneath its surface. Mix in the fantastic stories that popular culture throws at us and there follows a strong curiosity of what lies beneath.

How Do I Know What I Know?

It was this curiosity of our state secrets that drove me to a job in classified information. ███████████████████, I grew up with gems like █████████████████████████████████████ filling my head with elaborate fantasies of government cover-ups and clandestine globe-trotting. As a result of these stories, I dreamed of a job full of twists, turns, constant excitement, danger (not the type where anything really bad would ever happen), beautiful women, secret ninja moves taught by the government, guns, and tours through Area 51.

Even as I got older and faced the real possibilities of starting non-secret careers, my desire to work with classified information was always in the back of my mind. I got to the point where working perfectly respectable jobs in ████████████████ left me feeling like something was missing. Who wants to ██████████████████ when I could be cranking out hush-hush negotiations with North Korean ambassadors or chasing spies through posh cocktail parties while wearing a tuxedo? I resolved once and for all to chase my curiosity and get in on those elusive secrets.

So long story short, I eventually made it. It is not important how I landed my job or how long it took me. The point is, for the past

███████████████████, I have worked with classified information. My responsibilities primarily consist of ███████████████████

██████████████████████████ I am not going to say I have been let it on all the secrets (I do not really think anyone has), but I have worked on ████████████ of Top Secret, Sensitive Compartmentalized Information (SCI), and Special Access Program (SAP) projects. I wanted to be in on the secrets, and got what I wished for in spades.

So what did I learn when I finally started getting invited to the meetings? What did I see after I got the keys (or key cards, more accurately) to the closed doors? What was waiting for me when I finally got orders to travel to a secret facility? The answer to all three questions is the same: *Reality.* I, along with many of my generation, had been conditioned to think of state secrets as grandiose, other-worldly, and mystifying. I learned very quickly that reality is not quite like that. It never is, is it?

Hollywood Versus Reality

I would like to be as clear as possible: no matter what level of clearance you are privy to, or any other country's secrets you are trusted with, you will never, ever, ever, ever go to any base, laboratory, or compound and find aliens in the basement. They do not exist. None of that stuff that we see in movies exists, nor does anything that happens in the movies ever transpire. Anyone reporting to work thinking that they will walk in and find the War Room from Doctor Strangelove will only find cube farms and busted coffee makers. There are no extraterrestrial remains under the Pentagon. There are no Illuminati initiation rituals going on in the Situation Room. There are no time machines anywhere and there never will be. There are no secret agent fights on top of the Lincoln Memorial and there are *absolutely* no secret passageways in any of these old D.C. buildings that lead anywhere cool.

I am pretty sure, or at least hopeful, that this is hardly earth-shattering news. I'm not saying that any right-minded adult would actually believe that the government is concealing Stargate underneath the Reflecting Pool. I am saying that one of the main reasons why so many people have the wrong idea about state secrets is that fantasy tends to be much more visible and entertaining than reality. This makes sense. It's definitely in Hollywood's interest to promote sensational stories about classified matters. Usually only the public knows that major operations are conducted out of their sight, leaving an immense void for sexy fantasies to frolic in. On the other hand, for those who work with classified information and truly understand its nature, their best interest is to talk about it as little as possible. With such lopsided messaging, it is easy to form the wrong impression.

For the most part, I do not think that Hollywood's stories about classified projects are bad (irresponsible pieces like ███████████ aside). Some genuinely entertaining productions are coming out, and, myself aside, I know of plenty dedicated professionals who chose their line of work having been inspired by them. However, I believe it is important that the public comes to better understand the true nature of state secrets, just as I did. Just because secret operations are not as popular culture presents them does not make them any less exciting or vital to a nation's well-being.

If there is one take-away from what I am saying it is this: classified information is an absolutely critical component of a nation's security and advancement. Whether the public chooses to accept it or not, the government and its affiliates work every day for the overall well-being of this country and its citizens. For the most part, they do a pretty good job. Without classified operations made possible by classified information and classified materials, this sector would not be able to do a good job. No one has to believe this if they do not want to, but it is the truth. Take it or leave it.

Why We Have Secrets

I am going to keep my discussion within the context of the United States, since U.S. secrets serve as the basis for almost all of my experience. However, I am confident that classified material plays just as vital a role in any other country as it does in the U.S. Any poker player who shows his hand prematurely will lose. Any business that reveals all of its strategies and does not protect its innovations will fail. Any developed nation that does not keep its most important efforts classified will not be able to effectively advance its interests and well-being and protect its people.

We need to keep these secrets for many reasons. Diplomatic negotiations could not progress if every facet of the discussion were known and thus opposed by diverse pockets of critics. Interests are too varied to make everyone happy. Our economy would suffer if proprietary technology, valid currency circulation, key financial information, and fraud investigations were not safeguarded. While I recognize that crime and drugs are a huge problem in the U.S., it would be a much bigger problem if law enforcement agencies, and definitely not just DEA and FBI, by the way, were to have their efforts foiled by criminals being tipped off to their plans.

Also, let us not forget that there are a lot of bad people in the world called terrorists, and they want to kill you.

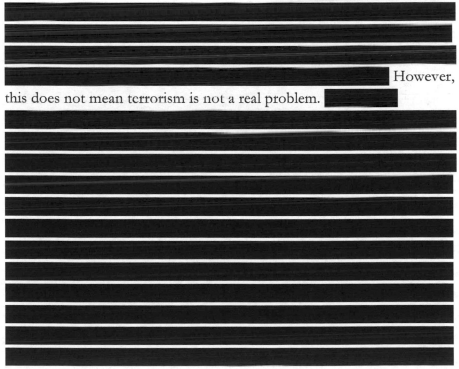

However, this does not mean terrorism is not a real problem.

██
██
██
██████████████████████████████.

State secrets do not guard massive conspiracies involving Bigfoot and James Bond; they guard the everyday security that the vast majority of our citizens takes for granted. Classified programs with organizations such as ██
██
██████████████████████████████████ prevent our enemies from poisoning our water supply, shutting off our power, destroying our roadways, cutting our communication lines, and invading our computer systems. More important, joint efforts of these agencies and more have prevented our enemies from acquiring technology and materials necessary to build nuclear weapons. Fewer, if any, of these missions would have succeeded had the hostiles learned their specific details.

Classified operations have many complicated aspects but without a doubt the most important are the men and women who make them happen. Analysts and linguists spend staggering amounts of time poring over terabytes of data, hours of recordings, and volumes of documents looking for the tiniest scraps of information that could turn out to be game-changing intelligence. ████████████████████████████
██
██
██
██
████████████████████████. Police officers, soldiers, and special agents work tirelessly and train to get beat up, shot at, blown up, tortured, drowned, frozen, pepper-sprayed, and sleep-deprived all to protect their country and fellow citizens. Keeping secrets safe lets them accomplish their missions and come home in one piece. Were it not for tightly guarded secrets, I do not believe this country would have been

successful in exfiltrating hostages from hostile nations, stopping huge shipments of dangerous narcotics from crossing our borders, killing the most dangerous terrorist in the world, or thousands of other important missions that never made it onto CNN.

Why Secrets Must Remain So

Since I have no problem saying that keeping state secrets saves lives, I also have no problem saying this: not keeping them kills. Leaks kill. This is not, in any way, hyperbole. ██████████████████████

██ love to claim that they champion truth above all else and any attempt to stop the leaks is nothing more than Big Brother trying to stifle free speech and dodge accountability. This is where I view popular culture's portrayal of secrets as damaging. People who buy into all the fantasies of the *X-Files* and *V for Vendetta* let themselves be convinced that all secrets must be sinister. They refuse to believe that classified operations are anything more than vehicles for oppression and injustice. I know that not all supporters ███████████ are paranoid conspiracy theorists. I recognize that some are just ideologically opposed to the ideas of getting involved in other nations' armed conflicts, ███████████████

██
██

████████████████████, or simply keeping secrets from citizens of a democracy.

To an extent, I agree with this. I completely understand the idea that a government, just like any other major entity, needs to maintain a certain level of transparency. I agree that actions significantly affecting a nation need to be subject to accountability and that flouting responsibility should never be justified for the sake of preserving secrecy. ██████████████████████████

Millennials Speak.

███
████████████████████████████████. There is absolutely
nothing wrong with questioning the actions of government, especially
when those actions come with extremely heavy consequences. However,
I am not the one to decide which controversial operations are shelved
and which ones are green lighted "for the greater good" (you hear this
phrase a lot in this line of work). It is not up to any one official, no
matter how high-ranking he or she may be. In fact, I am sorry to say
this, but it is certainly not up to uninformed, uninvolved individuals who
base their conclusions solely on ideology. I am not trying to sound
dodgy or condescending, but when I hear those who have no experience
with what can be at stake with these operations screaming bloody
murder about conspiracy and oppression, I have a hard taking them
seriously, much less caring about what they perceive to be right and
wrong.

Officials who give the "go" on these operations get a bum rap as
being robotic and devoid of compassion in their decision-making
(██). If there
is any individual in this profession who somehow enjoys generating
conflict, misery, death, and collateral damage, I have yet to meet him. I
hope I never do. The officials I know of that pull the trigger on these
decisions (literally and figuratively) are regular people with families,
consciences, and keen understandings of consequence. They fully
understand that their decisions can carry life-changing and life-ending
results just as well as they understand that these situations rarely come
with perfect, cut-and-dry solutions. Even the best-case scenarios almost
always have some pretty serious downsides. They are usually very
serious. These people make it their business to know every minute detail
of the case, they weigh the input of their colleagues, and they never ever
take these tough decisions lightly. ██████████████████████
████████, these decisions do keep them up at night.

146

Little Expenses: Loose Lips Sink Ships

I do not believe that anyone who works on classified projects would disagree that citizens should speak out loudly against government actions they find unacceptable. However, risking the lives and well-being of innocent people and their protectors by leaking information or spreading leaked information is never the answer.

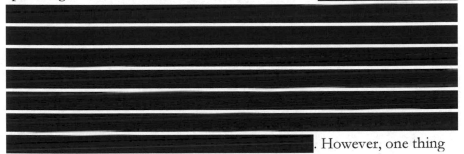

. However, one thing everybody can and should know is that compromised secrecy always worsens the situation. For those who harbor anger toward any government that keeps secrets from its citizens, just know that problems that require secrecy are bigger than any one of us, and those closest to this reality remind themselves of it every day.

Aside from dealing with the heavy consequences of classified projects, a career in state secrets has plenty of other drawbacks. For one, you can never talk about what you do the way you want to.

. The more people who think you have access to secrets, the bigger target you are for the enemy. Whenever I travel or even if I just hang out in a bar, I usually tell people I ▮▮▮▮▮▮▮▮▮▮▮. By the way, D.C. folk, here is a tip: whenever you are hanging out at happy hour and someone volunteers that they "work for the government but can't tell you what [they] do," they are lying. You're welcome.

Conclusion

I hope you do not think that I am trying to make this stuff sound sexy and glamorous. It is not. At all. It is stressful, lonely, and sometimes as infuriating as yelling into an empty room. Again, it is not at all what popular culture tells us. That said, I am probably going to stay with this job the rest of my life. Even when I do not like it, I always believe in it. I truly believe that, without state secrets, many of this nation's greatest victories and many of modern humanity's finest moments would never have taken place, and I am honored to be a part of it. I am never going to be Fox Mulder, and that does not bother me one bit. I never found the aliens in the basement, but I have definitely found what I was looking for.

Blending the Old School and the New School: The Intersection of Social Networking with Old Fashioned Grassroots Organizing

Paula Fynboh

Social media is flattening the world. Facebook alone has over 1.2 billion global users and more than 150,000 people from around the world join Twitter every day. It is almost impossible to imagine today's global events without the reach of social media. Take, for example, the summer 2009 Iranian protests and the Green Revolution. These protests were held in response to accusations of election fraud by the opposition after the reelection of incumbent president Mahmoud Ahmadinejad. Twitter, a tool that was not even around during the previous Iranian elections, dramatically influenced the coverage of the event and shifted the debate by sharing the real-time stories of everyday Iranians to the world. Twitter made it possible this time, even after the sitting government attempted to censor all of the country's media to cover up its brutal crackdown of the protests, to get the story out to the world. It also served as a means for those involved in the protests to organize and coordinate with one another.

Twitter's role in giving voice to the struggles of everyday Iranian citizens was so important that the U.S. Department of State encouraged the company to delay planned upgrades that would have caused temporary outages of the service during the protests.[i] Twitter users put a human face on the protests and played a crucial role in influencing how major news outlets, such as CNN, covered the elections.

After the January 2010 earthquake in Haiti, SMS text message technology brought immediate news of the earthquake and provided aid workers with tools to find the missing, and also, within moments, brought information about how people could help and triggered an unprecedented global response.

Did this happen just because of the social media tool or due to how social activists and everyday citizens used the tool? In my experience, the most successful grassroots campaigns do not look to social media tools alone as the solution. Rather, effective movements take advantage of emerging technology to implement tried and true ways to capture people's attention and inspire action. These methods include personalizing the issue, incorporating an easy point of entry for those who care about the issue, and helping those who care feel less isolated and helpless and more united and connected. As with most things, this is less about the tool itself, but more about how it is used.

I have heard more than one friend, relative, and client complain about social networking and say things like, "I just don't get it. I really don't care what someone made for dinner last night or if you went to the gym today." This is one side of social networking but it can also be so much more. Take the Haiti and Iranian election examples in this essay. Today we can use social networking to break up with someone in 140 characters or less, post a picture of our pets, *and* deliver vital information that might have been censored or never received the light of day without the tool. Social media tools can make us feel we know more about each other as well as the people in Iran and Haiti. That builds connections and makes us care. It all depends on how we choose to use it.

There is an emerging bible of tips and tools for effective use of social networking, such as how many times to post during a day, which hour of the day posts get the most hits, and how to use celebrity endorsements effectively. Everyone has an opinion on this issue and if I tried to include these rules here, they would be outdated before the book even went to press. Rather than talk about the rules and applications for social media, I will argue that social media is less about the tool itself and more about the intention behind it. Rather than focus on which social networking platform we choose or which rules apply where, we should discuss how we use social networking to engage, tell our stories, and connect with others.

Yet, more often than not, when I conduct trainings for non-governmental organizations (NGOs), community groups, and corporations about how to integrate social media with their organizing and engagement work, they often want to focus on the rules and platforms, because rules and checklists are tangible. They are more tangible than relationship-building and personal connection, which make social media effective. Through my work, I have begun to think differently about "the rules" of successful social networking. Social networking is less about knowing the specifics or seeing it as an "end all, be all" and more about considering how to use it as a tool to authentically engage with others. The bigger question is not how many times will I or my organization post a day, on what topic and in which social media platform, but rather, how will this tool help me better engage with the people around me in a meaningful way? How will it help me or my entity further the values that are important to me, build a community based around these values, and inspire people to action?

When it comes to making an impact in the world, it is less about the platform and more about building and sustaining authentic relationships. I have come to believe that while social media will continue to grow and evolve, the tried and true principles of relationship building and grassroots organizing stay the same. The secret is to discover how to incorporate relationship-building with social networking and how social networking can enhance and build authentic relationships.

I try here to offer some insight to this question. I have combined the Top 5 Tips of Grassroots Organizing that I have learned along the way with some thoughts on how they can be combined with social media to further build connections and inspire action around the world.

Tip #1: Relationships Matter

After the 2008 U.S. presidential election, many groups I worked with starting to ask for "The Obama." "We want that," they said. "We want to do what the Obama campaign did."

They were referring to the slick online campaign. The 2008 Obama presidential campaign was the first time social networking had really demonstrated its muscle in a major election. Many people concluded, "That's it! That's what we've been waiting for!" Social networking became the shiny new object everyone wanted, and we fell under the illusion that to run a successful campaign we just needed a really cool Facebook application, a sweet website, and a smart phone.

People ignored relationship building behind the fancy tools. Facebook "likes," just like lawn signs in the old school days, do not matter in a vote count. What matters is the number of people who actually show up and vote. The best way to get people to vote is to influence someone close to them to have a conversation about the issues that matter to them and then ask them to vote. Social media does not get people to the polls; social media leverages personal relationships to get people to the polls.

Social networking was able to identify a base of people who cared about the Obama campaign. The campaign then communicated with these folks and cultivated relationships with them. Much of this was complemented by old-fashioned grassroots organizing, including door-knocking and phone banking. Once the relationship was built, the campaign asked these people to reach out to their base, the people they had personal relationships with, including family members, friends, co-workers, classmates, and neighbors, and have a personal conversation with them about voting.

While social media supplied the platform to identify supporters, communicate, and mobilize Obama supporters in 2008, it was heavily complemented by old-fashioned conversation and relationship building.

As activists in today's world, we should not ignore the many tools available to us to connect with people, or the power of relationship building. We must continually ask ourselves how this tool can communicate a message, and how it can help us build a relationship and authentically engage with others.

Tip #2: Tell Your Story.

Storytelling is not just for campfires and bedtimes. Telling a real and personal story puts a human face on an issue and can be more influential that any facts, figures, or fancy pie graphs and is a grossly underused medium for building support and persuading others.

Grassroots organizers long suspected what the power of a story can do, but recently, research is beginning to validate this. The magazine *Fast Company* interviewed psychologists Melanie Green and Tim Brock, whose studies show that stories physically change the brains of people who become absorbed in them. As their research suggests, it seems that entering "story" worlds "radically alters the way information is processed." The article's author, Jonathan Gottschall, noted, "When we read dry, factual arguments, we read with our dukes up. We are critical and skeptical. But when we are absorbed in a story, we drop our intellectual guard. We are moved emotionally and this seems to leave us defenseless."

I once worked on a legislative campaign with a volunteer advocate who had been affected by cancer. I remember bringing her with me to the State Capitol to meet with her Senator on a Citizen's Lobby Day. She was so nervous about having a conversation with her elected official that she was visibly shaking. I tried to reassure her that she did not need to have all the answers; she just needed to tell her story. As we began the meeting, she forgot all her talking points, but proceeded to pull out her family photo album and showed the Senator the people in her life who lost their lives to cancer. A brother. A nephew. A mom. A best friend. That is the power a story can have, and emerging social media tools can help us tell our stories more creatively and to more people faster than ever before.

Two powerful and creative uses I have seen recently in blending social media with old-fashioned storytelling to bring awareness to an issue or a cause come to mind: "First World Problem Tweets as read by Poverty Stricken Haitians;"[ii] and Global Voices' activity[iii] in partnership with youth in Medellin, Colombia. In the first example, Haitians read a first world problem tweet while the camera films poverty and crumbling infrastructure behind them. In the latter example, Medellin youth make short videos featuring places and locations that define them, including a soccer field once built and donated by Pablo Escobar in exchange for the community's silence during the drug trade. This soccer field has now evolved into a place where youth perform public service outreach, conduct anti-gang initiatives, and organize on behalf of their community.

In both examples, photos and videos captured the viewers' attention and left us with a lasting impression that could not be accomplished through the statistics of poverty or crime alone. Stories move people and help build connections and facilitate understanding, even across cultures, geography, and distance.

Tip #3: Make the Ask.

Do you know the number one reason why people do not get involved, even in causes they care about? This is because they have not been asked. No matter how deep our relationships and how compelling our story, there is just no substitute for making "the ask"; that is, simply asking someone to contribute their time, talent, or money to a cause you care about.

I was a Girl Scout in grade school and we sold cookies. Every year, the top cookie salesgirl won a prize. I really wanted to win. My mom was a teacher and I sent my cookie order form with her to put in the teacher's lounge. I thought having my order form laying on the table in the teachers' lounge would help me clean up the competition and win that prize. Unfortunately for me, I was about to learn my first lesson in grassroots organizing. One of my rival Girl Scout competitors showed up at school early that day and went to each and every room and personally asked the teachers to buy cookies from her. Mrs. Koppel bought 32 boxes from her. I lost the competition, but gained some valuable experience that would serve me well later in life: always make a direct ask, and a personal ask is the best ask of all.

Regarding technology, a link or "click here to volunteer" or "click here to donate" button are often standard. Emerging social media tools can now track if you like a post, re-tweet a tweet from an organization or a cause, or even if you like a post or re-tweet a tweet from a friend on behalf of an organization or cause, and dump your name into a big database that can be used later to get you to vote, make a donation, or participate in a call to action. Social media is making the art of "list building" easier every day. However, as technology easily allows organizations and causes to capture our information and send us numerous emails later, the number of requests also become easier and easier to tune out or ignore.

The remedy? The old fashioned personal ask. If we want our base to support the issues we care about, a request to join a Facebook page cannot hurt, but people have a really hard time saying no to a face-to-face request. We should use social media to cast a wide net and identify our low-hanging fruit, but if we really want to create some action on behalf something we care about, we also need to follow-up personally.

Tip #4: Make it Easy

I get a lot of push back on this one. Those of us leading the cause, whether it is working intimately on a campaign or heading an organization, willingly drink the Kool-Aid all day long. We live and die by progress and setbacks and we care so passionately that we forget that not everyone shares our dedication. The truth is, most people won't spend hours or even an hour every day doing what we ask them to advance our cause. However, they will usually do something if we ask them, and also if we make the ask easy.

I once ran a Facebook campaign to get a pair of super cool red boots. My husband challenged me and said if I could get over 200 Facebook friends in a six-hour period, he would buy me the boots. Done and done. However, ironically it was the same day one of my old campaign colleagues also launched a Facebook campaign in support of public schools. My Facebook campaign kicked her campaign's ass, again not because my boots were more important than public education, but because my ask was simple, tangible, and measureable.

When engaging people into your work, whether online or offline, start with the easy asks: "Will you join our Facebook page?" Or, "Can you make one phone call to a decision-maker in the next 2 days?" Then, give them all of the information they will need to follow through: the link, talking points, the number, etc. Never forget to tell them why their action, no matter how small, makes a difference. Once someone contributes their time, monetary donation, or effort, no matter how small, thank them and then ask them to perform a somewhat harder ask. Keep asking, and thanking and explaining how their efforts are making a tangible difference or helping your campaign achieve your goal. Give people permission to say "no" at times and don't make it a contest of who is the most dedicated. Often we have no idea what other demands are facing our volunteers, campaigners, and supporters. Small acts add up. Finally, keep note of who is taking action. These people are our emerging leaders.

Social media tools can help us track volunteer and supporter efforts. We can see who opened emails, who clicked "take action" links, who forwarded the email or text on to friends and who liked or re-tweeted our posts. This is an organizer's dream. Embrace it. Use the data and technology to learn about your campaign's volunteers and supporters and use this knowledge to reach out personally to these people and say thank you. Take them out for coffee or do something else to get to know them and build your relationship with them and their connection to your cause or campaign.

Tip #5. Celebrate and Have Fun.

Last, but not least, Internet mêmes are popular and spread so fast because they are funny. They make me smile and sometimes even laugh out loud, even when I am alone. I do not care more about talking cats and hearing Cookie Monster sing "Call Me Maybe" than I do about restricted access to freedom of speech, repressed voter rights, and global hunger, but let's face it. The world can be a tough place and sometimes we just need to laugh and find something to be happy about.

Long-term, sustainable movement building, as well as grassroots organizing and relationship building, in my opinion, need to take the same approach at times. The issues we are fighting for are serious, but if we do not stop to acknowledge our progress and celebrate our successes, even if seemingly small, and laugh and celebrate together, we will not be able to sustain ourselves or our work for the long haul.

I am not saying we should all sneak a "Rick Rolling" link into our organization's next online Call to Action newsletter, but I do think it is increasingly important to stop, reflect, and celebrate often. We need to find ways to give ourselves and each other hope to keep fighting the good fight. Maybe host a contest to engage our volunteers' talents and creativity, showcase our many stories and successes, or encourage photo uploads from volunteers to put a face on your campaign. Focus on thanking and celebrating the number of people who are also taking action with us instead of dwelling too heavily on the ones who are not.

Conclusion

A lot has been said about the characteristics of the Millennial Generation, including that we are a generation that likes to be connected. I wonder, however, if we are really that different from generations before us that way, or if only now we have the tools to help us connect faster, easier, and on a greater scale. After all, organizing and movement building is about doing something together rather than alone.

Social media is letting us know each other and connect with each other like never before. It is how I became a part of this book project. It is breaking down the walls of censorship and geography, and helping democratize the media by expanding whose story is told and how. It is connecting the storytellers and the listeners. The most exciting thing about that is that we can be part of it.

I really enjoy when my Instagram or Facebook friends post pictures of their pets or what they made for breakfast on their wall. It gives me a little insight into what is important to them in that moment. It also gives me clues into their world and how I can better connect and engage with them. I have built stronger personal relationships with people over my yoga posts, my Boston Terrier posts, and yes, even my political and social cause posts. At times, my posts have inspired my friends to take action, just as theirs have done so for me. Most important, it has helped me further build my community, and that is one of the true sources of power for change: People.

As young people and community activists, we might not (yet) have the money or the influence of big weapons companies, oil companies, and the manufactured food and chemical companies of the world that so many of us hold up as examples of power, but we are connected. We might not own media companies and industries, but we have found a way to work around them. Our connections, both online and in-person, can complement, integrate, and build upon each other in extraordinary ways and through these connections, we invite more people to the table who can also share their stories, make an ask, and give us hope.

People power is a legitimate form of power. It can compete with money and we can have it. Plus, we also have social networking tools that are free, personal, and largely accessible, making us less and less dependent on traditional media to get our stories out there, increasing our access to decision-makers and others, and giving us the ability to connect across space and time.

---

[i] Reuters. "U.S. State Department speaks to Twitter over Iran." June 2009. Accessed November 15, 2012. *http://www.reuters.com/article/2009/06/16/us-iran-election-twitter-usa-idUSWBT011 37420090616*.

[ii] *Time*. "#FirstWorldProblems, as Read by Poverty-Stricken Haitians." October

2012. Accessed November 15, 2012.
http://newsfeed.time.com/2012/10/10/firstworldproblems-tweets-as-read-by-poverty-stricken-hatians/.
iii *http://www.globalvoicesonline.org.*

Part 3

Essays on Food, Consumption, and Global Health

Building a New Global Food System

Sara Nawaz

"It would be great if we could feed the world sustainably, but we can't," my friend informed me. "If we want to feed everybody, the reality is that industrial agriculture is the only way." While this is a common belief among my peers, its falsehood is becoming increasingly apparent. Finding sustainable alternatives to industrial agriculture is not only possible, but it is already happening.

In this essay I argue that we, as Millennials, must rethink the global food system. After tracing its current failures, I argue that the possibility of a sustainable, equitable global food system is within our grasp. While I focus largely on the possibilities for production, I note that alternatives are also needed in other aspects of the food system, such as consumption and distribution. I suggest that food sovereignty movements in the Global South can serve as inspiration for movements in the Global North, which often tend to focus only on creating change through consumerism. Additionally, I provide and discuss two examples of marginalization by and resistance to our current food system: Chester, Pennsylvania and the northern Cauca, Colombia.

The Global Food System is Broken

By 2050 we will need to produce 70 percent more additional food to feed the projected world population of 9 billion people, compared to our current 7 billion. Yet additional food is only part of the equation: human behavior is changing our climate. Currently, agriculture contributes 32 percent of total greenhouse gas (GHG) emissions; if we continue emissions business as usual, feeding another two billion people will certainly increase GHG emissions.[i] GHG emissions are not the only problem with modern agriculture.

Biodiversity is shrinking. According to the Food and Agriculture Organization, a United Nations specialized agency, the world's top 10 crops (rice, wheat, maize, soybeans, sorghum, millet, potatoes, sweet potatoes, sugar cane/beets, and bananas) supply over three-quarters of plant-based calories, dominating the world's cultivated lands.[ii] Rice, wheat, and maize account for more than half of all plant-based calories and 85 percent of the total volume of world grains produced. Shrinking biodiversity makes crops more susceptible to pests. Furthermore, monocropping, or growing a single crop over a number of years across a wide area, necessitates strings of new crop varieties engineered by powerful multi-national corporations (MNCs). Because these engineered crop varieties are especially vulnerable to pests, they contribute to a vicious cycle of chemical use.[iii] But food-related environmental risks are not limited to agriculture. Factory farms, where most meat in the United States is produced, use massive amounts of water and create huge cesspools of animal waste and contamination. Industrialized livestock production also involves tremendous amounts of animal suffering and excessive degrees of antibiotics and hormones used.[iv]

In addition to concerns of sustainability are those of equity and social justice. The global food price index has reached all-time highs in recent years: food riots across the developing world in 2008 serve as evidence of the suffering that price increases bring to many of the world's poorest.[v] Perversely, a country's thriving export market does not make it immune to hunger. Costa Rica grows flowers, melons, and strawberries, Kenya and Botswana export beef to Europe, and Lesotho grows asparagus.[vi] While the increased national incomes from such exports might theoretically help alleviate hunger, this is often not the case in these countries. Just because a country grows a lot of food does not mean its people are not hungry.

This grave situation arises from today's corporate "food regime." According to Philip McMichael[vii], a leading scholar in the study of the global food system, the term "food regime" is the structure of production and consumption of food currently dominant in the world. The first global food regime lasted from the 1800s through the Great Depression and involved importing food from the Colonies to Europe. The second regime was the reverse, where food was exported from the Global North to feed industrialization in the Global South. Today, McMichael asserts, the current food regime is corporate: agrifood corporations, involved in nearly every world food system, monopolize market power. These corporations, which include Monsanto, Archer Daniels Midland, Cargill, and Wal-Mart, use their enormous market power to affect trade, labor, property, and technology rules, gearing them in support of oligopolistic industrial agriculture. Many free market-oriented, public institutions support or ally with this corporate force: the World Bank, International Monetary Fund, the World Food Program, USAID, the USDA, and others.

The concept of a "food regime" does not mean that every aspect of a global food system has been entirely incorporated into a corporate, industrial approach; much of the developing world is still farmed by smallholders. The predominant global trend is a move towards a corporatized, industrialized model. Discussion of a "corporate food regime" is not about allocating blame to markets or corporate greed. Instead, it is about recognizing that a corporate food regime has come to characterize and dominate our current global food systems. Until we recognize this regime as a root cause of global hunger and as a key contributor to climate change, we will not be able to fully address these issues.

The Development and Export of the Corporate Food Regime

In the U.S., the industrial form of agriculture that developed following World War II is one dominated by chemical fertilizer and pesticide-based, low labor, and highly mechanized farming of wheat, corn, and soy. This form of agriculture developed as a result of deregulation and weakening of antitrust laws at the time, leading to a concentration of market power in the hands of a few firms. These firms have used their wealth to exploit American democracy, supporting legislation that maintains the status quo in their favor. A few examples of their hijacking American democracy include irrigation costs subsidized with public-funds, the passage of a tariff on Cuban sugar to keep it out of the U.S. market (which led to the expansive use of notoriously unhealthy high-fructose corn syrup), and preventing the Food and Drug Administration from testing for meat contamination until after processing.[viii]

The Global North has exported the American model to the Global South. Legally-binding trade agreements have played a central role in this process, privileging profit-making over labor and environmental laws, domestic economies, and local food systems. Foreign food aid has also played a role, paving the way for new export markets for Northern products under the guise of humanitarianism. The financialization of food, which has subjected global food commodities to risky speculation, has exacerbated fluctuations in food prices and increased food prices.[ix] Last, this industrialized model of agriculture has been imposed on the Global South through decades of development projects intended to benefit the developing world and lift them out of poverty. Market-based and modernized agriculture has created adverse economic and social outcomes in many countries host to these projects, usually at the expense of the poorest while benefitting the wealthy and degrading local ecosystems.[x]

The Replacement for Industrial: Agroecology

Many agriculture and development policymakers today still argue that, despite the growing threat of hunger, the only answer is to intensify industrial farming. However, a consensus is emerging around an alternative answer to feeding the world. It is both environmentally sustainable and more empowering of the individual poor. The recognition that a global food regime change is desirable and possible is gaining traction.

The International Assessment on Agricultural Knowledge, Science, and Technology for Development (IAASTD)[xi], a 2008 global report authored by 400 scientists and policymakers convened by the UN's Food and Agriculture Organization (FAO), asserts that such a change is needed. Although it was not publicized in the U.S., the report signals a key shift in the consensus regarding the potential for more sustainable approaches to food production to serve as the primary approach to dealing with the global food problem.

The IAASTD makes several points. First, it questions the use of industrial agriculture and genetically modified (GM) foods as answers to food crisis. From the authors' perspective, focusing on GM foods as the answer to world food problems misses the point: GM foods promote a production system that emphasizes monocultures rather than diversified, resilient, and sustainable farms. Second, it argues that agriculture must be understood not narrowly as a way of increasing food production, but in a more complex way. They argue that food production has a "multifunctional" social role and is a component of an intricate ecosystem. While organic farming utilizes some of these understandings of ecosystem complexity, "agroecology" is an alternative approach to agriculture that fully embraces this complexity. Finally, the IAASTD argues that smallholder agriculture, because of its ability to serve its holistic nutritional, environmental, and social role, must be the answer to the food crisis. Solutions will not come from the top-down but from the bottom-up.

Agroecology is not just an alternative for the world's poor; it is a proposed solution for feeding the entire world. Studies have shown that small peasant and family farms are more productive than plantation agriculture, per acre. The reason for the common misperception of the opposite, it appears, is that because smallholder agriculture usually involves farming multiple crops in the same field (polycultures), the yields of single crops are lower than those of monocultures (when measured per acre).[xii] According to De Schutter, the UN Special Rapporteur on the Right to Food and Miguel Altieri, the world's leading agroecologist, the issue is not whether agroecology has the potential to feed the world, but instead how to scale up agroecological methods so that this approach can achieve this aim.[xiii] In addition to higher yields, agroecology is better at sequestrating carbon dioxide emissions, is more water-efficient, uses fewer pesticides, and increases ecosystem services.[xiv] Importantly, because high biodiversity is compatible with high yields, agroecology increases species richness and abundance.[xv]

For these reasons, agroecology is crucial for slowing and mitigating climate change, in addition to reducing fossil fuel inputs and thus emitting fewer greenhouse gases. Since it creates greater resiliency to extreme weather events, it involves a mixture of trees along with other plants and organic soil, and requires less tillage but results in greater crop diversity. Higher biodiversity also protects against the weeds and pests that are likely to arise from increasing temperatures.[xvi] Lastly, its soils and biomass could potentially sequester 1.2-3.1 billion metric tons of atmospheric carbon per year.[xvii] In short, agroecology is "climate-proof."

To promote agroecology, policy approaches should involve a number of different mechanisms between market, state, and civil society. For example, Payments for Agroecological Services, a form of Payments for Ecosystem Services (PES), is a model in which "the potential public beneficiaries of ecosystem services at the local, national, and global scales fund the research and development, extension work (i.e., farmer education, usually supported by government agencies), and affordable credit required to scale agroecology up to the level required for the growing global population."[xviii] Such a PES solution attempts to remedy markets' failure to create private sector incentives for providing the public goods needed to develop agroecology. Thus, PES involves a transfer of resources in order to create incentives that gear land use decisions to better manage natural resources. An important component of such solutions is, "polycentricity" or the involvement of institutions at multiple (local, regional, and global) scales.[xix] However, the recognition of the importance of land sovereignty is essential to many policy approaches in the Global South.[xx] This means the ability of a people to control their land, for example, to protect against land grabs. Any PES solution must ensure and protect this sovereignty for its beneficiaries.

Beyond agroecological production, a re-envisioning of the entire food system is necessary. The broader food system includes not only production but the entire food process from consumption to waste disposal (although the latter is not discussed in this essay). In the U.S., market-distorting government farm subsidies and a lack of regulation of the U.S. food industry contribute to the persistence of its broken food system.[xxi] Changing production methods is not enough: the entire food system must be re-conceptualized.

Agroecology: An Answer, but "Only for the World's Poor"?
While there is a growing recognition in the U.S. of the problems with industrially farmed food, much of the American alternative food movement misses the mark. People are realizing that food produced, processed, and transported by the current industrial system may not be as healthy as consumers are led to believe. It also leaves a larger environmental footprint compared to food that is locally sourced and sustainably produced. Yet rather than aspire to question the existing corporate regime, this alternative movement aims to make us better consumers. We are told that the way to effect change is to better allocate our dollars towards better choices.

This has two problems. First, such movements disempower those who do not have many dollars to allocate. This includes people who have money to spend and omits people who do not. It further marginalizes the marginalized. Second, this line of reasoning assumes that the only way people can create change is as consumers rather than as political actors. While Michael Pollan has been one of the key voices in exposing the problems with the U.S. food industry, his approach is exclusionary. He wrote, "Not everyone can afford to eat high-quality food in America, and that is shameful: however, those of us who can, should."[xxii] Yet as Guthman stated, "…the existence of alternative food allows relatively well-off consumers to 'opt out' of conventionally grown food…commodified alternatives to regulatory failure tend to accentuate class inequality rather than ameliorate it."[xxiii] "Alternative" food movements can exacerbate inequality by creating two-tiered systems and reinforcing economic inequalities, among others.

As our generation shapes our own food movements, I believe that we as Millennials in the U.S. and elsewhere should regard the food sovereignty movement as an inspiration. Groups advocating food sovereignty can serve to remind us that in order to create change, we must aim to challenge the roots of the problem we want to solve: in this case the corporate food regime. Unfortunately, many of the alternative food groups that began with a more systems-challenging, radical approach have in recent years lost that edge. They have settled for being alternatives to the current food system rather than a force for its overhaul.[xxiv] These new projects, centering only on market-driven solutions, can be differentiated from the experiments earlier in the century that emphasized a re-envisioning of the atomized individual consumer as a political actor: worker-owned cooperatives, communes, and community gardens.[xxv] An example of such cooptation is the corporate takeover of organic food. As organic food has become more popular, it has become incorporated into the industrial, corporate food system. Today, organic no longer means local or non-industrial, and organic foods can contain a long list of non-organic substances.[xxvi] It too has been hijacked.

In Latin America, social movements such as *Vía Campesina* and the Landless Workers Movement in Brazil (*Movimento dos Trabalhadores Rurais Sem Terra*, MST) are addressing this need for systemic change. *Vía Campesina* has launched several campaigns for farmers, seeds, peasants' rights, and agrarian reform. The MST advocates for land access for poor workers, land reform in Brazil, and activism geared to deal with the social issues that prevent land possession for the poor.[xxvii] Part of this approach involves advocacy of the concept of "food sovereignty," which asserts that access to determine your community's food system is a fundamental right. Under the current food regime, most food choices are made for us, not by us. Rather than advocating for individuals to make "better" choices, we need to work as communities to question the underlying politics, culture, and economic structures that largely determine what ends up on our plates.

Challenging Food Regimes: Developing Progressive and Radical Food Movements

Holt-Giménez and Shattuck offer compelling insights into the food movements that are challenging our current food regime[xxviii]. They assert that we can understand the corporate food regime as comprising two main facets of thinking: neoliberal and reformist. The neoliberal approach centers on a discourse of "food enterprise" and has a "corporate" orientation. This approach emphasizes the need for a continuation of the corporate model discussed above. The reformist approach, the other facet of the corporate food regime, uses a discourse of "food security," oriented towards continuing the project of development. Its approach to the food crisis is basically the same as the neoliberal one but emphasizes food aid as well. While the reformist approach recognizes the problem of food insecurity, it reinforces the corporate agenda at the root of the problem. For example, in its 2008 *World Development Report*, the World Bank advocated the incorporation of smallholders into agribusiness value chains.[xxix] While such an approach might have beneficial impacts, it does not challenge the system of power relations that underpins the poverty of many groups.

On the other hand, two kinds of food movements aim to tackle the roots of this power imbalance, recognizing the environmental and social problems of the corporate model. Holt-Giménez and Shattuck categorize these as "progressive" and "radical."[xxx] The progressive approach uses a discourse of "food justice" and orients itself towards empowering communities marginalized by the current system. In responding to the food crisis, its approach is one of emphasizing the right to food and social protection and more sustainable, agroecological forms of production. The radical approach, which uses a discourse of "food sovereignty," orients itself not just towards empowering populations, but towards reasserting their entitlements to the land and natural resources needed to make food systems truly meet their own needs. Its approach to the food crisis is just as much about democracy and self-determination as it is about food. Both the progressive and radical approaches offer important contributions to reformulating the world's food systems.

Challenging the Corporate System: What Can it Look Like? Two Case Studies

Consider these two versions of hunger. In the northern Cauca, a region in the southwest of Colombia, lush green expanses of sugarcane extend as far as the eye can see. Here, afro-descendant communities have been pushed off their lands and, as biofuels production increases, so does food insecurity. That is, the popularity of plant-based alternatives to fossil fuels has displaced farmers so that more land can be used to grow crops used to create these fuels, which have been heavily subsidized by the U.S. government, among others. In Chester, Pennsylvania, outside of Philadelphia, boarded up windows and graffiti signal a depressed ex-shipbuilding city. Chester is what is referred to as a "food desert"; there hasn't been a supermarket for the population of about 35,000 in over a decade.[xxxi]

At first glance these places seem unique, and they are. They both have very different histories and local cultures. Yet despite the differences in appearance, the marginalization of both communities is a result of the current global corporate "food regime." Factors such as geography, domestic politics, and national wealth have very little to do with the food issues in both communities. They are emblematic of current situations currently found the world over. Yet they are both also examples of the kind of pushback that is also possible.

Both communities have begun the process of developing powerful alternatives, which I will explore. Such food struggles must involve addressing not *only* food issues but, more broadly, issues of the systemic marginalization of the communities. For many activists in the northern Cauca, this involves struggles to prevent land grabs by mining MNCs; for many in Chester, solutions must involve addressing environmental justice issues. In the face of this regime that depends on atomizing individuals, they both depend on collective operations to provide the strength to create opportunities for a different logic.

Chester, Pennsylvania, USA

A short ten-minute drive from Swarthmore, a wealthy Philadelphia suburb where I attended college, the city of Chester is located in the second-hungriest Congressional district in the U.S., behind the Bronx. It is also the poorest place in the state of Pennsylvania. Chester, a 65 percent African-American, low-income community, is considered a "food desert" because businesses, which left when poverty rose, do not wish to set up shop there. Residents can only buy food from convenience stores and fast food restaurants.[xxxii] However, in the face of this scarcity of food, obesity rates are high. Chester is emblematic of the struggles of inner-city residents across America.

Obesity is now a rising problem in many of these areas. According to Guthman, rich people and poor people eat the same amount of calories: thus, she argues, it is not excessive consumption that causes obesity, but environmental toxins that disrupt the endocrine system or "obesogens" that cause obesity[xxxiii]. These toxins are present in the hormones given to industrially-raised and slaughtered cattle. They are also present in commonly-used pesticides and fungicides and are used in the transportation of meat and produce. As Wallace points out, a variety of social and economic forces have hurt Chester.[xxxiv] These include a poor education system, which is one of the worst in Pennsylvania and funnels students into prisons. The community is also rampant with ecological violence. Chester houses four waste-treatment facilities, which cause a host of health problems for residents, including cancer, respiratory problems, and kidney and liver disease.[xxxv]

In attempt to fill this gap, to make the "food desert" bloom, the Chester Co-op was established. A member-owned and run store, the Co-op is able to offer fresh produce to the community at an affordable price. Founded by a Chester native, it employs locals and teaches them business management while maintaining a democratic environment.[xxxvi] At the same time, Chester residents are working more broadly for grassroots environmental justice. They formed the Chester Citizens Concerned for Quality of Life (CRCQL) and have found some success in keeping out the Soil Remediation Systems (SRS), a company that treats petroleum-contaminated soil by burning it, which was trying to open up in Chester. While the case did not make it to the Supreme Court, it was seen as a major initial environmental racism lawsuit. In 1997, Chester residents have had further successes, keeping out other chemical companies from Chester including Cherokee Biotechnology, and in winning a lawsuit against the Delaware County (DelCORA) sewage treatment plant that won Chester a $200,000 settlement that was used to set up a lead poisoning prevention program.

Northern Cauca, Colombia

The northern Cauca is a historically afro-descendant area located a one-to-two hour drive from Cali, one of Colombia's major cities. There is a high incidence of poverty in the north of the Cauca, with 41.63 percent of the population living under the government poverty line.[xxxvii] The irony in the northern Cauca is that, among verdant fields, poverty and malnutrition are growing. In the northern Cauca, 14.5 percent of the population experiences chronic malnutrition.[xxxviii] According to Juan Carlos Morales González of FIAN Colombia, 43 percent of households face food insecurity, broadly defined as lack of physical, social, and economic access to food that meets basic nutritional needs.[xxxix] The consolidation of land tenure is central to this problem: a number of factors including large-scale development projects and an industrial-oriented development agenda have led to growing food insecurity. Sugarcane plantations have taken over much of the land, using it for biofuel production. As land has been lost and unemployment has risen, many residents of the northern Cauca have left to live and work in Cali.

In summer 2012, I spent two months in the southwest of Colombia conducting fieldwork for my Masters of Philosophy in Development Studies, learning about food sovereignty projects being undertaken by a variety of community organizations. For example, the traditional farm at Pílamo is a piece of land collectively farmed by 40 families according to the traditional, agroforestal methods, set up in part by the social movement, the *Proceso de Comunidades Negras* (PCN). This social movement has been active nationally in pursuing social justice, helping secure the Law 70 in 1993 that granted afro-Colombian communities cultural and territorial rights.[xl]

In the community of La Toma, near the town of Suárez, the PCN along with others have succeeded in fighting more broadly to defend their territorial rights from the threat of multinational mining companies. In fact, La Toma is the only instance of a community that has taken back the rights to their lands. In 2002, Ingeominas, the Columbian government institute for mining, gave 99 hectares of land to a private title without first conducting a process of free, prior-informed consent with the communities as mandated by law. The government soon ordered that 1,300 families be evicted from these lands.[xli] Working with the NGO Sembrar, the PCN leaders of La Toma took the case to the International Court of Justice in 2010 and succeeded in ordering the government institute for mining, Ingeominas, to stop all mining licenses in La Toma until FPIC was carried out.

By lauding such movements for food sovereignty, I do not mean to idealize particular initiatives. In the northern Cauca, the process of attaining food sovereignty is only just beginning; perhaps because of this, it often means many different things. In some places, "food sovereignty" means a backyard garden; in others, it means a plantain-processing plant; in others it means a return to the traditional agroforestry practiced by peasants in previous centuries; for others, it must be accompanied by extensive demands to the state for land reform and land rights. I do not mean to imply that all the groups who use the term "food sovereignty" are necessarily advocating a systems change. We should not idealize the struggles that local social movements face in creating truly radical projects. And, we should not idealize the idea of "resistance," ignoring that resistance is always part of, and never wholly separate from, the thing that it is resisting.

Conclusion

In this essay, I have argued that it is possible to feed the world in a way that is both environmentally sustainable and beneficial to the many smallholders who depend on it for their livelihood. I have also criticized U.S. alternative movements for their almost exclusive focus on the role of the consumer, ignoring the many other ways we can create a new food system. Instead, I suggest that the food sovereignty movements occurring in the Global South might serve as a source of inspiration for us in the North. I look to the examples of Chester, Pennsylvania and the northern Cauca, hoping to highlight the power of both "progressive" and "radical" food movements.

While I have hardly scratched the surface of this vast topic, my goal has been not to make specific recommendations or conclusions, but rather to emphasize the need to rethink our assumptions about the ways that we might create a better food system. As we look back on the evolution of a food system that does not work, we as Millennials must step up to the challenge of dreaming big enough to truly envision a new one.

---

[i] World Bank. "Climate Smart Agriculture and the World Bank: The Facts." 2012. *http://climatechange.worldbank.org/content/climatesmart-agriculture-and-world-bank-facts.*

[ii] FAO. "Food Security: Concepts and Measurements." Trade Reforms and Food Security: Conceptualizing the Linkages. 2003.

[iii] Miguel Altieri. "Ecological Impacts of Industrial Agriculture and the Possibilities for Truly Sustainable Farming." 2000, In Fred Magdoff, John Bellamy Foster, Frederick H. Buttel (eds). *Hungry for Profit: Agribusiness' Threat to Farmers, Food, and the Environment.* New York, Monthly Review.

[iv] D. Nierenberg. "Happier Meals: Rethinking the Global Meat Industry." *Worldwatch Paper* 171. *http://www.worldwatch.org/node/819.*

[v] FAO. "World Food Situation: FAO Food Price Index." 2013. *http://www.fao.org/worldfoodsituation/wfs-home/foodpricesindex/en/.*

[vi] Farshad Araghi. "The Great Global Enclosure of Our Times: Peasants and the Agrarian Question at the End of the 20th Century." 2000, In Fred Magdoff, John Bellamy Foster, Frederick H. Buttel (eds). *Hungry for Profit: Agribusiness' Threat to Farmers, Food, and the Environment.* New York: Monthly Review.

[vii] McMichael, Philip. "A food regime genealogy". 2009. *Journal of Peasant Studies* 36 (1): 139–169

[viii] W. Hauter. *Foodopology.* 2012.

[ix] Robert Kaufman. *Bet the Farm.* 2012.

[x] More and Better Campaign. "Peoples' Framework for Action to Eradicate Hunger." 2009. *http://www.moreandbetter.org/en/news/peoples-comprehensive-framework-for-action-to-eradicate-hunger-first-draft-available.*

[xi] World Bank. "International Assessment of Agricultural Knowledge, Science and Technology for Development." 2008.

[xii] Peter Rosset. "The Multiple Functions and Benefits of Small Farm Agriculture In the Context of Global Trade Negotiations." Food First. 1999. *http://www.foodfirst.org/en/node/246.*

[xiii] M.A. *Altieri* and C.I. *Nichols.* "Scaling Up Agroecological Approaches for Food Sovereignty in Latin America." *Development* 51(4), 2008. pp. 472–480.

[xiv] J. Pretty, et al. "Resource-conserving Agriculture Increases Yields in Developing Countries." *Environmental Science and Technology* 40(4), 2005. pp. 1114–1119.

[xv] P. Batáry, A. Báldi, D. Kleijn, and T. Tscharntke. "Landscape-moderated Biodiversity Effects of Agri-environmental Management: A Meta-analysis." Proceedings of the Royal Society B: Biological Sciences 278(1713), 2011. pp. 1894–1902.

[xvi] O. De Schutter. Report Submitted by the Special Rapporteur on the Right to Food. UN Human Right Council, New York. 2010.

[xvii] R. Lal. "Sequestering Carbon in Soils of Agro-ecosystems." *Food Policy* 36 (suppl. 1), S33–S39. 2010.

[xviii] J. Farley, A. Schmitt, J. Alvez and N. Ribeiro de Freitas. "How Valuing Nature can Transform Agriculture. *Solutions* 2(6), 2012. pp. 64-73.

xix K. Andersson and E. Ostrom. "Analyzing Decentralized Resource Regimes from a Polycentric Perspective. Policy Sci 41, 2008. pp. 71–93.

xx S. Borras and J. Franco. "A 'Land Sovereignty' Alternative? Towards a Peoples' Counter-Enclosure." TNI Agrarian Justice Paper. 2012.

xxi J. Guthman, *Weighing In.* 2011.

xxii M. Pollan. *The Omnivore's Dilemma: A Natural History of Four Meals.* 2006.

xxiii Guthman, 2011, p. 152.

xxiv P. Allen, M. FitzSimmons, M. Goodman, and K. Warner. "Shifting Plates in the Agrifood Landscape: The Tectonics of Alternative Agrifood Initiatives in California." *Journal of Rural Studies* 19, 2003. pp. 61-75.

xxv Guthman, 2011.

xxvi Pollan, 2006.

xxvii MST, 2009.

xxviii E. H. Giménez, A. Shattuck. "Food Crises, Food Regimes and Food Movements: Rumblings of Reform or Tides of Transformation?" *Journal of Peasant Studies* 38: 1, 2011. pp. 109 — 144.

xxix World Bank. "Agriculture for Development: World Development Report." 2008.
http://web.worldbank.org/WBSITE/EXTERNAL/EXTDEC/EXTRESEARC H/EXTWDRS/0,,contentMDK:23092617~pagePK:478093~piPK:477627~theSite PK:477624,00.html.

xxx E. H. Giménez, A. Shattuck, 2011.

xxxi M. Wallace. "Eat Well, Seek Justice." 2011. *Swarthmore College Bulletin.*
http://media.swarthmore.edu/bulletin/?p=766.

xxxii Lubano, 2010.

xxxiii E. H. Giménez, A. Shattuck, 2011

xxxiv Wallace, 2011.

xxxv Delco Alliance for Environmental Justice. "Environmental Racism in Chester, Pennsylvania." 2007. *http://www.ejnet.org/chester/index_links.html.*

xxxvi Wallace, 2011.

xxxvii Government of Cauca. "Statistical Information for the Department of the Cauca." 2005.
http://www.ikernell.net/gobernacion/4dm1n1str4c10n/portal/estadisticas.php.

xxxviii Government of Cauca, 2005.

xxxix FAO, 2003.

xl A. Escobar. *Territories of Difference: Place, Movements, Life.* Redes. 2008.

xli Z. Arboleda-Mutis, "'Enemies of Progress, Enemies of Development': Black Communities' Territorial Claims in Northern Cauca, Colombia." MA Thesis. Institute for Social Studies, The Hague, Netherlands. 2012.

The Effects of Large-Scale Land Acquisitions on Global Food Security: The Case of Brazil

Mieke Dale-Harris

925 million people in this world suffer from hunger[i] but not due to a lack of food being produced. According to the same source the global agriculture sector currently produces enough food to feed everyone on the planet, all seven billion of us, at 2,720 calories daily.[ii] That is almost a third more than the commonly accepted 2,000-calorie a day intake considered necessary to live a healthy life. Instead, global food insecurity is a result of a lack of access to nutritious foods. Why is this?

In this essay, I use the example of Brazil and argue that food insecurity resulting from lack of access to food is a result of rural development policy. These policies do not successfully diminish financial and/or land poverty and produce an unintended consequence of hunger. Second, I argue that food insecurity is largely a result of widespread and increased emphasis and enthusiasm for growing "cash-crops", crops that are grown specifically for profit, normally as export crops rather than for domestic consumption. The most popular of these are soybeans, corn, and sugar, of which Brazil is currently a leading exporter, among others.

Food security and the politics of the global food system is a topic that will gain increasing importance in the next few decades. Social media is making the world smaller and waistlines are getting bigger in some countries, yet many go hungry in others. I believe that this will be one of the defining issues of the coming decades and that the Millennial Generation is the global cohort primed and ready to confront it. But as a student of this topic, I also believe that underlying causes of the existing problems in our global food system are little understood.

What is Food Security, or Insecurity?

The 1996 World Food Summit Plan of Action defined food security as existing "when all people, at all times, have physical and economic access to sufficient, safe and nutritious food to meet their dietary needs and food preferences for an active and healthy life."[iii]

The problem lies in the abnormally complex dietary needs of human beings. Unlike most other animals, we require a nutritiously diverse diet to physically and mentally develop and therefore lead life to its maximum potential. If these dietary needs are not met we will suffer from malnutrition, which affects many facets of our health, especially in youth and children.

Malnutrition results from an unbalanced diet, where certain nutrients are lacking, consumed in excess and/or in the wrong proportions. It can lead to stunted growth, dramatically lowered immune systems, mental impairment, obesity, cancer, and more. Often its effects are contradictory. This is what is commonly referred to as the "double-edged sword of malnutrition"[iv] when chronic under-nutrition coexists with obesity in countries, families or even individuals.

Malnutrition and food insecurity are primarily associated with developing countries where death from under nutrition is a daily occurrence. According to a United Nations Food and Agriculture Organization report,[v] 97.7 percent of the 870 million chronically under-nourished people worldwide are from developing countries, which is a shocking 3 out of every 20 persons.

Nevertheless, malnutrition and food insecurity are not only poor country problems. However, unlike in most developing countries, much of the food insecurity of developed countries does not result from restrictions to food, but a lack of access to healthy foods. An increasing cultivation focus away from fruits and vegetables and other traditional staple diet crops toward certain cash-crops has allowed western consumers to put processed food on the table at increasingly lower prices.[vi]

This in turn has resulted in a shift in food accessibility; in that low-income families in developed countries are not at risk of dying of hunger, but are susceptible to mal-nutrition related illnesses due to their heavy consumption of foods that contain lots of calories but not sufficient nutrients to meet their dietary needs.

The persistence of food insecurity in developing countries and its appearance in some developed countries since the 2008 financial crisis have made many institutions, governments, and individuals doubt whether current policies and trends surrounding the production of food are taking us in the right direction. The question on the lips of many of the less conservative agricultural followers is, "Are the products of agriculture industrialization and commercialization really alleviating global food security and increasing accessibility to nutritious foods?"

Industrial Agriculture

For farming, agricultural industrialization means a rise of large-scale land acquisitions (LSLAs). LSLAs refer to investments made into either buying or leasing large areas of agricultural lands. There is not a fixed size that defines LSLAs, but they are usually a thousand hectares or more, and therefore contrast radically with the small-hold farms of between <1 and 100 hectares (a little less than 250 acres). Investments into LSLAs have been steadily increasing over the last half-century, but they have been brought to public attention by a recent acceleration. According to a 2011 World Bank report, between 2007 and 2011 private investors and governments bought a staggering 111 million hectares of agricultural lands in the form of LSLAS.[vii]

But unfortunately, the rise of LSLAs has not brought with it a rise in global food security. In fact, the number of hungry people increased by approximately 235 million between 1995 and 2009,[viii] leading some organizations to suggest that a large-scale farming model is not the key to future global food security.[ix]

This essay aims to provide an overview of the effects of LSLAs on global food security. Brazil´s experience is of particular interest as the country has a long history of industrialized agriculture and is Latin America's biggest economic success story. In addition, I will assess whether this large-scale farming model is suitable for Sub-Saharan Africa, which has the highest rates of food insecurity in the world and is the current target of the majority of LSLAs. A minor section will then observe the effects of LSLA-based farming models on the food security of the countries implementing them.

Brazil and Food Security

Ever since the arrival of Portuguese colonialists Brazil has been an agriculture-based economy. With the rise of globalization, the "Green Revolution," a burst in agricultural technology, from pesticides to tractors to tube wells and the research surrounding it, and the advent of free trade policies in the 1960s and 1970s, the country managed to enter the world food market. This expansion was aided by a loosening of government laws concerning foreign investment and exports, which in turn boosted exports and provided new incentives for the large-scale farming of cash-crops.

A further boost was given to the Brazilian large-scale farming sector by government designed schemes. The first of these was Alto Paranaiba settlement program (PADAP), and the second, was the Japan-Brazil Agricultural Development Cooperation Program (PRODECER) introduced in 1979. Not surprisingly, during the implementation of these projects the Brazilian population was continually being reassured that the rise of LSLAs was just what the country needed for economic growth, environmental protection, increased rural employment, alleviation of rural poverty, and national food security. This would not be the case.

The first of these promises has been more than successfully met. The average annual growth of Brazilian agricultural productivity was 3.3 percent between 1975 and 2002 and a remarkable 5.7 percent between 1988 and 2002, over triple that of the United States between 1948 and 2002.[x]

This rapid agricultural growth turned Brazil into a major global competitor in the exportation of food products, especially of soybeans, sugar, and meat. Such products now account for as much as 42 percent of exports and contribute to around one-third of total gross domestic product, or GDP.[xi] Moreover, this rapid rise has not gone un-noticed by the world; Brazil is now the world's single country largest producer and exporter of agriculture products.[xii] Brazil's finance minister announced that due to the country's economic growth statistics, Brazil has replaced the UK as the world's sixth largest economy, causing a stir in English media.[xiii]

However, this agricultural boom seemed to do little for the country's food security. In the late 1990s Brazil still had very high indexes of poverty and food insecurity, and hope of change was marred by its infamous reputation of extreme inequality. In 2003 the World Bank found that 35.8 percent of the population continued to live below the national poverty line. This is about 20 percent more than the poverty levels experienced by countries with similar GDPs. Furthermore, while there was economic growth of 125.9 percent between 1992 and 2005 the country's poverty rates dropped by a scant 0.6 percent between 1995 and 2003, and in 2010, 65 million Brazilians, which equates to a third of the population, still faced food insecurity.[xiv]

In part, Brazil's lack of correlation between rising GDP and alleviation of extreme inequality can be directly connected to the increase in LSLAs and the un-productive, or even negative, disruption they caused rural inhabitants. Since the first boom of the century in the 1960s the rise of LSLAs has produced in Brazil one of the most concentrated landownership economies in the world. In 1992, 2.6 million hectares of rural lands were in the hands of foreigners and by

2008 this had over doubled to 5.6 million hectares.[xv] In 2011 it was determined that just 1.5 percent of rural landowners effectively occupied 52.6 percent of all agriculture lands.[xvi] One Brazilian newspaper, *Folha de SoaPoalo*, even calculated with data provided by the National Institute for Colonization and Agrarian Reform (INCRA) that between 2007 and 2010 the equivalent of "22 football fields of land were bought every hour by foreigners."[xvii]

Land Inequality and National Income

This land distribution inequality is reflected in national income inequality. According to the 2010 census over half the population earn below the monthly minimum wage of R$510 ($245.77). Twenty-five percent of the population have a monthly income per capita of below R$188 and 50 percent below R$375.[xviii] The money is going to the top 20 percent of earners who in 2009 accrued an astonishing 58.9 percent of total national earnings.[xix]

Such prolonged inequality is undesirable on ethical grounds and does little to improve national food security. It has been shown that in countries like Brazil with high levels of poverty, protracted inequitable development "adversely affects growth and health outcomes," impedes further development and results in even more inequality.[xx] This means that while Brazil´s middle and upper classes prosper a large chunk of the poor stay at exactly the same level.

LSLAs have directly contributed to Brazil's current state of high inequality and thus prolonged food insecurity. Their negative impact on rural development through involuntary-displacements of rural inhabitants has restricted land access for many peasants and agricultural employment opportunities in general. By pushing people off their lands they take away the food sovereignty of the needy. They deprive them of their main source of food security without providing a viable alternative in the form of employment.

In the two decades following the advent of the "Green Revolution" and free trade in the early 1960s it is estimated that millions of peasants were displaced by LSLAs.[xxi] In the 1970s alone soybean production grew from 172,000 to 2.3 million hectares in the regions where grown most. It was responsible for the displacement of 300,000 people in the state of Rio Grande and 2.5 million people in Parana, compared to a gain of 170,000 the previous decade.[xxii] Similarly, the implementation of PROCEDER "caused the near extinction of indigenous communities living in affected areas."[xxiii]

To date, land displacements have proven to be inherently interlinked with LSLAs and are considered largely to blame for rural inequality and employment instability in affected countries. Large-scale farming investors often claim that the intervention will have a positive effect on rural employment, and therefore on development and food security. However, research on the jobs currently generated by industrialized large-scale mono-crop farms tells a very different story. While family farming in the tropics creates about 35 jobs per 100 hectares, plantations of oil-palm and sugar generate 10, eucalyptus 2, and soybean a measly half job per 100 hectares. One source cited that for every 11 persons displaced by soybean plantations in the tropics just one job (temporary or permanent) was created.[xxiv]

Furthermore, the farm-based employment that is created by LSLAs is characterized by its temporary and extremely low-skilled nature. This employment at large is poorly-paid and in some areas child labor and the antiquated system of forced labor still exist.[xxv] Mass unemployment caused by involuntary displacements puts further downward pressure on farm employment wages as desperate peasants will work "from sunrise to sunset for a completely inadequate salary" of $1.41 a day since "they have no alternative because they have no land of their own."[xxvi]

Therefore, rather than alleviating poverty, LSLAs subject increasing numbers of peasants to food insecurity through working poverty at below $2 per day. This goes directly against FAO advice of using decent employment as the "main channel" with which to promote upward growth and relieve rural food insecurity via the reversal of inequality trends.[xxvii]

LSLAs and Brazil's Development

Escalating land prices due to increased interest in farmland from wealthy investors was a further limitation on Brazilian rural development. Farmers who were not reliant on low-skilled labor before displacement but possessed food sovereignty from their own lands were unlikely to be able to afford similar areas of fertile land in the near future.

Such unrealistically high land prices result in restricted access to land and thus high landlessness. Restricted access to land threatens the food security of many peasants as it prevents them from supplying their own food, which for many is their traditional and only method of survival. It is a widespread phenomenon in developing countries, where 200 million rural inhabitants, equivalent to 20 percent of the world's poor, do not have access to sufficient land to make a living.[xxviii]

Not surprisingly, it is also a prevailing problem in Brazil. In northern Brazil, which receives many displaced migrant farmers from mid-western regions, about 40 percent of the rural population is landless.[xxix] Many families are forced to move to cities as they repeatedly fail to muster the resources necessary to feed themselves. However, recipient cities struggle to create employment at the rate of migration. Consequently, migrant families often end up living in a state of income poverty and food insecurity in one of Brazil's many growing *favelas* (city slums), where violence, disease, and hunger are the daily norm.

President Luis Inácio Lula da Silva tried to reverse many of these effects during the first decade of the 21st century. Like many left-wing Latin American presidents of the millennium, he put at least some of his greed for agriculture taxes aside. He made desperate attempts to reign in the counterproductive large-scale farming model that was dominating his countryside and doing nothing for the poor and food insecure of the country. After winning elections in 2002 "Lula" introduced schemes targeted at improving food security by restricting land access for foreign investors and increasing it for northeastern peasants. He also implemented the effective *Fome Zero* (Zero Hunger) program. Much of *Fome Zero's* rural success resulted from its focus on increasing the livelihoods of small-hold farmers.

Exporting Brazilian Agricultural Policy to Sub-Saharan Africa
Despite this recognition that LSLA policies did not initiate equally-distributed rural development that lowered indices of unemployment, poverty, and food insecurity, the Brazilian government is not holding back on international LSLA investments. In line with 75 percent of the world's current LSLA investments, Brazil's focus is aimed at Africa and in particular Mozambique.

Due to its large strips of undervalued fertile land, cheap labor, and relaxed regulations, Sub-Saharan Africa is the target of the boosted enthusiasm for foreign investments in LSLAs. This increased enthusiasm is a symptom of capitalist greed and developed countries' desire to ensure their national food security in the face of a repeat of the 2007-2008 global food price crisis, when along with other core crops, corn and soybeans rose by 125 percent and 107 percent, respectively.[xxx]

However, increased food security for either the recipient or implementing countries is doubtful. Evidence from Brazil and other countries that have received influxes of LSLAs indicates the unlikelihood that such intervention in the Sub-Saharan Africa farming sector will provide relief to high rates of poverty and food insecurity via rural development. In fact, an analysis of the current state of Mozambique and its Sub-Saharan Africa neighbors denotes that heavy LSLA investment in this region will result in even more devastating rates of national food insecurity, in a continent where food insecurity is already at a global high.

A statement drawn up by an association of Mozambican peasants, heavily opposed the ProSavanna project, an LSLA scheme that is due to be introduced over 14 million hectares of arable land by the Brazilian, Japanese, and Mozambican governments. This statement is mainly based on an assessment of the effects of agrarian capitalism in Brazil and above anything condemns the inevitable result that the impending LSLAs will "transform Mozambican peasant farmers into their employees and rural laborers."[xxxi]

Like Brazil before its agrarian revolution, rural Mozambique predominantly consists of small-hold farmers. These farmers sustain the food security of their own families and/or the regional, provincial and/or national population. It is these farmers with ample experience in their trade that LSLA investors will use to fill their low-skilled and low-paid temporary or permanent employment positions. Those who have been made unemployed by LSLAs, either through literal displacement or dramatically increased pressures on their profit margins, will have little choice but to accept such a measly offer. Although this will help, in some perverse form of the word, to alleviate LSLA-generated unemployment, it is unlikely that this employment will be sufficient to meet growing demand.

The displacement of Mozambican small-hold peasant farmers by LSLAs will therefore directly threaten the country's rural food security. The farms that once provided for the nation's diverse nutritional needs will be replaced by monoculture cash-crop farms aimed at the export market. For medium-sized farms this will result in lower incomes. For smaller ones it will replace food sovereignty with either inadequate laborer incomes or unemployment.

In Sub-Saharan Africa, LSLA proposals nearly always underestimate the scale of resulting farmer displacements. Feigned "confusion" over idle lands is a common problem, which stems from the fact that 90 percent of land in the region is farmed without legal property rights, but instead through informal tenure systems.[xxxii] This confusion is most likely feigned as there is nothing surprising in the fact that fertile land is being farmed in a region where food insecurity is rife.

Mozambique has not escaped such pretense. The "idle" lands earmarked for LSLAs by investors are reportedly not idle at all, but instead occupied by "millions of peasants" who use the fertile soils and abundance of water to feed their families.[xxxiii] This indicates that, following ProSavanna's implementation, the figures of adversely affected farms and displaced workforce will easily surpass those that reflect the individuals benefited from by industrial farm employment.

Furthermore, Sub-Saharan Africa has been identified as having a growing rural workforce. If decent rural employment is not generated in the near future this new workforce will face vulnerability to food insecurity due to low-income poverty and/or no land access.[xxxiv] Moreover, increased rural unemployment will only serve to reduce already low agriculture wages by increasing employers' bargaining power.

Globally, extreme working poverty (below $1.25 per day) is associated with agriculture employment practices. 62 percent of Sub-Saharan Africa's working poverty is experienced in rural regions, and in general, Africa's farming employment rarely generates more than $750 annually, a scant $2.40 daily on a 6 day week.[xxxv] This is barely enough to feed oneself a healthy nutritious diet and definitely not enough if further expenses have to be met and additional family members have to be fed.

Where do the Displaced Farmers go?

Rural-urban migration is a commonly found solution to this problem. However, even rapidly industrializing countries like Brazil can rarely effectively cope with the pressures of rapid urbanization, so the slowly industrializing countries of Sub-Saharan Africa have no chance. Already an estimated 90 percent of new rural settlements in Africa are taking the form of slums.[xxxvi] Increasing this number will only take us further away from reaching the Millennium Development Goal of eradicating hunger and poverty.

The neglect of small-hold farmers by LSLAs drives rural-urban migration by reducing rural food sovereignty and not generating sufficient and decent rural employment to meet growing demand. The life of a peasant farmer is a precarious one, but the food sovereignty it provides is generally preferable to reliance on unstable and low-income agricultural work. Therefore, if living standards and food security are to really advance in rural Sub-Saharan Africa, governments, both national and foreign, need to invest in the region's small-hold farmers. By doing this with land titling, provision of infrastructure, education, and other schemes, peasant farmers could continue to possess food sovereignty and expand to a level where they have complete food security and a real income.

Enabling farmers to earn a real income provides a means to improve land productivity, through employed help and/or increased use of fertilizers and technology. This in turn boosts rural development through provision of employment, either directly or via increased consumption of both farm and non-farm related products.

Moreover, support of small farmers not only serves to feed the rural poor. Evidence indicates that such a strategy can also be what is best for national food security. Even in countries with heavy influxes of LSLAs, small farmers continue to be the backbone of the national food supply. For instance, in Brazil 70 percent of nationally consumed food continues to come from small-hold farmers who cultivate just 30 percent of arable lands.[xxxvii] This is because the major cash-crops currently cultivated by LSLAs only constitute a very small proportion of a well-rounded nutritious diet and are often not even grown for human consumption. One commenter has pointed out that Brazilian soybean production "has proved considerably more efficient at feeding European cattle than maintaining the livelihoods of poor Brazilians."[xxxviii]

Non-Food and Specialty Crops

In 2011 only 20 percent of the maize grown in the U.S., the largest producer of maize in the world, was consumed directly by humans as food. The remaining 80 percent went in almost equal shares to either ethanol production or animal feed. Soybean contribution to global food security is also much less than its potential. Over half of the 7,000 tons of soybean imported into the UK daily, mostly from Brazil, is used for livestock food.[xxxix]

This demand for meat, and therefore the production of feedstuffs, which is predicted to swiftly increase with the development of China, India, and other countries with expanding middle classes, is consuming millions of "ghost hectares" in developing countries. Although meat is a good source of protein, its daily consumption, which is the trend in middle and high-income countries, is not necessary for maintaining a well-rounded diet and thus food security. Therefore, the devotion of large expanses of arable land to feedstuffs, in countries where meat is a rare luxury and there is a daily struggle to find sufficient nutrients to feed the population is not only out of place, but does nothing to alleviate their national food insecurity.

The 99¢ hamburger is another major criticism associated with large-scale cash-crop farming and its effect on the world food security. Intentionally or not, this farming model has pushed investments away from perishable goods like fruits and vegetables, otherwise known as "specialty-crops," and toward imperishable products that contribute to low-cost processed foods that are high in sugars and fats.[xl]

Corn and soy decreased in price by 32 percent and 21 percent, respectively, between 1996 and 2006.[xli] Meaning that, "While the costs of sugars and fats have become cheaper, healthier options like fruit and vegetables have become more expensive, rising nearly 40 percent over the last 20 years."[xlii] In other words, the products of LSLAs do not provide for the dietary needs of either the developing countries where implemented or the developed countries implementing them.

The soybean alone is put into numerous products. It whitens bread, makes emulsifier (E322), and replaces saturated fats. It is an ingredient in doughnuts, instant soup, chocolate, sausages, margarine, and much more. The soybean is also the father of the infamous trans-fats. Trans-fats were once hailed as a healthy alternative to saturated fats. However, it has since been discovered that they are nearly twice as bad for the heart and are estimated to cause between 30,000 and 100,000 deaths annually.

Conclusion: Killing Us with Cheap Food

Unfortunately, trans-fats are just one example; corn and/or soya are used in most unhealthy processed foods in various forms of fats and sugars. They have been specially picked for this role for their dirt cheap

191

production and malleable nature, which makes them fantastic for food producers but potentially lethal for consumers. Ever cheaper processed foods wrapped in psychologically "alluring" packaging, means that where the poor used to suffer from under-nutrition they now suffer from obesity, or both. It seems an unlikely coincidence that the surge in products made with corn and soya over the last couple of decades occurred at the exactly the same time as the obesity epidemic in the U.S, which in turn lead to an increase in the debilitating and threatening disease of diabetes.[xliii]

In Bristol, a fairly well-off British city, 41 percent of families are "forced" to buy cheaper high-calorie but low-nutrient foods as healthy foods have become unaffordable[xliv]. This is not a localized problem. In the U.S. in 2009, $1 could buy 1,200 calories of potato chips or 875 calories of soda, but just 250 calories of vegetables or 170 calories of fresh fruit.[xlv]

All this indicates that repressed rural development is not the only adverse effect of LSLAs. In their current state they are not even providing food security for the middle-high-income countries implementing them. By diverting attention away from nutritious crops and focusing almost solely on a small-range of cash-crops they are pushing down the prices of unhealthy and fatty processed foods, for which there is an abundance of ingredients, and increasing the prices of nutritious foods. This contributes to malnutrition and food insecurity.

The world population is predicted to reach the phenomenal size of 9 billion inhabitants by 2050. This will mean more mouths to feed and more employment to provide. Evidence shows that a continuation of the current trend for LSLAs is not relieving, and maybe even exacerbating global food insecurity in the present, so what hope does it have for the future?

LSLAs, and the support system surrounding them, have so far been unproductive at alleviating poverty and thus food insecurity in developing countries, and detrimental to the nutrition, and thus food security, of peoples in developed countries. They do not help to relieve rural poverty in developing countries as they stunt rural development by feeding problems of inequality, restricted land access, and lack of employment or decent employment. This has been the experience of a number of Latin American countries and there is little reason to think that it will play out differently in Sub-Saharan Africa.

In addition, they harm food security of all countries by directing production away from nutritious crops toward certain cash-crops that are above all ultimately used for fuel, animal-feed, or unhealthy processed foods. This new form of food distribution has led to rising prices in both developed and developing countries of healthy foods and decreasing prices of fatty foods that are likely to result in malnutrition and in particular obesity. It is therefore vital that rather than press on with this system in face of dramatic population rise, we create a farming system that meets both alimentation and employment needs. This will involve ensuring that rural production provides nutritional foods to meet local, urban and international demands. It means putting the emphasis back on high labor-intensive farming of foods that end up on our table in near enough their original form. If we cannot do this we will see a struggle for food and against poverty in the future that could well escalate into a war. There is already enough of that.

[i] United Nations. "The State of Food Insecurity in the World 2010." Food and Agriculture Organization (UN-FAO). 2010. *http://www.fao.org/docrep/013/i1683e/i1683e.pdf*.

[ii] United Nations. "Reducing Poverty and Hunger, the Critical Role of Financing for Food, Agriculture, and Rural Development." Food and Agriculture Organization, International Fund for Agricultural Development, World Food Program. 2002. *http://www.fao.org/docrep/003/Y6265e/y6265e00.htm*.

[iii] United Nations. "Food Security Statistics." Food and Agriculture Organization (UN-FAO). *http://www.fao.org/economic/ess/ess-fs/it/*.

[iv] L.T. Leatherman and A. Goodman. "Coca-colonization of diets in the Yucatan." *Social Science and Medicine*, 61, 2004. pp. 833-846.

[v] United Nations Food and Agriculture Organization. "Decent rural employment for food security: A case for action." 2012. *http://www.fao.org/docrep/015/i2750e/i2750e00.pdf*.

[vi] Moltzen 2009; Starmer et al. 2006.

vii World Bank. "Rising Global Interest in Farmland; Can it yield sustainable and equitable benefits?" 2011.
http://siteresources.worldbank.org/INTARD/Resources/ESW_Sept7_final_final.pdf.
viii *http://www.worldhunger.org.*
ix GRAIN 2008; UN-FAO 2012).
x United Nations Industrial Development Organisation. "Agribusiness for Africa's prosperity." 2011.
xi Ibid.
xii J. Almeida. *Brazil in Focus, Economic, Political and Social Issues.* NOVA Publishers. 2008.
xiii P. Inman. "Brazil's economy overtakes UK to become world's sixth largest." *The Guardian.* 6th March 2012.
http://www.guardian.co.uk/business/2012/mar/06/brazil-economy-worlds-sixth-largest.
xiv Mundi Index Database. 2012; World Bank, IBGE, and TKN databases)
xv R. Hackbart. *Aquisição de imóveis rurais por estrangeiros.* Brasilia, INCRA. 2008.
http://www.senado.gov.br/comissoes/CRA/AP/AP20080305_Rolf_Hackbart.pdf;
A.U. Oliveira. "A questão da aquisição de terras por estrangeiros no Brasil: um retorno aos dossiês." *AGRÁRIA,* São Paulo, 12, 2010. pp. 3-113. Accessed through: "Land Grabbing, Agribusinesses and the Peasantry in Brazil and Mozambique." Land Deal Politics Initiative. 2012.
http://www.cornelllandproject.org/download/landgrab2012papers/Clements_Fernandes.pdf.
xvi DATALUTA. Banco de Dados da Luta pela Terra. *Brasil: Relatorio.* 2011.
http://docs.fct.unesp.br/nera/projetos/dataluta_brasil_2010.pdf.
xvii Folha de S.Paulo. "Estangeiros compram 22 campos de futebol por hora." 2010.
http://www1.folha.uol.com.br/poder/824211-estrangeiros-compram-22-campos-de-futebol-por-hora.shtml.
xviii J. Leahy. "2010 census shows that Brazil's inequalities remain." *Financial Times.* 2010.
http://www.ft.com/intl/cms/s/0/71352352-112c-11e1-ad22-00144feabdc0.html#axzz2FK1JoAn6.
xix World Bank Database. 2012.
xx World Bank, (2004). Inequality and economic development in Brazil; D. Benjamin, L. Brandt, and J. Gile. "Inequality and growth in rural China: Does higher inequality impede growth?" *Economic Journal,* 121 (557), 2006 pp. 1281-1309.
xxi C. Welch. "Globalization and the transformation of work in rural Brazil: agribusiness, rural labor unions, and peasant mobilization." *International Labor and Working-Class History,* 70, 2006. pp. 35-60.
xxii A.C. Diegues. "The Social Dynamics of Deforestation in the Brazilian Amazon: An Overview." United Nations Research Institute for Sustainable

Development (UNRISD). 1992; M.A. Altieri and E. Bravo. "The ecological and social tragedy of crop-based biofuel production in the Americas," in R. Jonasse, (ed.) *Agrofuels in the Americas*. Food First Books, Oakland, CA. 2009. pp. 15-24. *http://www.foodfirst.org/files/pdf/Agrofuels_in_the_Americas.pdf*.

xxiii La Via Campesina. "Land Grabbing for Agribusiness in Mozambique: UNAC Statement on the ProSavanna Program." 2012. *http://viacampesina.org/en/index.php/main-issues-mainmenu-27/agrarian-reform-mainmenu-36/1321-land-grabbing-for-agribusiness-on-mozambique-unac-statement-on-the-prosavana-programme*.

xxiv E. Holt-Giménez. "Biofuels: myths of the agro-fuels transition." *Food First Backgrounder*, 13(2), 2007. *http://www.foodfirst.org/node/1711*; Welch, 2006.

xxv FOA, 2006.

xxvi B. Dangl. "Land as a centre of power in Bolivia." Toward Freedom. 2006. *http://www.towardfreedom.com/americas/938-land-as-a-center-of-power-in-bolivia*.

xxvii United Nations Food and Agriculture Organisation. "The State of Food Insecurity in the World." 2012. *http://www.fao.org/publications/sofi/en/*.

xxviii Global Land Tool Network, United Nations Human Settlement Program (UN-HABITAT). "Secure Land Rights For All." 2008. *http://www.responsibleagroinvestment.org/rai/sites/responsibleagroinvestment.org/files/Sec ure%20land%20rights%20for%20all-UN%20HABITAT.pdf*.

xxix S. Santos de Souza. "Land Reform, Regional Planning and Socio-economic Development in Brazil." Darwin College, University of Cambridge. 2010. *http://www.dspace.cam.ac.uk/bitstream/1810/229766/1/THESIS_SAULO.pdf*.

xxx Global Research. "Financial speculators reap profit from global hunger." 2008.

xxxi Diegues, 1992.

xxxii Dangl, 2006.

xxxiii Diegues, 1992.

xxxiv FAO, 2012.

xxxv Ibid.

xxxvi Diegues, 1992.

xxxvii INESC, 2008.

xxxviii SAFE, 1999.

xxxix Lucas, 2011.

xl Moltzen, 2009.

xli Starmer et al., 2006.

xlii Moltzen, 2009.

xliii Ibid.

xliv *The Bristol Post*. "Thousands of Bristolians struggle to pay for food. November 23, 2011. *http://www.thisisbristol.co.uk/Thousands-Bristolians-struggle-pay-food/story-13929710-detail/story.html#axzz2OkkOTIL6*

xlv Ibid.

The Millennial Generation and Changing Our Culture of Consumption

Nick Santos

The last two decades of environmentalism have been a mixed bag of stagnation in the United States. Our scientific understanding of our impacts on ecosystems, resources, and human populations through environmental pollution and destruction has increased dramatically. This understanding has moved rapidly into the general population and created real desire to reduce environmental impacts. Simultaneously, our ability to tackle these issues at the highest levels of government has deteriorated due to increased political polarization. Environmental conservation, once the realm of conservatives through market-based solutions, has become an issue solely championed by the political left. Grassroots solutions have resulted in some success but lack the key, economy-wide implications that top-down, federal regulation can have.

This is a bird's eye-view of the governmental side of environmentalism today. For individuals, generally increasing income and populations in the United States, and, importantly now, abroad, mean that we are consuming far more than we did even 20 years ago despite our increased environmental awareness. According to the WorldWatch Institute, an organization focused on global sustainability, private consumption expenditures in 2000 had quadrupled over the previous four decades and are only increasing along with the corresponding resource consumption.[i] With another two billion people on this planet by 2050, we can expect this problem to grow as well.

Our consumption presents a monumental challenge. It is an issue that is at the very foundation of our growth-based economy. As a result it will require a solution that shows immediate results but plans for the long term. Current efforts in the sustainability movement may seem to address consumption, but have thus far remained focused on more environmentally-efficient growth. Our lack of sufficient action leaves us overtaxing almost every natural resource that we have learned to use. We absolutely must find ways to consume significantly fewer resources. If we do not, we face the collapse of some of these resources and ensuing global instability.

In this essay, we will explore the deep-rooted issues underlying consumption, the very human difficulties of finding a solution, and some potential ways forward. I argue that regarding consumption, our current attitudes and methods will not solve the problem, and we need a new way of thinking about what we consume and how to consume less. As a Millennial, I have seen very little concrete environmental progress in my lifetime, in part owing to our inaction on climate change and its ramifications. It is easy to look at these issues and the current political climate and believe that the future holds more of the same. But we have options, so long as we stop ignoring them, and we can mitigate our environmental problems while strengthening our economy and our quality of life.

For Millennials, these problems are now ours to solve, whether we like it or not. We are not inherently better in addressing environmental issues than previous generations. Far from it: we are the next iteration of a consumptive culture. But other cultural changes occurring in this generation, such as advanced information systems, extensive sharing, global engagement and increased governmental participation, enable opportunities for addressing these problems that were unavailable a generation ago. Our acceptance of these opportunities may help us be a generation of progress.

Consumption to Our Core

Step One in the Alcoholics Anonymous recovery program is admitting to yourself that you have a problem that you are incapable of solving without a significant change. In the developed world, we have yet to truly admit that we have a consumption problem. With environmental problems, we must acknowledge them in order to have the incentive or will to address them. The global consumer class is growing rapidly, far more quickly than our efforts to reduce consumption can keep up with. On its own, this increase has no inherent problem. More people outside of the U.S. are achieving a standard of living that we in America would describe as comfortable. The problem lies in the limits of our biological world to provide the resources required for this growth and the existing mass of consumers. Growth of the consumer class constitutes a tradeoff, between wildlands and croplands, biodiversity and homogeneity, and sometimes even between resources like food and fuel. Deforestation, waterway contamination, and resource depletion are all largely driven by increased demand for products. We are unsustainably consuming everything we have left.

The indirect nature of these problems makes them difficult to grasp in their entirety. Big picture estimates predict that we would need more than four Earth-like planets to support a planet where everyone consumed as much as Americans.[ii] Clearly, this is an unsustainable trajectory. We must scale our resource usage down to a level that meets what our one planet can provide. We can scale back through smarter growth patterns for developing and middle-income countries combined with changes and reductions in consumptive patterns in the already high-consuming countries.

Americans in particular seem to resent the idea of giving up much of anything significant in the name of sustainability. We often see our privilege as the product of our hard work rather than circumstance, or worse, imperialism. But what if we could be equally as happy with less? Would we still see reducing consumption as giving something up? Research suggests that in the United States our collective wealth and expenditures have not made us happier than countries with less wealth. The Happy Planet Index, published by the New Economics Foundation, weights "experienced well-being," life expectancy, and ecological footprints of nations. The result is a measure of happiness weighted by environmental cost (see graph).

The United States consistently ranks low on the index, 105th in 2012, in large part due to its high income scores and high ecological footprints corresponding with its happiness, whereas other nations get similar happiness with less income. Further, within our society, we level off in terms of happiness around $75,000 per year per household. That is, additional income beyond that does not appear to make us report more happiness; returns on wealth in the form of happiness diminish.[iii] That additional income is then inefficiently used, and maybe we would be willing to forgo using it on consumption in favor of environmental conservation.

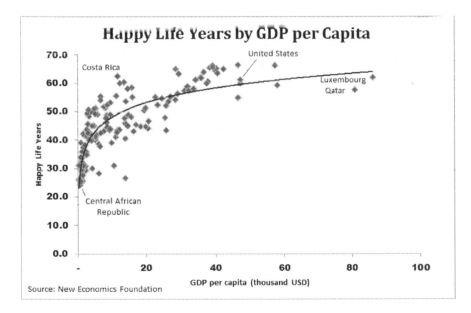

Crossing the Next Set of Hurdles

In the United States, we spend a massive amount of effort on the sustainability problem, with minimal results compared to its scale. Our best efforts today seem to operate on the assumption that with the right information, people will make environmentally beneficial decisions. This simply and unfortunately is not true and has not played out that way; we have the classic problem of translating our awareness into action. As a result, a large segment of our society is aware of major environmental problems and is somewhat aware of its own role in creating and perpetuating these problems. Acknowledgement is an important first step, but we need to cross several more hurdles of translating that knowledge into reduced and smarter consumption before we call it progress. Millennials, being the next generation tasked with addressing these issues, are primed to lead us over these hurdles. But we need a plan of action that, so far, our society has been unable to produce.

A primary component of this plan of action will involve stronger motivators for change, or stronger use of existing motivators. Current motivators are psychologically weak: things like our children's future, rainforest destruction, and health of people in developing nations. They are concepts we may identify strongly with, but are often indirect and mostly unseen by us, the end users of products and services. When we do see these impacts and results, they are often so disconnected in time from our actions that it fails to imprint a strong connection with our own involvement in the problem. This makes these issues poor motivators for behavior change. Humans require a strong relationship between our action and the resulting change in order to deeply connect them. Education alone is not enough, and moving to action is hurdle number one.

The second reason we have yet to find a viable strategy or path to reducing consumption is that changing behavior is a fundamentally difficult task. Large-scale behavior change campaigns must be flexible enough to adapt to the needs, desires, habits, and training of billions of individuals. So far, when sustainability efforts have focused on behavior change, they have gone for the problems simple and generic enough to appeal to a large segment of our population; think swapping incandescent light bulbs for more energy efficient ones. This lowest common denominator approach gets some results, but understandably takes us to a shallow level of behavior change. Going deeper with subgroups and individuals to enable more meaningful reductions in consumption is the second hurdle.

Understanding Our Own Behavior

The common component of both hurdles is our own psychology. Our existing behavior is easier to complete, presenting a challenge to adoption of new behavior. Essentially we act out consumption through habits. Similar to how political incumbents are heavily favored against their opponents in a reelection, our existing behaviors tend to win out against efforts to replace them with new ones, without regard for their merit. And here is the truly difficult problem: billions of us have already learned consumption in the current form. We are skilled over-consumers.

Purchasing behavior is one of these incumbent behaviors that are difficult to unlearn once taught. When and how we shop for groceries, and other goods, is acted out of habits learned in our youth. Unless you look at every item on the shelf, you are applying a set of filters to help you narrow down your attention to what matters. If we hope to reduce our impact as consumers, we will all need to drop these filters, at least temporarily, to see the universe of possibilities again and choose new options. This behavior is not specific to groceries and shopping alone, but we commonly act it out in those venues.

As a result of these habits and filters, we must understand that some portion of our lifetime impact is already written into the future. Often, we can only change so many behaviors at once, so we move slowly through changes. This slowness means that significant time passes from the time we are first aware of our impacts to the time we finally act to reduce them. We can, and for many reasons should, queue up these changes in order to tackle them individually with the result being incremental, but not rapid, progress. The exception to this rule includes, for example, life-changing events such as moving or other momentous shifts that force reevaluation of basic tasks such as where you shop. We can make events like moving a tool for change if we recognize the opportunity.

Using this Knowledge to Our Advantage

These lags between knowledge and action mean that the better option is teaching it correctly the first time to the next generation. We must raise each successive generation with a stronger sustainability ethic than the last. Remember, once learned, these ethics are very difficult to change. This mantra of doing better for each generation is common across many social issues, and for good reason. Yet, it is often limited to preserving lifestyles for future generations. We must now include the next generation in the solution through their higher adaptability to change. To begin, however, we must change culture in the current generation, which comes down to changing our own behavior.

To change our own behavior to align with our values, we must work at the small group level, and even the individual level. For this reason, I will not provide precise prescriptions to fix our environmental problems here. It is too big a group in too small a space. By organizing into groups, we gain a number of advantages. Teams inspire, motivate, and help keep up momentum. Teams allow us to find strategies that resonate with our lifestyles. Teams also prevent isolation and can guide us to better information and strategies when other members learn lessons first. If you are interested in reducing your consumption, I encourage you to start by finding at least a partner, if not a small group, to work with and keep the challenge going.

We can also use the same technology that is employed to sell us more products to hack our own behavior and buy less. The biggest innovation in advertising in the last decade or more, in my opinion, is the refinement of demographic targeting. Rooted in the information advertisers can gain about us from our Internet usage patterns and information we provide online, advertisements today use a staggering amount of information about each of us to determine what products we might like and what ads to show us. This same sort of profiling, willingly shared, can help us identify potential strategies to reduce consumption. When combined with motivation systems such as "gamification," or turning behavior change activities into games with basic reward systems, this information can help us self-organize into groups, find impact reduction strategies that are personally achievable, and execute the strategies.

This is just scratching the surface. Plenty of room exists in this space for others to innovate and iterate. These are strategies I believe many Millennials could be ready for by virtue of our acceptance of technology and social change and our understanding of environmental problems. Each strategy can work with a subset of the population, but we need more ideas to gather a broader base and succeed in changing culture. Reaching sustainability requires all hands on deck and all ideas executed.

In the long run, we will need a new economic model, something akin to a steady state economy, if we hope to reach sustainability. A growth-based economy simply provides too large of an incentive to consume more. We will need to figure out exactly what this new economy looks like if we hope to reach sustainability. This is an area we are only beginning to talk about. The subject needs far more research on what the economic foundation will be, what its new drivers are, and what needs to be in place during the transition to ensure some level of stability. I do not have that answer yet, unfortunately.

Basics of Consuming Less

Any piece of writing criticizing consumption that fails to offer anything on how the reader can begin consuming less tends to fall on deaf ears. While implementation is much larger than one article, I have found that a few important components need to be in place for individual success in reducing consumption. As we saw earlier, consuming less is all about changing how we think, and how that leads into what we actually do. First, we need to recognize that the cost of doing business has changed. When we must buy something, we can no longer prioritize price above all else if we wish to remain committed to our sustainability ethic. Environmental performance of the products we must buy becomes a top factor, while price becomes a lesser factor. Price is not a not always a predictor for sustainability, but by and large the cheapest goods have environmentally and socially detrimental effects that cascade down the supply chain. If you enter a purchase ready to pay more for an environmentally responsible, but sometimes costlier, product, you will be more prepared to hold up under price pressure and stick to your social and environmental values.

The second factor regarding purchasing is where our money goes. Primarily, we must stop giving our money to companies that put it to work against us. For example, if I give my money to a corporation with a poor track record on workers' rights, environmental destruction, and product health, I expect that my money is working against my values. This is not a new concept. Boycotts have been a common tactic for quite some time amongst groups looking to change the practices of companies. We now need to recognize that even in the absence of a large group, our purchases add up and our choices to move money elsewhere matters. This goes hand in hand with buying goods made with environmental costs in mind. If we factor in both environmental performance of a product and the practices of the companies we do business with, we can create a better market for responsible products.

A Young Field

The issue of seriously reducing consumption remains a young field. The sustainability movement has set the stage for us to think about a culture of less, but we have yet to lay the foundation or create the cultural change required to do more than simple actions. This responsibility, as I said before, will require Millennials to rise to the challenge, prove our environmental credentials, and lead us to an era where sustainability is more than talk and token actions.

We have a huge task ahead of us as a generation, a nation, and a planet. We need to recognize that the pace of policy is quite slow and that a movement in our culture is necessary to succeed in our core environmental goals. We will need to move beyond the work that our parents' and grandparents' generations did with environmental lifestyles and policy. We need to remember what sustainability means: consuming resources in a manner that allows their continual harvest and beneficial use by the entire ecosystem. This will require significant changes in our own thinking, lifestyles, culture, and economy. We will need to learn how to change our own behavior if we hope to make any of these changes. We have the innovative capacity to do this, but we will need to engage far more people and turn true reduction of consumption into a cultural value.

If these recommendations end up feeling shallow, I encourage you to engage in a longer conversation with me – my email address is at the beginning of this book.

---

[i] WorldWatch Institute. "The State of Consumption Today." 2011. Accessed February 25, 2013. *http://www.worldwatch.org/node/810.*

[ii] Footprint Network. "United States of America Factsheet." 2012. Accessed February 25, 2013.
http://www.footprintnetwork.org/images/trends/2012/pdf/2012_unitedstates.pdf.

[iii] D. Kahneman and A. Deaton. "High income improves evaluation of life but not." *Proceedings of the National Academies of Sciences.* 2010.
http://wws.princeton.edu/news/Income_Happiness/Happiness_Money_Report.pdf.

Global Health in the 21ˢᵗ Century

Paxton Bach, Anne-Marie Jamin,
and Kimberly Williams

In this essay, we begin by defining Global Health and exploring its
unique context of development. We then examine several dominant
factors shaping the health of our planet today. With this understanding
the urgency to embrace Global Health as a paradigm of hope for our
future becomes clear. Later, we explore why Global Health is intimately
significant to our generation and the direction we believe it will take in
the near future. As part of the globally aware and integrated cohort that
is the Millennial Generation, we believe that the makeup of our
generation reflects the nature of Global Health. We are capable of
advancing an effective Global Health agenda in the coming decades.

Global Health: Why is it Important?

Global Health has emerged as a guiding concept in academia, policy,
development, and philanthropy. It has captured the interest of heads of
state and the international organizations that set global agendas, in
addition to students, volunteers, health professionals, and lobbyists who
must implement these agendas within their own complex realities. We
argue that as globalized factors continue to transcend national
boundaries, and make public health "Global Health," the paradigm of
Global Health offers the best vision for our planet's future. The
prioritization, development, and implementation of Global Health

initiatives must come from a deep understanding of Global Health and how it has developed. It must also derive from a thorough comprehension of the current and dominant factors influencing health on our planet. Narrowing health inequities, addressing the rapidly increasing interaction between humans, animals, and the environment, tackling the rising double burden of disease, improving the persistent social, economic, and political determinants of health, and strengthening existing health systems are some of the greatest challenges that the health of our nations face today. Only in identifying and understanding these global and local realities can we have an honest discussion of where we are heading and move forward.

Interpretations and values assigned to Global Health continue to steer the course of health on our planet through global agendas, Global Health initiatives, volunteerism, medical tourism, part time Global Health work, ethical education, and so on. The use of the term "Global Health" has become much more prevalent in the past few decades. Both factors make understanding the term much more important. This growing interest in Global Health is demonstrated by the significant increase in *PubMed's* Global Health-related articles from 155 in the 1960s to 39,759 between 2000 and 2005.[i] As a relatively recent concept, a broad range of definitions is currently being used to capture the meaning of Global Health. Given the proliferation of definitions and usages of Global Health, it is important to ask which are truly innovative and which are merely readjustments of traditional public health principles. To provide a vision for our contemporary reality we should understand why this new concept emerged and why older concepts were deemed inadequate.

What is Global Health?

In establishing what Global Health signifies it is first necessary to identify its roots. The term Global Health evolved from basic principles established in two different fields: public health and International Health. While it has maintained some elements from its conceptual predecessors, it remains distinct in its values and approach. The public health discipline was the first to draw focus to population-based approaches, prevention strategies, evidence-based decision-making, social equity, emphasis on serving vulnerable populations, multidisciplinary and interdisciplinary collaboration, and the understanding of health as a public good.[ii]

Public health also demanded a profound understanding of the conditions in which people grow, live, and work, and their impact on health. These conditions are also known as the social determinants of health. International Health developed into the application of public health principles in improving health abroad, particularly in low-income countries.[iii] International Health typically refers to the efforts of high-income countries to help low-income countries address salient health issues. As such, the framework of International Health is intimately tied to the political science discourse of international relations, and takes states, their governments, and their sovereignty as its primary starting points.

International Health initiatives have typically followed a macro level, top-down design in which heads of state and development institutions, located far from the communities they seek to assist, identify health priorities and create solutions. The solutions are often vertically applied, operating completely independent from existing health systems. These initiatives are also often disease-specific, attempting to address a specific disease in isolation from the complex determinants of health within communities.

The rise of globalization in recent decades, however, has required the development of a unique concept to understand, frame, and address health on local and global scales. Drawing on the fundamental principles of public and International Health, the concept of Global Health began to emerge. It recognizes that increasingly, determinants of health transcend national boundaries and require a global response.[iv] It acknowledges that a growing number of free trade agreements, increased cross-border human mobility, technology transfer, and trade among others, have blurred national boundaries and have generated globally integrated systems of production and trade. Commodities, however, are not the only things that do not recognize national boundaries. Infectious diseases do not respect invisible lines on a map. Climate change, pandemics, factors affecting chronic illness, and the resistance of bacteria to antibiotics are all increasingly problems that transcend borders, requiring a collaborative, multi-sectorial response. These factors necessitate a truly global concept when considering human health.

What conceptually sets Global Health apart from International Health is the recognition that we must work together towards health equity. The world is not comprised of separate human populations that can each be treated in isolation by their own individual governments. It is only by improving the health of the most vulnerable populations globally that we can improve the health of populations in both high and low-income countries. Global Health is not about high-income countries helping low-income countries; it is about working and learning together to address universal issues that affect the health of our inextricably linked global population.

How We Got Here

One of the most influential documents in the development of Global Health is the Declaration of Alma Ata, created at the International Conference on Primary Health Care (PHC) in 1978. It challenged the traditionally dominant approach to health service delivery that relied on technology and disease-specific interventions. Alma Ata signified a philosophical shift in values, drawing on the traditional values of public health to emphasize health equity, social justice, and community empowerment as vital components in international efforts towards developing and maintaining the health of individuals and communities. It recognized that the magnitude of this endeavor could only be accomplished through engaging local communities and local resources, employing culturally appropriate technology and using evidence-based decision-making. Also intrinsic to a PHC approach is the understanding that action must be taken to address the underlying social, cultural, and political determinants of health to develop an environment that protects and promotes health. Applied globally, with international, national, and local actors working in harmony, the PHC approach aimed to bring to fruition the Global Health vision of tackling health problems as one integrated world with a common humanity, each person entitled to health as a basic human right. In this spirit, the motto that emerged from Alma Ata was "health for all."

The complexity of implementing a PHC approach as an integrated global effort, however, proved a significant obstacle. Two years after the Alma Ata was created, in 1980, Walsh and Warren discussed the challenges associated with the application of PHC solutions to Global Health issues.[v] PHC solutions require not only health care reform but also a global system reform where all sectors influencing the development of communities - education, agriculture, transportation, trade, among others - must effectively collaborate. These solutions also require efforts on behalf of international organizations, such as policy decentralization, long-term commitment, and flexibility.

The results of PHC initiatives often take longer to manifest and are difficult to measure. In the face of these challenges, Walsh and Warren (1980) proposed a selective approach to PHC, "treating those few diseases responsible for the greatest mortality in less developed areas."[vi] Under the literary guise of PHC, this selective approach actually shifted global focus backwards to a vertical disease-specific approach. Top-down approaches, where institutions like the World Health Organization (WHO) create a program and attempt to implement it globally, do not always work. These bureaucratic and slow-moving institutions lack the flexibility and adaptability to change course once they have started. Many of the dominant Global Health initiatives and strategies of today have emerged from this selective PHC ideology: the Millennium Development Goals; the Global Fund to fight Acquired Immunodeficiency Syndrome (AIDS), Tuberculosis, and Malaria; The President George W. Bush Emergency Plan for AIDS Relief (PEPFAR);

210

and Roll Back Malaria, among others.

Albert Einstein once said that insanity is doing the same thing over and over again and expecting different results. Yet in 2013 we find ourselves surprised, once again, that vertical disease-specific approaches are not producing the desired results. They have been criticized as "delivering diminished returns [as] the AIDS epidemic has peaked, both in terms of deaths and new infections, non-communicable diseases (NCDs) are increasing and the climate change crisis is an ever-present threat."[vii]

Thus, we argue that the Global Health of today must shift its focus from a one-size-fits-all, top-down approach to community-specific. Emphasis must shift from global to local. Narrowly-defined, disease-specific approaches must give way to community strengthening. In an increasingly globalized world marked by rapid urban development, corporate farming, large scale food production, and international trade, we find ourselves at a critical point. Our habitat continues to expand, reducing boundaries to wildlife and the subsequent emergence and re-emergence of wild, zoonotic disease. As our actions have an increasingly significant impact on our environment, our environment will have a significantly greater impact on us. We have hit a tipping point in which it is crucial to reframe our commitment to improve Global Health.

The following sections will briefly explore some of the dominant challenges shaping the health on our planet today. A discussion of these challenges will emphasize the critical need to embrace Global Health as a dominant academic and policy paradigm and provide contextual insight and direction for the future.

Minding the Gap

It is unacceptable that a child born in some countries today can expect to enjoy a life expectancy of more than 80 years while in other countries the same child will face a life expectancy below 45 years.[viii] This life expectancy gap is a contextual force driving Global Health. Across the globe, significant differences in health persist between and within countries. Those living in poverty face exponentially greater challenges to living healthy lives, which results in a higher prevalence of illness and a lower life expectancy. These deplorable differences, referred to as health inequities, largely frame the context of Global Health today. Many think these inequities persist because of individual, controllable factors such as health behaviors, personal choices, and access to medical services. Conversely, as emphasized by the WHO, inequities stem primarily from systemic factors: the conditions in which people live, work, and grow.[ix]

Where someone is born is beyond their control. Poverty is not an individual characteristic, but a property of a global system that produces and reproduces it. These social determinants of health - housing, employment conditions, socioeconomic status, and others - are shaped by political, social, and economic forces. To reduce the gap of health inequities then, we must address these root causes. We must acknowledge the devastating impact of current political, social, and economic policies, and begin to reframe them in the interest of health for all. Now more than ever, we must remind ourselves that health is a fundamental human right, a matter of social justice, and that we must act now. We must mind these gaps.

Confronting the Interconnectedness of Human, Animal, and Environmental Health

The ever-increasing interaction between humans, animals, and the environment is one of the prominent forces shaping the current context of Global Health. Avian flu (H5N1), mad cow disease, the rise of bacterial antibiotic resistance, climate change, and H1N1 all provide evidence of the growing impact of this interconnectedness on the health of our planet. When approaching this complexity of health on a global scale it is imperative to incorporate innovative concepts and strategies.

The concept of "One Health" or "One Medicine" recognizes that our health as humans on this planet is inextricably linked to the health of animals and ecosystems. The concept of One Health promotes "a worldwide strategy for expanding interdisciplinary collaborations and communications in all aspects of health care for humans, animals and the environment."[x] One Health expands the call of health for all beyond the traditional boundaries of human bodies and invisible lines on a map to the ecosystems that sustain us and the animals upon which we depend. This concept, coined in the mid-19th century by Rudolf Virchow and William Osler, is far from novel. Calvin Schwabe reframed it in a modern context in 1984[xi] and today the One Health approach requires the collaboration of public health professionals, veterinarians, clinicians, environmental officers, and occupational health physicians, among other sectors. This approach is crucial to understand the complex context of disease development and to inform appropriate prevention and control measures. Through an inter-sectorial and evidence-based-approach we can begin to address the determinants of health and the development of communities, creating healthier environments for individuals at local and global levels.

To illustrate how embracing the concept of One Health is relevant and critical to the vision of Global Health, we can look at the example of zoonotic disease. The prevalence and unique nature of zoonotic disease is a significant concern because it continues to take millions of lives every year and accounts for a significant proportion of the global burden of disease.

An evaluation conducted by Taylor, Latham and Woolhouse found that 61 percent of the 1,415 pathogens recorded worldwide are zoonotic[xii]. Zoonosis is a pathogen that can be transmitted between humans and animals, and lends itself to the emergence of new diseases and re-emergence of old diseases once thought of as well-managed.[xiii] That is, emergence refers to a newly identified or newly evolved pathogen, and re-emergence refers to a significant rise of a pathogen's incidence in a region[xiv] where it once was considered under control.

Within the current context of globalization, many factors exacerbate the emergence and re-emergence of zoonotic disease. The global movement of food and goods, climate change, environmental pollution, the pervasive use of antibiotics, migration from rural to urban centers, and destruction of wildlife habitats all promote pathogen emergence and re-emergence. For example, as we continue to encroach upon wildlife habitats through urban development, contact between humans and animals has become more frequent. This contact greatly increases the risk of disease transmission between species. As animals become more resilient to an increasingly selective environment, so do the diseases they transmit to humans through microbial adaptation. Furthermore, the environmental pollution caused by urban development such as open landfills and manure dispersal has increased the risk of exposure for animals to diseases they can then transmit to humans.

The spread of zoonotic disease highlights the interconnectedness between humans, animals, and the environment and the subsequent need for a One Health inter-sectorial and collaborative approach. In articulating, prioritizing, and addressing Global Health issues like zoonotic disease, we must embrace innovative concepts such as One Health that are in line with the values of Global Health .

The Double Burden of Disease

Global Health can lend its vision to another pressing challenge that many call the double burden of disease. Low, middle, and high-income countries struggle with the issue of treatment of the malnourished, who are most vulnerable to infectious diseases and the over-nourished, who are most vulnerable to poor cardiovascular health. How does a country such as South Africa deal with this double burden? Initially, the country's health system was not fully equipped to deal with infectious diseases and now, in the same hospitals, they struggle to adequately treat under- and over-nourished patients. This double burden illustrates the unequal distribution of wealth between countries and within countries. It was often assumed that economic development and increased gross domestic product corresponds to a reduction of infectious diseases within a country. There has been some reduction, but as a result of global travel and the rapid cross-border movement of goods, global outbreaks of infectious diseases such as H1N1 are more frequent and can have greater global impact than in the past. The health care systems of high-income countries, like those of low-income countries, are ill equipped to deal with chronic disease.

In the latter half of the 19th century there was a large focus on sanitation and public health measures as a way to prevent disease. However, with the rise of the germ theory of disease and improvements in medical technology, many health systems shifted to emphasizing acute care, while marginalizing prevention and public health.[xv] This faith in reductionism has stopped us from focusing on the bigger social and economic issues that got us to where we are today. We believe that the discipline of Global Health can begin to forge new paths via innovative models that focus on a disease-free lifespan and compress the amount of time individuals spend sick over their lifetime. This disease compression would free up finances from disease treatment that could be to be spent on other sectors to improve health, such as education and housing. Innovate ideas and models that focus on health, not illness are needed to ensure the affordability of health care in the future.

Development to Sustainability: The Future

Another factor that requires consideration in contextualizing Global Health is the acknowledgment that finite global resources demand sustainable development. In establishing global and local priorities of development, it is imperative to consider the ecological and social legacy we impart to future generations. The Millennium Development Goals (MDGs) created by the United Nations focus on factors to eradicate poverty and its diverse consequences. Some of the goals are health-focused, but many of them attempt to address broader issues of health such as the social determinants of health. The MDGs have guided international development policy since 2000. They have stimulated an unprecedented global prioritization of select targets and indicators. However, progress has been far from uniform. As we continue to move forward we have realized that the initial MDG goals are fundamentally flawed. They are focused on macroeconomic targets, especially for low-income countries, and not on the interconnectedness of the planet. They heavily emphasize the development of low-income countries and fail to acknowledge that health on our planet requires a critical look at how we pursue unfettered development. These goals are set to expire in 2015 and be replaced by the Sustainable Development Goals (SDGs).

The SDGs are currently being developed. They are intended to transition to a more green economy and, most important, to set targets for all nations, not only low-income countries. The transition from the MDGs to SDGs is meant to bring more countries into the fold and broaden the scope of the agreements. There is growing recognition among international leaders that we are beginning to run up against some planetary limits and that our current paradigm is not going to work much longer. It is hoped that the SDGs will address these concerns by setting standards and goals for development that can direct national policy in all countries. Health plays a vital role in these negotiations because it is an issue that is cross-cutting. The most successful MDGs have largely been the most concrete and measurable ones. Evaluation and measurement is a big challenge throughout creation of the SDG.

But sustainable development is not new. The Declaration of AID effectiveness, signed in Paris in 2005, is another important step in the movement towards sustainable development.[xvi] The Paris Declaration, as it is commonly known, outlines a commitment to strengthening existing health systems, harmonizing and aligning strategic development priorities, and emphasizing ownership by those who will benefit and utilize the global development system.[xvii]

In the past two decades we have witnessed over 18 billion U.S. dollars[xviii] of funding of only a few diseases, such as treatment for HIV and AIDS. Research has shown that highly active antiretroviral therapy (HAART) treatments can be implemented very effectively to treat some of the world's poorest people in some of the most remote regions. However, this vertical programming, which is based on one disease, even if integrated into an already existing health system, or horizontal programming, is imperfect. It is imperfect not because of the risk of increased resistance to HAART but because it fails to address the root of the problem. It is narrowly defined and absorbs a large portion of limited resources and interest. This single disease-based approach has created a two-tiered healthcare system based on disease and a potential loss of faith in the health system by those who need it most.

We understand the trend in moving from development to sustainability, but we worry that this might mean an abandonment of everything that we have accomplished so far. This shift from development to sustainability is beneficial because it demonstrates an awareness of the broader picture, but it is unlikely to be the one solution to all our problems. The Global Health approach addresses root causes and emphasizes flexibility. We are concerned that the SDGs may fail in both regards.

Where Do We Go From Here?

We currently see a rapidly growing movement of young adults committed to incorporating Global Health in their careers. New educational programs are being created across Canada and in other high-income countries. Enrollment in existing graduate school programs has exploded, and overseas volunteering has become its own industry. What has sparked this newfound interest, can we expect this trend to continue, and can it be harnessed to achieve meaningful progress?

An argument can be made that the swell signifies a new era of social accountability: a commitment to eradicating the inequities that we see around the world. It may represent a sign of frustration at the status quo. Or, it could be interpreted as an apology of sorts from a new cohort in response to so many years of colonization, marginalization, and conflict. A more cynical perspective might also suggest that it is merely adventure-seeking from a new generation, nothing more than a passing fad. In any case, it is an important question to address as we build a vision for the future.

Across the Millennial Generation, we argue that a major contributor to this newfound commitment to Global Health is simply the growing interconnectedness of our world. In an increasingly multicultural and global society, our peers have been surrounded by an awareness of cultures and conflicts from around the planet. Thanks to our personal relationships with refugees, immigrants, Aboriginal peoples, and many other groups who have experienced marginalization, the inequities seen on television now resonate with many like never before. Additionally, we are in a time of unprecedented access to information, allowing us constant exposure to international politics and global injustices. Via television, the Internet, and social media, we are privy to stories of suffering in a way that no previous generation has ever experienced, and are afforded intimate access to the lives of those working in the field.

Through these mediums we can now take inspiration from those who have dedicated themselves to engendering change. It is not surprising that many from our generation are choosing to model their careers accordingly. There are, of course, many reasons that Global Health is gaining attention. However if we accept that this interconnectedness truly is a major driver behind this growing interest, a significant reversal in the trend is as unlikely as a return to the pre-Internet age.

If an increased profile for Global Health is here to stay, the question then becomes how to support this interest, as the hazards of engaging in Global Health work are well described. From personal safety, to disruption of local communities, to sheer ineffectiveness, it is a field rife with opportunities to harm rather than help. Therefore we should take precautions to ensure that this newfound interest is channeled appropriately, so that those choosing to continue on in this field are equipped to perform their work safely, ethically, and effectively. It is exciting that those gravitating towards this type of work seek out proper training, as reflected by soaring enrollment, and the availability of fundamental education should be a priority for any programs developing future Global Health workers. This is particularly important given that we now define "Global Health" in much broader terms than what was previously known as "International Health." Recognizing that the inequities in our own backyards are just as much a Global Health issue as those seen on an international stage, we should encourage opportunities to integrate Global Health into day-to-day practice at home or abroad, rurally or in urban centers.

The Way Forward

A dream as expansive as "health for all" is almost unimaginable given the disparities that surround us, but that is precisely why it should be sought. The highest attainable standard of health, as defined as physical, social, economic, and spiritual wellbeing, is enshrined in the 1948 Universal Declaration of Human Rights. It would be disingenuous and hypocritical to not make it a sincere priority. We believe that while the barriers are vast and diverse, situations complex, and each story impossibly unique, progress is attainable.

A Global Health approach is a paradigm for tackling inequity and a philosophy encouraging vision, cooperation, creativity, and adaptation. Concepts such as One Health and sustainability in development and issues such as zoonosis and the double-burden of disease highlight some prevailing ideas and concerns in an ever-evolving field, but it is the momentum of a new generation that we find truly encouraging. It remains to be seen where this movement can take us. However, to maximize our opportunity the responsibility falls on us to continue to equip ourselves with the necessary vision to recognize the inequities present in our respective fields, with the skills required to combat them and the will to correct them.

The Global Health Domination

The WHO was founded in 1947 and has been the leading institution doing Global Health work since then. However, has the WHO lost its power, just as the power of the nation-state has eroded due to increased global influence of actors such as transnational corporations?[xix] Does this then leave an important space for individuals to not only advocate for Global Health, but to be Global Health, to push the envelope of where we are headed?

Why do we do it? Why does our Generation care so much? Three of us have seen it firsthand. Anne-Marie bicycled from Canada to Guatemala to raise money for an indigenous women and children's clinic. Along the way, her faith in communities was renewed as random strangers cheered her on. Kimberly volunteered at a student-run medical clinic housed in one of the biggest homeless shelters in Canada. She listened with horror but was inspired by the incredible lives that those in her community have experienced. Those encounters were very similar to the stories Kimberly heard from patients in rural Uganda during her thesis research, assuring her of the universality of Global Health. Paxton spent a year representing Canada at the International Federation of Medical Students' Association. During his term he witnessed medical students from over 100 countries coming together to discuss the health of the most vulnerable populations, and how to hopefully make it just a little bit better.

We are overwhelmed on a daily basis by the energy of those who care about this entity that we call Global Health. This slight enigma is our passion. We work at it, not because the definition is clear to us, or the future of this discourse is certain, but because it binds our generation and it makes us feel even in the midst of tragedy that there is hope. There is hope that the complications that arise in our lifetime and in the lifetime of those who follow, may find a solution. That is why to us, it is the paradigm of the future. It is a Global Health Domination.

---

[i] T. Brown, M. Cueto and E. Fee. "The World Health Organization and the Transition From 'International' to 'Global' Public Health." *Am J Public Health.* 96(1), January, 2006. pp. 62–72. doi: 10.2105/AJPH.2004.050831.

[ii] J. Koplan, C. Bond, et al. *Towards a common definition of global health.* Lancet. 373: 1993-1995. doi: 10.1016/50140-6736(09)60332-9. June 2009.

[iii] Ibid.

[iv] Ibid.

[v] J. Walsh and K. Warren. "Selective primary health care: An interim strategy for disease control in developing countries." *Social Science and Medicine.* 14, 1980. pp. 145-163. doi:10.1016/0160-7995(80)90034-9. p. 145.

vi *Ibid.*

vii The Lancet. "Global health in 2012: Development to sustainability." *The Lancet.* 379, January 2012. p. 193.

viii Commission on Social Determinants of Health. "Closing the gap in a generation: Health equity through action on the social determinants of health. Final Report of the Commission on Social Determinants of Health." Geneva, World Health Organization. 2008.

ix Ibid.

x G. Rabozzi, L. Bonizzi, et al. "Emerging Zoonoses: The "one health approach." *Safety and Health at Work.* 3, 2012. pp. 77-83. *http://dx.doi.org/10.105491/SHAW.2012.3.1.77.* p. 82.

xi Cardiff, R., Ward, J., & Barthold, S. "One medicine-one pathology': Are veterinary and human pathology prepared?" *Laboratory Investigation.* 88, 2008. pp. 18-26. doi: 10.1038/labinvest.3700695.

xii L.H. Taylor, S.M. Latham SM, & M.E.J. Woolhouse Risk factors for human disease emergence. *Philosophical Transactions of the Royal Society London* – B, 356: 2001. pp. 983–989.

xiii Rabozzi et al., 2012.

xiv L. Christou. "The global burden of bacterial and viral zoonotic infections." *Clinical Microbial Infections* 17, 2011. pp. 326-330. doi: 10.1111/j.1469-0691.2010.03441.x.

xv F. Marvasti and R. Stafford. "From Sick Care to Health Care: Reengineering Prevention into the U.S. System." *New England Journal of Medicine,* 367(10), 2012. pp. 889-891.

xvi Organisation for Economic Co-operation and Development. "The Paris Declaration on Aid Effectiveness." OECD: France. 2005.

xvii Ibid.

xviii The Global Fund. *Global Fund Distributions. By Region, Country, and Grant Agreement (in USD equivalents).* The Global Fund: Geneva. 2012.

xix Michael Mann. "Has globalization ended the rise and rise of the nation-state?" *Review of International Political Economy.* Vol. 4, Iss. 3. 1997.

Part 4

Essays on the United States

Taxes in America

Benjamin Ross

Our new Constitution is now established, and has an appearance that promises permanency; but in this world nothing can be said to be certain, except death and taxes.

— Benjamin Franklin, Letter to Jean-
Baptiste Leroy (November 13, 1789)

Benjamin Franklin's infamous statement has been used in combination with the threat of legal force for generations to pacify citizens into dutifully, and often unquestioningly, paying dues to the government in the form of taxes. The prevailing assumptions in America are that taxes are an unavoidable necessity and absolute certainty (as Franklin proclaims), are used as the government's primary funding source, and have held this esteemed position since the founding of the country. These assumptions, however, are only partially true.

In this essay, I take a libertarian approach to the theory, history, and impacts of taxes in America. I provide a short history of taxes in the United States with a focus on the income tax. I begin with an explanation of the concept of taxation, cover the Founding Fathers' general opinions on taxes, and then end with the passage of the Sixteenth Amendment. Next, I move to the role that the income tax has played on the economic, social, and political landscape of America. I cover ways the income tax has changed the government's role in society, primarily through unchecked growth. Lastly, I discuss the role taxes will play in the future and some impacts they will have upon the way of life in America. Throughout the essay I argue that direct taxation, particularly through the income tax, has allowed government to outgrow the limits placed upon it by the Constitution, and that this growth is a primary contributing factor to many problems plaguing the country today.

What are Taxes?

In their most elemental form, taxes are one of several means to fund government activities, including selling government assets, imposing import tariffs, borrowing from other countries through the sale of government-backed securities, and printing money. Conversations regarding taxation primarily focus on the personal income tax, the largest and most imposing tax that most individuals pay. Personal income taxes are, however, a singular weapon in the robust arsenal of tactical taxation weaponry owned and operated by all levels of the American government.

In all, seven categories of taxes are imposed in America and, aside from income taxes, they include property taxes, consumption taxes, corporate taxes, payroll taxes, inheritance taxes, and capital gains taxes. The overall number of individual taxes imposed, however, is unknown. The size and range of the American government's taxing capabilities have steadily expanded to a point where each and every economic activity committed by an individual or business is subject to taxation by one or more governing authorities. Not surprisingly, the definition of economic activity also resides under the jurisdiction of the government and covers any action that remotely resembles an economic exchange, even through the most obtuse and tenuous reasoning. Simply stated, the American government can and will tax anything it wants.

One theory behind taxation is that a rising tide lifts all boats and by spreading the wealth, the government can create a level playing field with equal opportunities for all Americans. The historical and current result of government spending, however, is the creation of false economies and inconsistencies within the marketplace through excessive waste. Public representatives as a whole have a negative track record of spending others' money responsibly. The free market concept of capitalism is negated when a government thinks it can spend citizens' money better than they can.

Taxes, then, become a tool used by the government to micromanage society and promote desired behaviors. For example, if the government wants to encourage the purchase of blue trucks, it will tax red ones or provide subsidies for blue paint manufacturers. The marketplace, then, becomes flooded with a supply of blue trucks without an equivalent demand. To correct the situation, the government must create the demand through offering tax incentives for the purchase of blue trucks. In the end, it is better for the government to allow the free market to perform freely by not getting involved.

The amount of wealth in an economy is tied directly to the amount and availability of its resources. Similar to the first law of thermodynamics, the amount of wealth in a system is finite and cannot be created or destroyed, but merely changes form. Taxes are only constructive to an economy when they are used to improve the means of accessing, improving, or selling resources. If tax money is spent in other ways, the system as a whole will not prosper, but merely grow and, eventually, even the growth will stop. America is currently in the latter stage of declining prosperity and economic growth, with most of its wealth and resources now leaving the country, and taxes have played a lead role in the decline.

The Origins of American Taxation

It can safely be said that taxes were not well-regarded in America at the time of the country's founding. One of the most memorable scenes of American history is that of Boston's own Sons of Liberty dumping barrels of British tea into Boston Harbor while Massachusetts was still a lowly colonial possession of the British crown. The Boston Tea Party, as it would become known, was a reaction to taxation policies imposed by Britain and was a key event in what would eventually lead to American independence via the American Revolution. The phrase "taxation without representation" was coined to exemplify the unfavorable feelings of Americans towards paying taxes to a government they had no part in and who did not represent their interests.

Once American independence was gained, details regarding the structure of the government were ironed out between the states through the Articles of Confederation. The Articles of Confederation were later replaced by the Constitution and subsequent amendments that remain the theoretical supreme law of the land. The division of duties and authorities between state and federal governments were broadly defined in the Constitution intentionally to leave room for future debate and interpretation, but the main function of the federal government was the protection of the peoples' rights and property against enemies foreign and domestic, including the government itself. Regarding taxation, the Constitution states the following:

Article I Section 2 Paragraph 3:

> ...direct Taxes shall be apportioned among the several states...according to their respective Numbers....

Article I Section 8 Paragraph 1:

> The Congress shall have power to lay and collect taxes, duties, imposts and excises, to pay the debts and provide for the common defense and general welfare of the United States; but all duties, imposts and excises shall be uniform throughout the United States....

Article I Section 9 Paragraph 4:

> No Capitation, or other direct, Tax shall be laid, unless in
> Proportion to the Census or Enumeration herein directed to be
> taken.

Since it was assumed at the time of the Constitution's birth that people
were citizens of their resident state first and their federal government
second, federal taxation powers were "few and defined" according to
James Madison, the Chief Architect of the Constitution. Powers not
delegated to the federal government were reserved to the states in the
Tenth Amendment and allowed for taxing privileges by the states
individually if they chose. Nowhere in the Constitution is an income tax
mentioned because, at the time, America was a young nation with little
monetary income at an individual level. What was earned as money was
considered property and property was protected under the Constitution.
A direct tax, then, would be seen as a government claim of ownership
upon private property. Americans were generally cynical of central
governments and reacted to attempts to assert influence or control over
their lives with scorn and often rebellion. Taxation was seen as a
hindrance to the freedom and prosperity of a nation and as an
unnecessary burden that most Americans could not afford and simply
did not want.

The prevailing attitude among the Founding Fathers, early
representatives, and the American citizenry was that the imposition of
taxes should be limited to consumption taxes in amounts that would
provide what was minimally necessary for the government to function.
According to Thomas Jefferson, to be just, taxes should be determined
and overseen by the people and based upon current economic
circumstances, attitudes towards the government, and basic functional
needs. They should be uniform and consistent in nature and limited to
what can be comfortably spared. Jefferson's tax philosophy relied

heavily upon consumption taxes and import tariffs since the tax burden would fall most heavily upon the rich who could most easily afford to pay them. While Jefferson realized and often advocated the need for taxation in a progressive society, he recognized the inherent dangers and warned that any wasteful spending or unneeded government offices or services should be eliminated immediately. He argued that taxes should be used to raise revenue for necessary services and nothing else. Jefferson's main goal regarding taxation was to avoid at all costs what history showed to be the eventual manifestation of an aggressive taxation policy: involuntary servitude of the people to their government.[i]

The First American Taxes

The first generations of independent Americans saw relatively little of their money going to the government through taxes. In general, the only taxes at the federal level were those placed upon the consumption of "vice" or "sin" goods and services deemed undesirable by society. Prior to the Civil War, nearly all federal revenues were derived from import tariffs, which are essentially taxes placed upon goods and material resources imported into America. While import tariffs did inflate the prices of effected items, they were used as a tool to protect American businesses by making goods and resources produced and sold within the homeland artificially cheaper. Many Americans also saw imported goods as superfluous luxuries for the rich, and those who could afford to accumulate such luxuries could easily pay the additional taxes and tariffs. Thus, import tariffs and consumption taxes could shift the burden of government funding to those consuming the most goods.

Debts accumulated from the War of 1812 brought about new forms of internal taxes such as the sales tax and the income tax. The income tax was not imposed and was quickly rescinded in favor of existing import tariffs that sufficiently funded necessary government activities and effectively paid the debt. Income taxes remained unpopular and would not be used for another 50 years when necessity demanded them. The secession of the southern states dealt a major financial blow to the federal Union government that relied heavily upon tariffs from cotton and other goods imported and exported through southern harbors.

In 1862, Congress enacted the nation's first income tax law and added additional sales, excise, and inheritance taxes to fund the Union's Civil War effort. It was at this time that the Bureau of Internal Revenue, which would later become known as the Internal Revenue Service (IRS), was established under the Department of the Treasury to collect tax payments. The income tax was progressive in nature and was used to keep the federal government solvent through the Civil War years, but was repealed in 1872 again in favor of tariffs and excise taxes. The federal income tax remained part of the national political discussion, and even had a short revival in 1894, but was eventually ruled to be unconstitutional by the Supreme Court in 1895.[ii]

Debts incurred from the Spanish-American War, decreasing tariff revenues during the First World War, and a growing desire to correct social inequalities by "soaking the rich" and placing the tax burden upon their shoulders led to the eventual adoption of the Sixteenth Amendment to the Constitution in 1913.[iii] The appropriately labeled "Income Tax Amendment" effectively gutted the Constitutional limitations placed upon the government's taxing ability by giving Congress the power to "lay and collect taxes on incomes, from whatever source derived, without apportionment among the several States, and without regard to any census or enumeration." Although the power granted to Congress through the amendment was truly terrifying to limited government advocates, proponents assured the population that the income tax was targeted at wealthy individuals and businesses and would be both voluntary and temporary.

Passage and Implementation of the Sixteenth Amendment
The text of the Sixteenth Amendment was intended to be the proverbial nail in the coffin for the income tax discussion by giving Congress practically unlimited taxation powers. Instead of clearing up the argument, the Sixteenth Amendment created new legal and

Constitutional difficulties that have yet to be resolved to this day. According to many researchers and legal scholars, the Sixteenth Amendment was never properly ratified by the requisite states that would render it invalid on its face. Furthermore, it has been argued that Constitutional Amendments cannot grant the government powers that are prohibited by or directly contradict those set forth by the original Constitution. To do so is a violation of the necessitous checks and balances system. Although the legitimacy of the Amendment was still in contention, Secretary of State Philander Knox declared it properly ratified and, thus, effective on March 1, 1913.[iv] The IRS was then revamped and again given the responsibility of collecting taxes.

Shortly after the adoption of the Sixteenth Amendment, the Supreme Court ruled through a number of separate cases that the Sixteenth Amendment did not violate the Constitution by altering the types of taxes Congress could lay and collect and could be enforced as written. Over the next few decades, Congress would task the IRS with building a tax code that was first published as the Internal Revenue Code of 1939. The Code was revised numerous times in response to the ebb and flow of government sentiment and government spending needs. Tax rates would rise until the beginning of World War II and would reach 94 percent for the highest income bracket in the years 1944-1945. Rates held mostly steady though the mid-1950s, but would fall incrementally over the next few decades. The low point of income tax rates would be seen in the late-1980s after President Ronald Reagan encouraged replacing income taxes with other less intrusive taxes.

With few exceptions, tax revenues received by the federal government rose every year throughout the 20th century. A growing population combined with increased federal tax revenues saw an expansion of the IRS in size, duty, and budget into a burgeoning agency with authorities that deride Constitutional checks and balances. The IRS now has the power to create tax regulations based upon their interpretation of tax laws, collect and examine private information submitted via tax returns, request and receive documents from banks and other organizations without the consent of the individual or business and without a warrant, distribute information to other government agencies, collect tax payments, investigate individuals and businesses suspected of "tax crimes," and seize the property of suspects through raids conducted with a SWAT-style team of armed special agents. The IRS now boasts over 110,000 employees, 650 offices in the United States, 12 offices outside the United States, and an annual budget approaching $13 billion.[v]

At 4 million words plus, the complication of the tax code baffles citizens and tax professionals alike, and makes it nearly impossible to conform to every measure. The sheer number of tax credits, deductions, and loopholes is mind-boggling, yet it continues to grow. The tax code works as a method for Congress to give favors to well-connected individuals, businesses, and industries at the detriment of other groups. As a whole, the tax code creates inefficiencies across the board that benefits the minority but hurts the majority.

Despite the size of the tax code and power of the IRS, numerous anti-tax groups vainly argue that the IRS cannot force the payment of income taxes since Congress never passed a law requiring this of individuals. Both the IRS and the Supreme Court have affirmed that the tax system relies upon voluntary compliance and assessment, yet individuals who fail to voluntarily comply with every rule and regulation of the tax code, whether intentionally or not, quite often find themselves facing involuntary confiscations, penalties, and punishments or, in a word, servitude.

The United States Federal Reserve

Another piece of legislation enacted in 1913 would work in tandem with the income tax to forever change the economic, social, and political landscape of America. Several small-scale financial crises and pressure from powerful bankers resulted in the creation of a central bank to direct the nation's financial affairs through the Federal Reserve Act. By delegating its Constitutional duty to control the supply and value of the nation's currency to the Federal Reserve, Congress placed the nation's financial future in the hands of a private corporate institution that operated in secrecy and was not subject to public scrutiny. Since its inception, the Federal Reserve has played a major role in exacerbating boom and bust cycles through its efforts to artificially control the nation's money supply. President Nixon's decision to take the United States off of the Gold Standard in 1971 gave the Federal Reserve absolute control of the nation's money supply, a money supply that was backed by nothing but debt that could be expanded infinitely.

For decades the federal government, in combination with the Federal Reserve, has been inflating numerous financial bubbles tied to housing by guaranteeing loans made in the private market to private consumers. The resulting reckless lending practices eventually burst the bubble and America, along with most of the world, fell into a deep recession in late 2007. Home and stock values tumbled, corporations failed, unemployment skyrocketed, and credit for loans dried up. Workers were laid off and many simply walked away from their homes and other financial obligations, leaving lenders holding the debt.

Large multinational corporations and banks suffered major losses from bad debts and had to be bailed out by the federal government to the tune of trillions of dollars. Rather than let the recession work itself out, the Federal Reserve would pump trillions of printed dollars into private banks through a method known as Quantitative Easing (QE) in an effort to inflate the faltering economy and encourage lending. How much money was spent and who the money went to was kept secret from the public and attempts to audit the Federal Reserve went nowhere. Profits of banks and large corporations soared, yet the trillions of dollars spent through QE did relatively little for the national economy and unemployment.

More than anything, the federal government's response to the recession, including the sponsorship and encouragement of the Federal Reserve's QE program, drove a deep wedge between the rich and poor in America. Faith and trust in the government hit near rock-bottom, with Congressional approval ratings consistently in the teens, and widespread social unrest spurned major grassroots movements that rallied against government and corporate corruption and cronyism. Both major political parties, Democrat and Republican, incessantly blamed each other for the nation's problems and, instead of uniting to fight the problems, preferred to fight each other through political and philosophical warfare carried out on the national stage. The parties preached the contradictory message that government is the problem but, if given control, their party could make government the solution.

American citizens, fed up with problems created and fueled by the government, find it hopeless to fight such a large and powerful monster and also turn to fighting each other. The people have splintered into polarized ideological factions and moderate representatives willing to work with the other side have been replaced with hostile party loyalists who refuse to budge. The political spectrum of representation has become heavily weighted on the extremes, while the fastest-growing political groups are moderates, independents, and Libertarians aligned near the middle.[vi]

What Would Thomas Jefferson Say?

Thomas Jefferson's recommendation to harmonize government spending and size with current economic and political circumstances has been effectively ignored. Instead of cutting unneeded government offices and services, reducing taxes, and slashing government spending, the opposite approach has been taken since the beginning of the recession. Government offices continue to expand in size and number along with the number of respective employees, although many jobs that would previously have been run by the government have been contracted out to private companies. Government contractors, which are private and semi-private companies funded entirely or partially by government contracts, have increased to allow the government to finance desired operations while keeping the number of actual government employees artificially low. Welfare assistance programs offered by the federal government have been forced to expand in size and to loosen qualification requirements to meet the demands of growing populations of unemployed and underemployed and an alarmingly increasing cost of living. The number of individuals and families receiving direct monetary assistance through various federal social service programs, such as Medicare, Social Security, Veteran's assistance, and welfare programs, has steadily risen since their inception with a major spike since the beginning of the recession. According to Plumer 2012, nearly half of all American households received a direct monetary benefit from the federal government in 2011, and the numbers have risen since.

The federal government, along with its respective agencies and offices, has ballooned in size, budget, and function in a manner that the Founding Fathers could have scarcely imagined. State and local governments have similarly followed suit and swelled their own ranks. The questions whether the government can and should be involved in an activity have been replaced by when and how will the government be involved. The limitations of powers and checks and balances systems of the Constitution have been eroded through legislative, executive, and judicial actions. The Constitution itself is treated not as the supreme law of the United States but as an antiquated collection of suggestions and opinions not applicable to today's world. Government roles and funding possibilities are only as limited as one's imagination. To cover the costs of all the offices and activities, government spending is at historic highs with nearly one and a half times as much going out than is coming in. More money is now spent by the government every year than it spent the entire first century of the country's existence.[vii]

The federal government is becoming increasingly desperate to finance its activities and is pumping furiously at every available well. Though federal income taxes remain relatively low by historical comparisons, the number and breadth of taxes at all levels of government have steadily risen, resulting in an overall increase in the total percentage of income being paid from the individual or business to the government.[viii] In areas with high state and local taxes, it is not uncommon for an individual to pay more than half of their income in taxes. Proposals for either tax cuts or increases, along with spending cuts or increases, instigate political fights to the death and, ultimately, legislative gridlock; yet new taxes get snuck into the dark corners of seemingly benign legislation and make their way into the law. And while revenues generated through the payment of said taxes are immense, the government continues to run budget deficits.

Where Are We Headed?

The current federal debt, totaling over $16 trillion, will soon surpass that of the entire 27-nation European Union. Estimates of America's unfunded liabilities, future monetary obligations that exceed the current funds available, range from a conservative $60 trillion to $200 trillion on the high end.[ix] Many unfunded liabilities promised in previous years, including Social Security, Medicare, federal employee benefits, and other entitlement programs, are now becoming due and are holding the American government and people hostage by draining public coffers. Mandatory spending is now greater than the amount of revenue coming in through taxes, but only accounts for two-thirds of federal spending. The remaining one-third is discretionary and must be borrowed from other countries or, as a last resort, printed directly by the Federal Reserve.

The process of inflation, or printing money backed by nothing, drives down the value of the dollar and increases the price of goods and services. The so-called "invisible tax of inflation" ultimately punishes money savers by driving down the future value of accumulated savings and rewards immediate spending. Payments from entitlement programs are tied to inflation and are systematically increased to keep pace with the cost of living. Thus, a vicious cycle is created in which the more money that is spent, the more money that must be spent. Instead of breaking the cycle and ending or phasing out unconstitutional entitlement programs, the government pays out money that does not exist and "kicks the can" down the road for future generations to deal with. The reckless style of spending, taxing, borrowing, and printing practiced by the federal government is wreaking havoc upon the finances of the country, leaving mountains of debt for future generations to be paid with interest, and, perhaps worst of all, allows the government to keep growing.

Citizens of America and beyond are dealing with the effects of an oversized and overextended federal government that is heavily involved in the political, economic, and social affairs of every citizen in the country. The IRS, with its ability to create and enforce laws and its willingness to prosecute individuals over seemingly trivial matters, has made it clear to the American people that they no longer work for themselves, but for the government that, in turn, works for the interests of the international banking cartel and large corporations. Accelerating growth of Constitution-based and independent political parties shows that many Americans have had enough of a praetorian government that operates outside of the rule of law and works to control every aspect of its citizens' lives through legal force.

Tax reform is used as a platform for candidates of both major parties to run on and has bipartisan support among the people. Numerous tax reform proposals, from a flat tax to a fair tax to a local-only tax, exist and could replace the income tax and the IRS overnight. If momentum can be gained by tax reform movements and candidates, enough pressure could eventually be put upon the Congress to redesign the tax code in a fair and equitable manner that the people would support.

Conclusion

As a member of the Millennial Generation, I find the current state of economic, social, and political affairs in America disheartening. The country is currently over-burdened by taxes, regulations, and a repressive government, with no end in sight. Debt accumulated through decades of imprudent spending and financial decisions must be paid eventually or the country will go bankrupt. Even with the numerous and seemingly insurmountable problems the country faces, there is still room for hope. The spirit of the American people is strong and able to overcome adversities. If the people realize that the problem is not with them but with the poor choices made by their government, they can unite to fight and release their potential. When the people start working together, they will force the Congress to work with them. When Congress and the rest of government work with and for the people once again, positive change will come. If they do not work together, however, the outlook is dire.

The future of taxation in America is unknown and is the cause for much concern. Debt and increasing unfunded liabilities guarantee escalations in future public spending, the funding of which has yet to be determined. Aside from borrowing from other countries, the options are limited. If the money is simply printed, a day of reckoning looms in the not too-distant future where hyperinflation and the eventual collapse of the dollar inevitably wait. History has shown that a people will not endure tyranny very long, and if the route of increased taxes is taken, it is only a matter of time before an already tax-saturated population revolts. Desperation could also lead to spending cuts of entitlement payouts or elimination of the programs altogether. This situation, it is likely, would also lead to revolts.

If America, a once great nation, continues along the path of attempting to tax itself into prosperity, it will find itself facing collapse as so many other nations have before it. Similar to a snake trying to eat its own tail is America in trying to tax itself into prosperity and equality. The decision to enact direct income taxes in 1913 has shown itself to be the single biggest mistake in America's post-Civil War history, yet with enough support from the people and a healthy application of pressure upon Congress, direct taxes could once again be eliminated. It is often said that America is too powerful to be taken down from the outside and can only be destroyed from within. The American government has become too large and powerful at all levels, and much of its power results from taxation. If the way to get rid of a stray cat is to stop feeding it, then the way to limit a government is to restrict its funding.

Whatever course is taken to mend the ship, it must be chosen fast, for it is quickly taking on water from thousands of tiny holes. Perhaps if Benjamin Franklin were here to assess the situation, he would conclude that the Constitution's appearance of permanency has been severely clouded, and the only thing that is certain in today's world is that America is suffering death through taxes.

---

[i] Jefferson, 1984.

[ii] Darrell Anderson. "The American Income Tax: Theft Under the Color of Law." 2006. Retrieved February 10, 2013. *http://www.simpleliberty.org/tait/*.

[iii] Douglas V. Gibbs. "Temecula Constitution Class: Income Tax - 16th Amendment." 2012. Retrieved February 13, 2013. *http://politicalpistachio.blogspot.com/2012/08/temecula-constitution-class-income-tax.html.*

[iv] Ibid.

[v] IRS, 2012.

[vi] Schmidt, Shelley, and Bardes, 2011.

[vii] The White House, 2013.

[viii] Henry Blodget. "The Truth About Taxes: Here's How High Today's Rates Really Are." 2011. Retrieved February 20, 2013. *http://www.businessinsider.com/history-of-tax-rates?op=1.*

[ix] Peter Ferrera. *America's Ticking Bankruptcy Bomb.* Broadside Books, New York. 2011.

The Student Loan Crisis and the Next Generation of American Capitalists
R.P. Thead

In the United States, is a college education worth the investment if you cannot pay for it? Are four years of undergraduate education worth possibly decades of debt? With the typical college student graduating with an average of $27,000 in student loan debt, and growing,[i] the student loan crisis will be one of the defining issues of the American Millennial Generation, which this essay will address.

First, I give a short history of the issue to put the topic into context. It is important to know how and why taking out loans to pay for higher education has grown into what is often referred to as a crisis. Later, I examine some long-term consequences of starting one's professional career, or post-college life while dragging two and three figure debt around like an anvil-sized stumbling block. A debt-ridden generation negatively affects home ownership demand, risk and debt aversion, and creates problems for consigners of tuition debt.

It's going to be a real mess. It already is.

Student Loan Primer

Consider this scenario. A graduating high school senior has been accepted into college and he or she lacks a scholarship or his or her family lack money to pay the tuition out of pocket. To pay for tuition, the family and/or student must take out loans to pay. Two types of loans are available to students in the United States: federal loans, which are tuition loans provided directly to college students by the federal government with different repayment terms; and private loans, which are tuition loans obtained from a private business such as a bank or other lender. These private loans have varying interest rates and repayment options; some require credit checks and collateral. Private loans are not provided or supposedly guaranteed by the federal government. The repayment terms are more attractive with federal loans.[ii] There are different types of student loans available and not all of them are created equal.

In the 1970s the U.S. government decided the country needed more college-educated people. To reach this goal, the government decided to provide increased and easier access to cheap loans for tuition so more people could attend college. The tuition loan market needed more liquidity. So the government established a Government-Sponsored Enterprise (GSE) to serve this purpose. A GSE operates as an "instrumentality" of the U.S. government, which means it operates with its own management and is autonomous from the government, as long as the GSE follows its charter, dictated by the government. Only the government can alter this charter or the core purpose of the GSE. The executives of GSEs are not politically appointed and do not require confirmation by Congress, unlike cabinet posts and heads of federal agencies.[iii]

This GSE established in 1972, then called the Student Loan Marketing Association (commonly referred to as Sallie Mae) was created to fill the tuition liquidity gap. That is, the government set up an institution whose sole reason to exist was to provide easy access to federal loans for students who want to attend college but need to borrow money for tuition. The federal government attempted to fill what it perceived as a gap in the domestic market for school loans. But, as of 2005, Sallie Mae was a fully private company, and its full name was Student Loan Marketing Corporation.[iv] Its status as a privately held corporation, versus an association, means that Sallie Mae can focus on

242

its primary objective: profits. Sallie Mae deals in both private and federal loans, acting as a basic loan collector for the federal government now that, since 2010, the Department of Education administers all federal student loans.

Sallie Mae also acts as a private lender to students who are ineligible for federal student loans or whose federal loan package is not enough to cover the full cost of tuition and living expenses at their college. Sallie Mae is not alone: more banks have moved into this lucrative market of tuition loan lending.[v]

This essay will not get too much into the business-side of profiting from student loans, specifics about interest rates, default rates, repayment options, cosigners, credit swaps, or the politics of federal aid debt.[vi] The loan amounts that students and cosigners have taken to pay for college have steadily increased since the late 1970s to the present day. According to the National Center for Education Statistics, college tuition alone increased more than 400 percent from 1980 to 2011.[vii] This of course does not account for living expenses and medical costs, which would increase the percent of college education costs even more. Therefore, Sallie Mae, the federal government, and private lenders are now loaning more money to meet rising tuition costs. Student loan debtors are anyone holding any sort of student loan debt, whether private or federal.

People go to college for many reasons, but the biggest reason is to get an education that will lead to a job and career. Using this rationale, taking out a loan to make more money is a rational economic choice. That is how capitalism works. The tuition loan is seen as an investment that will create economic benefits and returns to allow the student to be an economic actor in the U.S. national economy: buying cars, houses, clothes, food, and supporting the enormous consumer market. The student can repay the loan with money made at the job that was acquired because that student assumed that tuition debt. But what happens when there are no jobs? Or what happens when graduates saddled with tuition debt are unable to find jobs that allow them to meet the minimum payments on the loan?

Student Loan Debtors in the U.S. Economy

Since around 2007, life for graduating American college students got tougher when the U.S. economy began to falter, followed by economic fallout in 2008. The United States is now experiencing the largest, most persistent and deepest economic downturn the country has seen since the Great Depression. Official unemployment numbers have remained high and have been higher for young people.[viii] Although these numbers exclude many people who have given up finding work, these missing workers are significant. Additionally, the official unemployment rate does not include the underemployed.[ix] Having a job is good, but when it cannot cover the minimum payments on tuition loans, a risk that was intended to improve one's economic well-being, it is not enough. What can we expect for a future generation of capitalists who start a post-college professional career with an average of $27,000-plus in debt?

Some of the tuition loan repayment plans last decades, much like a mortgage on a home, which is the largest purchase most people will make in their lives. Mortgage-related debt is at the root of the nation's economic woes, which have spread all over the globe.

For decades, the housing market has been one of the major indicators of the United States economic health and still is for those who believe in the tenets of 20th century macroeconomics. If housing can be brought back, the rest of the economy will follow, or so it is argued. Or, if people are buying homes again, the economy must be doing well. A strong housing market has, for many years, been used a sign of economic confidence. But, houses and everything else are worth money. They only have value because it is assumed that in the future someone will be interested in buying that house, stock, bond, security, or car. Someone will attribute value to that item and want to purchase it. What happens to the housing market when an entire generation is unable or unwilling to assume a large debt responsibility like a multi-decade mortgage?

Student Loan Debtors and Future Mortgage-Holders

I will examine this in two ways. First, what if a percentage of this student loan-indebted generation cannot purchase a home? To get a loan for a mortgage, a person has to have credit. A bank must feel confident that a person borrowing to purchase a house will be able to repay that loan. What if an increasing percentage of future homebuyers have horrible credit because of their inability to meet the payments on their student loans? If a 22 year-old student graduating with $27,000 in student loan debt is only able to find part-time work, and cannot meet the minimum payment on his student loans, that person will not likely have much credit or good credit. The former student will need longer to repay a student loan, since the loans accrue interest.

It's impossible to make a big purchase if you cannot pay for it, or if no one will lend you the money. How long will a person need to repair his credit, much less pay down the student loan enough to consider assuming more debt in terms of a mortgage? This leads to my second point.

Once this person establishes himself as moderately financially stable, he is making student loan payments on time, finally moved back out of his parents' home if he was lucky enough to be able to "boomerang" in the first place, and has paid down enough of the loan, interest included, then he starts to see light at the end of the college debt tunnel. Will that person want to jump right back into some long-term debt like a mortgage? If not, then this aversion to debt has larger implications for capitalism than just the impact of decreased demand for home ownership. Home ownership, and the headache of a mortgage, is an essential part of a vibrant capitalist economy in the U.S.

Risk plays an important role in capitalism. Not all investments work out. Many successful entrepreneurs succeed because they have the stomach for risk. At its simplest definition, taking risk in capitalism means putting out money with no assurance that money will turn a profit or even be returned. Notwithstanding neoclassical economics and its assumptions or any other theories, if a generation's first financial investment involves assuming a large amount of debt with a dismal outcome for a number of years after graduation, then those debt-holders will be far more risk-averse when they finally hit their wealth-generating years, whenever those years happen. And, a larg(er) number of people unable or unwilling to assume home ownership because of a bad experience with large and long-term debt puts an additional strain on financing investments, risky and not. In addition, this is a poor first experience with investing.

One of the best ways to raise personal capital is to take out a loan against one's home, which is the most valuable and, at least before 2007, stable asset. Lack of this collateral may pose future problems for capitalists and capitalism. Loans against mortgages can raise money to do a number of things that require money you do not have, such as buy automobiles and invest in stocks. This unwillingness and/or inability to assume debt on any sort of investment may, in the long-term, hinder the overall competitiveness of the U.S. national economy for decades to come.

Are Student Loans Different from Other Types of Debt?

Unlike other types of debt, student loans cannot be discharged in bankruptcy. To an extent, this prohibition makes a lot of sense. When you take out a loan for a house and you cannot pay that loan back or on time, you lose the house. The bank or other loan holder has collateral and can take back the physical item that you purchased with its money. It is secure debt. This is not the case with an education. If someone is in the hole to Sallie Mae for $75,000 for a philosophy degree from a private liberal arts school and cannot make the payments, Sallie Mae cannot come to your house and take back all of the things you learned while in school. Arguably one of the reasons the United States has and has had such a competitive economy is due to its citizens' ability to discharge debt in bankruptcy and get back out there to fight another day.[x]

Except for college tuition, no other lending scheme will hand over tens of thousands of dollars to teenage students with no collateral or

246

assurance that the money will be repaid. With federal loans, the U.S. government assumes the responsibility for the debt. The federal government assumes the risk with loan repayment because an educated population and economically productive workforce is, according to some, a responsible way to spend the country's finances. The educated population is the return on investment. Loaning the money is better than outright paying for the education of citizens, or so goes the paradigm. With a loan, at least the government will get some of its money back, plus a little extra in interest. But private student loan lenders, such as post-2005 Sallie Mae, do not wear the same rose-colored spectacles as Congress or the Department of Education. Private businesses define returns on investment a bit different than the federal government.

For private lenders, tuition loans are no different than lending money to start a business or to buy a car or a house. They want collateral, and they are going to get their money back. As a result, many lenders require cosigners since the lenders do not think it is responsible to trust a teenager to make rational decisions regarding the efficient allocation of their resources, denominated in the tens of thousands, regarding a choice of major in school that will lead to a job enabling him to repay his loans. Private lenders are also very aware of the job market awaiting the borrowers once they have graduated and exhausted the loaned money. They have no forgiveness programs like the federal government.

As a result, a growing number of co-signing parents and grandparents are dealing with the effects of a weak job market. Assets can be seized and wages can be garnished. In what is becoming a bigger problem, private tuition lenders are garnishing social security payments for the cosigners eligible to receive the benefits. With a rapidly aging population in the United States and a constant political debate over entitlements, this could be a disaster.

Parallels can be drawn between the student loan crisis and the subprime mortgage crisis that sent the world and U.S. economy into a tailspin. Both have similar histories: the government created GSEs (government-sponsored enterprises) to fill what it perceived as a liquidity gap in a certain market. For the housing market, this includes the Federal National Mortgage Association (Fannie Mae) and the Federal Home Loan Mortgage Corporation (Freddie Mac). These quasi-government entities later became private, with an implicit assumption that since the government initiated the founding and initial funding of these two GSEs, that the government would back the debt. For the housing crisis, this turned out to be true. Will it also be the case for the student loan market?

Additionally, the housing crisis happened due to a number of factors, one being that investment entities were bundling and securitizing the mortgage debt, then trading it for profit. And, since this practice was possible, more debt equaled more profit, so it made sense to load up as many borrowers as possible with as much debt as they could, with little regard for creditworthiness. Sallie Mae and other private loan lenders operate in a similar fashion, although there is no true equivalent to credit default swap for student loan backed assets. If the lenders and collectors of student loan money decide to go on a financial gambling spree (see, credit default swap), will they do so because of an implicit understanding that the U.S. federal government will pick up the tab when the walls come tumbling down? The experience of Fannie Mae and Freddie Mac might be an encouragement to roll the dice. That is all for moral hazard, at least in this essay.

Last, just as the housing crisis was the result of a bubble or an intrinsically overvalued or inflated asset, the same can be said about higher education. People take out loans because they see value in the education they are getting in return for taking on debt; it is a good investment because it will lead to a higher quality of life after graduation. When many of the only jobs available to graduates do not require college-level training, the students are left wondering whether or not the student loan debt, and risk, was worth it.

Consider also the 400 percent increase in tuition in 1980–2011 mentioned earlier. A number of factors explain this increase, including increased emphasis on building more state-of-the-art campus housing, academic buildings, and athletic facilities to attract the best and brightest. The rise of private-sector compensation for many top university officials was common, with a professional university administrative workforce that now includes "deans" and "student affairs officers" governing as many non-academic issues as they can cram into their fiefdoms.[xi] There was also a decrease in federal funding for grants and scholarships. This last factor, however, connects with the housing-related economic downturn that started around 2007.

Rebranding Student Loan Debt as an "Education Mortgage"

In a literal translation, "mortgage" is a combination of the French words *mort* (dead/death), and *gage* (pledge). A mortgage is a death pledge. The term's common use derives from Sir William Blackstone's *Commentaries on the Laws of England*, an 18th-century essay collection that discusses and describes English common law at that time. Blackstone wrote, "Estates held *in vadio*, in gage, or pledge; which are of two kinds, *vivum vadium*, or living pledge; and *mortuum vadium*, dead pledge, or mortgage."

In the modern usage based on Blackstone's definition, a home mortgage, the death/dead (*mort*) part of mortgage references the life of the contract. The contract is dead if the debtor defaults on the payments and the property returns to the person/institution holding the paper on the loan. Alternately, the contract is also dead once the principal and interest have been paid and the debtor assumes full legal ownership of the property. This is a very simplified explanation of Blackstone's work, but we're talking about student loans and not 18th-century English Common Law.[xii]

I advocate that the term "education mortgage" be used when discussing student loan debt, as it more accurately describes the life of the debt. As mentioned earlier, student loan debt cannot be discharged in bankruptcy proceedings except in very rare cases. And while the U.S. government has done and is doing what it can to help those underwater home mortgage holders,[xiii] various bankruptcy proceedings are still a more realistic way to discharge debt for underwater property owners than those drowning in student loan debt. Student loans, then, are set up to quite literally follow the debtor to his or her grave if he never pays them. They are, even more than a home mortgage, a death pledge.

What Can be Done?

Can anything be done? From as long as I can remember, the importance and value of a college education was encouraged in primary and high school. It was simple logic: you go to college, you get an education, and you graduate and get a job. If you have to take on debt to pay for that education, do not worry because it is "good debt" and "an investment in yourself." Oddly, I am fairly certain that none of my teachers were on the payroll for any student loan lenders. But for that generation, the college-job-two cars-house life progression was understood. If the generation ahead of us had to take on a little debt along the way, it was fine. College was cheaper then and a college education stood for a lot more. What went wrong?

For one, the college-educated population is at a saturation point in the United States. A college education is no longer a commodity—what you study matters more and more. This is especially true regarding the jobs lost as a result of the Great Recession. Many of those jobs are never coming back. Things got bad, and companies adapted and became more productive and efficient. They needed fewer workers, and workers who were not affected learned to step up to the plate lest they be next. This excludes most public sector employees, such as teachers and school officials who did not warn graduating students about student loan debt. As a result, some students are questioning the time and debt investment in a college education.[xiv] Education for education's sake is different from crippling yourself economically for perhaps decades.

The United States now has a glut of educated, but debt-ridden, young people. The nation has a culture of non-violent settling of disputes through respected institutions, and the 20th century has shown that change can come through peaceful protest. But history has also shown that a large number of disaffected, hopeless, but educated youth with little to do who are capable of easily organizing themselves though social media and other avenues can present governments with "social unrest." The fall 2011 Occupy protests may be the generation's opening salvo in stepping forward and expressing its unhappiness with the status quo.

What can be done except write essays about the issue? To start, future student borrowers could be realistically educated regarding the situation they will encounter when they reach the other side of the stage after receiving their college diplomas. If high school teachers, advisors, and even college admissions staff are not explaining the post-graduation reality, there is little chance graduates will hear the hard facts on their own. A very expensive education, no matter how well students perform, does not guarantee employment. Private lenders certainly will not dissuade students from taking on large amounts of debt. Count the colleges out when asking prospective students to give a second thought to taking out large tuition debt. Recent news stories show a boiler room-type atmosphere for marketing and recruiting for new students, especially from for-profit colleges.[xv] And, the brave men and women serving in the U.S. military and their G.I. Bill tuition benefits have become an especially lucrative market for some schools. Yet you may not hear about this since some of these schools are owned by the country's oldest and "respected" newspapers.

The best we can hope is that the public school system will set students straight about student loan debt and the decreasing value of a college education. Some students are offered financial literacy courses at some point before they graduate. Maybe those courses would be a good place to have a real conversation about student loan debt, in addition to the regular topics of weekly budgeting and checkbook balancing. Students are educated about hard drugs, sex, HIV/AIDS, and forced to read Nathaniel Hawthorne novels at a very young age. There is no harm done in warning about the possible downsides to taking on tens of thousands of dollars, or more, of non-dischargeable debt.

Conclusion

The student loan crisis has long-term consequences in the United States. These consequences include a future housing market depression as student loan holders are unable to secure mortgages due to student loan-related credit issues. More ominously, a generation is being educated to be more risk averse about long-term debt, whether for a mortgage or future investments, as a result of their first real experience as debtor. Debt and the ability to escape debt and try again are very important for the U.S. liberal market variety of a capitalist economy.[xvi]

Any good, simple description of how student loan lending institutions profit from tuition loans can be easily compared to the subprime housing crisis that brought the U.S. and world economy to its knees in 2008. Now that student loan debt has surpassed total national credit card debt, and the total outstanding student loan debt now stands at more than one trillion U.S. dollars, perhaps the subject will receive more attention.[xvii] Yet much of the older generation, especially the older decision makers in the United States, see the student loan issue not so much as a crisis but rather as a young person's problem. They may reconsider their stance when some of them try to sell their home and find that no one is interested in buying it or lack credit to qualify for a mortgage.

If student loans were rebranded as "education mortgages" then the seriousness of the financial obligation will be better understood. It would not be difficult to leverage a term that people are more familiar with - mortgage - so they better understand the *death pledge* that is student loan debt. This is something. It is a start.

A few Twitter updates regarding #studentloans:

> I think I'd rather go to jail for not paying my student loans than have to deal with the people handling my loans. #NoHelpAtAll

Well after calculating how much I'll need in student loans I decided I'm most likely gonna start pushing drugs

Sallie Mae is like a needy ex-girlfriend that takes everything from u & still calls u for more until u're broke & u hate women #StudentLoans

Id be okay with the world ending in 2012...don't have to pay back my student loans" says my roommate haha

---

[i] Blake Ellis. "Average Student Loan Debt Nears $27,000." CNN. Accessed October 18 2012.
http://money.cnn.com/2012/10/18/pf/college/student-loan-debt/index.html.

[ii] For more information, *www.finaid.org* is a good resource regarding loan package repayment terms, in addition to its overview on private lenders.

[iii] Congressional Research Service (CRS). "Government-Sponsored Enterprises (GSEs): An Institutional Overview." 2007. Accessed October 8, 2012.
http://www.fas.org/sgp/crs/misc/RS21663.pdf.

[iv] United States Department of the Treasury. "Lessons Learned from the Privatization of Sallie Mae." March 2006. Accessed October 18 2012.
http://www.treasury.gov/about/organizational-structure/offices/Documents/SallieMaePrivatizationReport.pdf.

[v] Ibid.

[vi] I will be happy to discuss it with anyone who is interested (r.p.thead@gmail.com).

[vii] National Center for Education Statistics. "Fast Facts" Tuition Costs of Colleges and Universities." Accessed October 8, 2012.
http://nces.ed.gov/fastfacts/display.asp?id=76.

[viii] International Labour Organization. "Spotlight on U.S. Youth." Accessed November 29 2012. *http://www.ilo.org/washington/ilo-and-the-united-states/spot-light-on-the-us-labor-market/spot-light-on-us-youth/lang--en/index.htm.*

[ix] United States Department of Labor. "Economic News Release." Accessed November 29 2012. *http://www.bls.gov/news.release/empsit.t15.htm.*

[x] Michelle J. White, "Economic Analysis of Corporate and Personal Bankruptcy Law." National Bureau of Economic Research, 2005.

[xi] Glenn Harlan Reynolds. *The Higher Education Bubble.* Encounter Books, USA, 2012.

[xii] For more information: *Commentaries on the Laws of England in Four Books. Notes selected from the editions of Archibold, Christian, Coleridge, Chitty, Stewart, Kerr, and*

others, Barron Field's Analysis, and Additional Notes, and a Life of the Author by George Sharswood. In Two Volumes. Philadelphia, J.B. Lippincott Co., 1893. Vol. 1, Books I & II.

[xiii] Cases of negative equity on a home loan where the current real value of the home is worth less than the debt owed.

[xiv] Search "student loans" on Twitter.

[xv] Google search "Kaplan University recruitment tactics."

[xvi] Hall and Soskice. *Varieties of Capitalism: The Institutional Foundations of Comparative Advantage.* Oxford University Press, USA, 2001.

[xvii] Catherine Rampell. "Report Details Woes of Student Loan Debt." *New York Times.* Accessed October 8, 2012.
http://www.nytimes.com/2012/07/20/business/government-report-details-student-loan-debt.html?_r=0.

America's Religious Diversity: Challenge or Opportunity?

Sabith Khan

As a Muslim kid growing up in Bangalore, the most cosmopolitan city in India, I learned early on the value of respecting others' way of life and faith even if it differed radically from mine. Diversity was a way of life for me. After moving to the United Arab Emirates at the age of 26 and living there for two years, I became aware that living among a mostly Muslim population felt different. Although the move was a change from my life in Bangalore, the experience was not a culture shock, since Dubai had a community of South Asians.

All this changed three years ago. At the age of 28, I moved to study in the United States. Only then did I encounter the "Mecca of all religions": walking down Times Square and Fifth Avenue in New York reminded me that the world is a very diverse place indeed. But without a common framework of shared values and aspirations, keeping an incredibly diverse nation such as the United States together can be increasingly hard. Social and national cohesion must transcend religion.

Among sociologists and anthropologists, those great observers of society and religion, it is widely acknowledged that the "secularization" hypothesis is no longer valid: a grand narrative claiming that as societies modernize and progress, religious values lose their appeal. In the last few decades, religion has made a global comeback. Events such as the Iranian Revolution of 1979, the Satanic Verses controversy involving writer Salman Rushdie in 1988, the argued contribution of Roman Catholic Church to the fall of Communism in 1989, and global terrorist acts in the name of extremist sects of religion all have brought religion to public consciousness.[i]

Also widely acknowledged is that among the industrialized nations, the U.S. remains the most religiously observant nation. According to the Pew Research Center's latest survey on religion, just 16.1 percent of the U.S. population is religiously "unaffiliated." The remaining respondents claimed to have some religious affiliation or another.[ii] The Pew survey, based on interviews with more than 35,000 Americans, finds that religious affiliation in the U.S is extremely fluid while being diverse.

Perhaps the U.S is undergoing a "shift in consciousness" regarding religious acceptance. Just as the Civil Rights Movement in the 1960s led to guaranteeing the rights of African Americans to equal representation and, arguably, equality in society, I believe there is a similar movement happening socially, albeit in a much smaller and low-key manner: a movement for true universal acceptance of all religious groups in the U.S.

Religion, Civil Society and Changing Demographics

The U.S. is witnessing a demographic shift as well as a shift in consciousness, which is becoming apparent with public rhetoric about race, religion, and minorities. Since 1965 the U.S. has seen a huge influx of immigrants from across the world, in particular from non-western countries in Asia, Africa, and Latin America. This influx has significantly altered the racial and religious dynamics of the U.S.[iii]

While the country welcomed most immigrants without major opposition or barriers to integration in American society, the past ten years or so have witnessed a rise in the number of hate groups in the U.S. Many of these groups have based their work on xenophobic and religious ideologies. The shooting at a Sikh Gurdwara in Wisconsin in August 2012 is just one documented example of hate crimes committed out of religious intolerance.[iv] This trend of hate crimes has increased, especially since 9/11. It continues to grow, challenging the notion of the U.S as a land of freedom of religion and belief.

The Southern Poverty Law Center, a non-profit organization dedicated to studying these issues claims that the number of hate-groups in the U.S. has increased to 1,018 in 2012, a 70 percent rise since 2000.[v] This increase makes the issue of religious-based hate crimes not only salient, but also urgent, as far as guaranteeing the rights of minority religions, managing social tensions, and making the United States an immigrant-friendly nation.

In his 2007 book *America and the Challenges of Religious Diversity*, award-winning Princeton sociologist Robert Wuthnow took a close, hard look at the changing religious landscape in the U.S., and analyzed its impact on the American population. Using in-depth interviews with religious leaders, laymen, and people from what are sometimes referred to as the "new religions" in the U.S., such as Hindus, Muslims, and Buddhists, the book provides a compelling argument for greater interfaith dialogue. Additionally, Wuthnow used the book as a call for Christians to be more proactive in learning and accommodating these religious groups.

The book begins with two telling incidents to set the stage as to how Americans learn about other religious traditions and faiths. The deaths of Mother Teresa, the global icon of peace and charity in India, the country with the largest number of Hindus, and the death of Princess Diana, whose tragic death with her fiancé Dodi-Al Fayed, a Muslim, are each striking examples of confluence of religions. The fact that these events received global media coverage is significant.

The key argument in Wuthnow's book is that increasing religious diversity presents challenges to the existing American social fabric and that we must pay close attention to this issue. There is a call for greater interaction and also work between religious groups, while the author focused on encouraging Christian groups to increase their interfaith work. Anecdotally, I can attest to the need for this work, as I spent a year working in Washington, D.C. for an American Muslim organization that works with young Muslims. Although I witnessed some interfaith work being performed by non-profits in my own work, for the most part this work was symbolic, ad-hoc, and forced. Instead, what is needed is a more comprehensive approach to inter-faith dialogue.

The Pew survey mentioned earlier said over 28 percent of people in the U.S. left the religion they were raised with in favor of another religion or no religion at all. This accounts for much of the internal re-structuring of the religious landscape and hopefully creates space for additional accommodation within and among different religious groups.

The survey also states that while Protestantism is expected to become a minority faith in the U.S., the number of Catholics is also changing. Latinos, a quickly growing minority group in the U.S., 1 in 3 of which practice Catholicism, may account for any growth of U.S. Catholics in the near future. This Latino demographic accounts for nearly half of all Catholics 18-29 years. But immigration-based religious demographic change is not confined to Catholics. The Pew report also notes that immigration is adding to the U.S religious quilt with Muslims accounting for nearly 0.6 percent of the U.S. adult population and Hindus about 0.4 percent of the population.

This is also significant in the context of globalization. Wuthnow and other sociologists of religion have argued about the conflict between globalization and religion. Abullahi Al-Na'im is a good example regarding this debate. He observes that religion and globalization can exist side by side and that both are part of dynamic change. And since they both are part of globalization-based change, they feed off each other. Since the U.S. is the leader and principle architect of modern global capitalism and remains the largest economic engine in the world, any debates regarding the relationship between globalization and religion will include the experience of the United States.[vi]

Christian or Secular Nation?

The United States is perceived as a secular nation, though some adherents of Christianity would dispute this. Constitutionally the first amendment is understood as guaranteeing the right to freedom of religion and by implication, no particular religion is favored. However, the framework of society seems to be imbued with "Judeo-Christian values." Considering my background, I especially notice these values. Wuthnow agrees, too.

While maintaining the position that the U.S. has been shaped largely by a Christian notion, Wuthnow seems optimistic of the possibility of Christians and followers of other faiths working together. Other religions that fundamentally differ from the tenets of Christian religion were not considered by the U.S. Founding Fathers when they created the language of the U.S. founding documents. Only "flavors" of Christianity were seriously considered. And, according to Wuthnow and the data above, in general, the American public agrees.

Democracy Versus Authoritarianism?

Maintaining and respecting diversity in a pluralist, democratic society is a constant challenge with all the differing views on social and political issues. However, as Wuthnow, William E. Connolly, and other scholars have observed, it has been argued that a diverse populace could lead to a weakening of a national democracy, since an inclusive political order brings different people with varying understandings and backgrounds together, including some from authoritarian countries and cultures. This sort of narrow interpretation leads to a limited understanding of democracy and can decrease the level of democratic participation.

But if we look at the data, this sort of thinking can be easily debunked. Minority voting in the 2012 elections was very high. Latino voters helped President Obama win re-election, and a similar trend can be found among American Muslims, 89 percent of whom voted for President Obama in the 2008 elections.[vii] While a complete dataset regarding voting numbers for this past 2012 election is not available yet, I assume the data have not shifted significantly, although they have changed some. Both the Latino and Muslim communities appeared to have a record turnout in the elections, which is considered historic in many ways.

I believe that diversity strengthens democracy, but the above argument is put forth by people with a very exclusive notion of American society. While most immigrants who come from Asia, Africa, or the Middle East were not exposed to the form of democracy that exists in the U.S., or may not have arrived with ingrained sense of democratic culture, a significant number of Americans do not participate in democratic processes. Nor are they part of the country's social capital, the by-product from people interacting with one another, usually in the form of increased personal trust. Social capital in the U.S. has been declining in the past few decades, however. Robert Putnam's *Bowling Alone* has documented this change in America quite well. This argument is nevertheless salient and comes up in the context of immigrants from countries that are not democratic in parts of the world such as the Middle East and Africa.

One Exclusive Way or Multiple Paths?

Considering the opportunities for Americans to interact with and learn from other faiths, Wuthnow stated that many Americans have become "spiritual shoppers," often exploring other religious traditions and cultural practices such as transcendental meditation, yoga and other practices that are not theologically binding but expressions of their spiritual quest.

While religious diffusion is happening as more and more people spiritually shop, there is also a hardening of religious stances, a response from some hardliners to what they perceive as an intrusion into their way of life.

Between the "spiritual shoppers" and those with a very rigid "one-way" interpretation of life and religion are those who believe that multiple paths to god exist and that it is acceptable for one to worship and believe in whatever they like. This group is open to ideas, has had experiences, friendships, and social networks that are inclusive, and are generally more curious about other religions.

For all the progress that the U.S. has made regarding religious tolerance, there is a marked ignorance among Americans about religions that are not a form of Christianity. Until recently, even Mormonism, a 'local' or 'home-grown' flavor of Christianity, was under attack. Until his nomination as the Republican nominee for the 2012 presidential election and even after it, Mitt Romney could not shake off his faith affiliation and its negative connotation.

During my first year of graduate school at Syracuse University in upstate New York, I remember meeting a fellow graduate student who shared his work-space with me. After the initial pleasantries, my colleague asked me if I was Hindu, seeing that I am from India. I told him that I am Muslim, to which my friend inquired, "So, what religion do you follow?"

While this one-off incident cannot be extrapolated beyond this particular interaction (the person has since learned a great deal about my religion, and I have learned quite a lot about his), it does demonstrate that there are Americans who have never met or dealt with people from other faiths or backgrounds.

This is cause for concern, considering that the racial and religious demography of the country is constantly changing. These people are likely to be very concerned if they perceive or observe their neighborhoods being taken over by immigrants and outsiders who do not look like them and who have very different belief systems.

This is a natural human reaction, which must be addressed with wisdom and care.

A Secular Nation?

What does a secular nation do with religion? Push religion under the carpet, blot it out from public consciousness and pretend that it does not exist, or does it deal with its public expression? Does it acknowledge the fact that we are all different, that we dress, eat, and think differently and that it is okay for us to do so? How do France and India, both countries with secular constitutions, perceive and implement the project of secularism? How has the U.S. dealt with it?

In answering these difficult questions, I believe India offers a good, but not perfect, example of managing this diversity. While history has definitely helped build a syncretic mix of religious traditions, incorporating elements of Hindu, Muslim, Christian ideals to build the country that is present-day India, there is a strong tradition of tolerance, mutual acceptance of the "other," and even celebration of diversity that is woven into Indian social fabric. While not ideal in any sense, this symbiotic existence of the various religions in India is an example that can be drawn upon as an example.

There is an ongoing battle over social issues in several U.S. states; one of the more salient issues is same-sex marriage. Arguments over marriage laws are also a reflection of some of the values held by the religiously inclined. It is widely understood that the religious values and notions of what America represents are closely linked, much as a majority of the American public sees a country based on, if not governed by, Christian values.

Wuthnow asked, "How pluralistic should we be?" He answered by making a case for religious and social cooperation. He also advocated for Christians to reach out to people of other faith traditions and actively engage, rather than just "tolerate" them. He adds that the followers of Islam and Hinduism don't want to be just "tolerated" but rather actively "understood." He called for reflective pluralism with adequate thinking and consideration of what one believes in and where one's beliefs are coming from. He stated rightly that if exclusivists ignore all other religions and continue to live in a bubble, there will be a difficult future as the country becomes increasingly diverse.

I agree with Wuthnow's point, though there is a tendency within certain minority groups to "stick with their own" and not work with or among other faith groups. This trend must be countered by all sides. I think that non-profit organizations should take the lead in this undertaking, as they can be non-partisan and also neutral. They can act as honest brokers.

While interfaith organizations exist to educate and spread

information regarding commonality among faiths, more needs to be done to develop "strength of character" to deal with each other and live peacefully amid so much diversity. There is a call for building "personal relationships" with others if these efforts are to succeed. This may also tie in with Robert Putnam's and others' hypotheses who have worked on social capital formation: they suggest that sufficient "binding and bonding" between groups will lead to greater cohesion.

Conclusion

In my experience, natural friendship, love that develops between neighbors, co-workers and colleagues, far exceeds any organized or government-sponsored program. The social capital built through mutual association and proximity is far more significant. To capture the spirit of Putnam's book, I do not prefer to go "bowling alone." This may be a strategy that would work for minority religions in the U.S., as well.

While we can address solutions and possible models of how religious groups can work together, the deeper issues concerning theological differences are not addressed. How does one, for example, work with a church that believes that you are damned to hell because you do not believe in their creed? Or how does a denomination like the Mormon Church work with Episcopalians or Evangelists, who have had a troubled history with each other?

These are not easy questions to answer and the solution is not simplistic or straightforward. While some of the scholars and intellectuals quoted here offer some thoughts to start the conversation, I believe concerted efforts in public policy and civil society are needed to address these challenges. Only tolerance and acceptance can really answer these questions.

While opposing bigotry, narrow-mindedness, and racism is a life-long project that I believe we must all commit to, differences among people regarding many issues will remain. The point is not to expect everyone to think the same or strive for homogenous beliefs, but rather to make safe a country and world so that everyone can be acknowledged and accepted in our societies.

Perhaps the answer to managing the diversity of religious thought may lie in ensuring that others feel safe in our presence, and as the late John F. Kennedy said, "If we cannot end our differences, at least we can help make the world safe for diversity."

---

[i] Jonathan Benthall. *Returning to Religion: Why a Secular Age is Haunted by Faith.* London, I.B. Tauris. 2008.

[ii] Pew Forum on Religion and Public Life. *Religious Affiliation: Diverse and Dynamic.* February 2008. Accessed November 12, 2012. *http://religions.pewforum.org/pdf/report-religious-landscape-study-full.pdf.*

[iii] Ibid.

[iv] *CBSNews.* "Shooting at Sikh temple in Wis., at least 7 dead." August 5th, 2012. Accessed November 12, 2012. *http://www.cbsnews.com/8301-201_162-57486965/shooting-at-sikh-temple-in-wis-at-least-7-dead/*

[v] Southern Poverty Law Center. "What We Do." Accessed November 12, 2012. *http://www.splcenter.org/what-we-do/hate-and-extremism.*

[vi] Abdullahi Ahmed An-Na`im. *The Politics of Religion and Morality of Globalization.* Oxford University Press. 2005.

[vii] LatinoVoteMap.org. "Map." 2012. Accessed November 12, 2012. *http://www.latinovotemap.org/map/.*

Acknowledgements – from R.P. Thead

Special thanks to Kimberly Ly for assisting me with the genesis of the idea of this book, the talented musician and songwriter Wendell Kimbrough for the title suggestion, Andy Shuai Liu and Ioulia Fenton for their assistance in recruiting contributors, Alison Lake for helping me prepare the manuscript for publication, Jeri Walker-Bickett, Michael Kennedy, Gail Luxton, Oz Alturk and the Young Professionals in Foreign Policy organization, the team over at PolicyMic.com, and Will Coxwell for his generous *pro bono* legal assistance.

Also, this book would not have been possible were it not for our successful Kickstarter campaign, the core of which was a well-produced video. Many thanks to the crew who made that video happen: Ian Walker, Greg Baylon, Zach Williams, Stu Haight, and Jay Lujan.

Made in the USA
Lexington, KY
04 February 2016